THE FULL MONTE

other books by Paul Dishman

Water, War, and Wonder: A Photographic Exploration of the Balkans

THE FULL MONTE

A Fulbright Scholar's Humorous and Heartwarming Experience in Montenegro

(A beautiful little country you've never heard of, but really ought to visit.)

Paul Dishman, Ph.D.

AuthorHouse™ LLC
1663 Liberty Drive
Bloomington, IN 47403
www.authorhouse.com
Phone: 1-800-839-8640

© 2014 Paul Dishman, Ph.D. All rights reserved.

No part of this book may be reproduced, stored in a retrieval system, or transmitted by any means without the written permission of the author.

Published by AuthorHouse 03/11/2014

ISBN: 978-1-4918-4373-4 (sc)
ISBN: 978-1-4969-0657-1 (e)

Library of Congress Control Number: 2013923476

Any people depicted in stock imagery provided by Thinkstock are models, and such images are being used for illustrative purposes only.
Certain stock imagery © Thinkstock.

Because of the dynamic nature of the Internet, any web addresses or links contained in this book may have changed since publication and may no longer be valid. The views expressed in this work are solely those of the author and do not necessarily reflect the views of the publisher, and the publisher hereby disclaims any responsibility for them.

Photographs and artwork by the author.
Front cover: Bay of Kotor
Back cover: Mount Lovćen
Back cover photo of author courtesy of Bethann Freeland.

Contents

To my mother, **Phyllis**,
who couldn't go
and
To my wife, **Beth Lynn**,
who did
and made it all worthwhile

It was then we realized if you haven't driven in an isolated southern Balkan mountain range at midnight on a moonless night, down an unlit, winding, single-lane road, dodging old women dressed completely in black who were herding donkeys and sheep down the middle of the pavement, not knowing where you were because the GPS system showed your car in the middle of the Ionic Sea, and you did not know the local language, well, you really hadn't traveled.

And, up to that point, I guess we hadn't.

Slovenia
Hungary
Croatia
Romania
Bosnia and Herzegovina
Serbia
Split
Mostar
Prijepolje
Hvar
Prishtinë
Bulgaria
Dubrovnik
Kosovo
Montenegro
Shkodër
Macedonia
Vevčani
Orhid
Albania
Italy
Berat
Meteora
Turkey
Sarandë
Greece
Olympia
Athens
Santorini
The Balkans

BOSNIA
AND
HERZEGOVINA
Mostar
Prijepolje
SERBIA
Žabljak
MONTENEGRO
Kolašin
Nikšić
CROATIA
Dubrovnik
Ostrog Monastery
KOSOVO
Plav
Gusinje
Perast
Podgorica
Kotor
Cetinje
Budva
Sveti Stefan
Drobnići
Godinje
Skadar
Lake
ALBANIA
Bar
Shkodër
Ulcinj

INTRODUCTION

How are Things in *Crna Gora*?

Why in the name of God's green earth would anybody want to read a book about Montenegro? Much less one written by a pedantic professor. Most Americans have never heard of the country and those who have, cannot locate it on an atlas. Even if you have a map and know where to look, it still takes a magnifying glass to find it. To people in the United States, the word Montenegro sounds Spanish. When I would mention to people where we were traveling, they would all get a glazed look in their eye while they tried to remember where in the Carmen Sandiego it was. Most of our friends thought we were going to the capital of Uruguay. Others asked if it was one of those banana republics near Belize. A few were certain it was a Portuguese island off the coast of Africa.

It is not anywhere near those places. Montenegro is situated north of Albania and south of Bosnia-Herzegovina and is the smallest of the republics that made up the former country of Yugoslavia. It sits on the coast of the azure Adriatic sea across from its better-known neighbor, Italy. The two countries share a laconic love for leisure, passion, wine, sun, food, and family. When the Venetians came conquering down the sea's eastern coast, they sailed into the Bay of Kotor and were impressed with the dark pine trees that covered the mountains. They called the place *monte negro* or black mountain. In Serbian, it is *Crna Gora.*[1]

Montenegro is simply magnificent. Their Ministry of Tourism markets the country as having "Wild Beauty" and they have not exaggerated. It has Alp-like mountains, valleys of grape-filled vineyards, roaring river rapids, pristine (and

1 If you cannot get enough of Montenegrin history (and who can?), read *Realm of the Black Mountain* by Elizabeth Roberts. It is thoroughly researched and written by a former British diplomat to the area.

primordial) forests, fjords with almost vertical massifs that stretch up to the sky, and beach after beach that face into the setting sun. All of this in a country only fifty-five by eighty miles across—magnificence in miniature.

It is difficult to know which is more beautiful, the landscape or the people. Montenegrins are tall (they average over six feet)2, dark (from all the Mediterranean sun), and exceedingly handsome. And, that's just the females. The women have long black hair that accentuates their very long legs. They have baby-like complexions and killer smiles—Slavic sirens all. Because of their embracing nature and unbridled love of strangers, Montenegrin people have been described as "aggressively friendly."

The country sits at the crossroads of Western Civilization. Divided one way, it is the difference between Latin Catholicism and Eastern Orthodoxy. Cut the other way, it defines the historical border of occidental Europe and the oriental Middle East. It is a mix of Slavic, Byzantine, Moslem, and Albanian people, all living on top of Illyrian, Roman, and Ottoman ruins.3

I have always wanted to go to this little country. It is the land of my people.

My mother's father was born in a large stone house above one of those stony beaches. Hardship forced him to leave his family and immigrate to America. He married my grandmother, begat my mother, and never said a single word about his family or what he had left behind. I never knew him as he died before I was born. Thus, I never got to ask him the questions that he would not answer for my mother.

If grandfather didn't leave me many clues about his early life, he did bequeath me his face. My mother still looks at me wistfully, shakes her head,

---

[2] Montenegrin men are so tall, urinals are installed high on restroom walls. So high, that if you are only 5' 9"—you might not qualify.

[3] The Slavs arrived in the 6th century A.D. from somewhere near the Baltics and took over the joint. The Slavs were one of the civilizations that pushed the Romans back, in this case across the Adriatic. They arrived in what is now northern Serbia and then migrated again splitting into multiple factions that settled from the Black Sea to the Adriatic. Those who walked north were the Slovenes, those who headed west became Croats and both eventually came under the influence of the Roman Catholic Church. Those who strayed south to the coast were Serbs and were eventually converted to the Orthodox movement coming up from Constantinople. The odd thing about the Slavs is all the previous invaders—the Huns (as in Attila), the Goths (the original ones, not the ones we have today), and the Turkish Avars came, pillaged, looted, and left. Not the Slavs, they stayed. There are two sociological theories about this. One believes the Slavs found the Balkans immensely more appealing than where they had come from, as it was warmer. (They were previously known as the Cold Slavs.) The other theory is that Slavs were inherently lazy, and the trip back was just out of the question. The Montenegrins believe the latter.

and says how much I look like him. He must have been a very handsome man. At least as handsome as you can be when you are a short, balding man with bushy eyebrows over a large schnozz—all part of my Montenegrin inheritance.

Mother kept our little known heritage alive as best she could. When I was in elementary school and we were assigned to make a country map out of flour paste, she told me not to raise my hand until the very end of the list so I would get Yugoslavia. (This was before there was a Zaire or Zimbabwe.) When we wrote reports about world leaders, she told me to pick Josef Tito, the man who ruled the country with a velvet fist from 1945 until his death in 1980. (This had to have raised some eyebrows in the north Dallas, staunch anti-communist, John Birch neighborhood in which we lived.)

Therefore, I wanted to make sure that my trip was really going to happen before I called and told her.

"Mom, I've been named a Fulbright Scholar."

"What? Oh, son, that is so exciting!"

"And you'll never guess where I am going—to Montenegro!"

"Oh, my heavens! I can't believe you're going there. I have wanted to go my whole life! You know my father was from there. Where will you be living? When are you leaving?"

"We will be living the capital, Podgorica. We're not leaving until January."

"How long will you be gone?"

"It's just for six months, Mom. We will be back in June."

"This is so wonderful! I am so excited for you! Where did you say you were going?"

Mother had contracted Alzheimer's disease six years earlier and her memory degradation was fairly slow but constant. We would have the same conversation over and over. It was like being stuck in Bill Murray's *Groundhog Day* but in shorter, five-minute loops.

She has a great attitude about her disability. She constantly tells us she loves us and laughs over things she cannot remember. With her disease, what used to be so important is not anymore but little things can become significant. The brunt of care taking has fallen upon my sister as she lives two miles away from mother and I live five hundred times that. My sister is at my mother's home constantly, much more often than my mother remembers she is. She takes care of mother's finances, hires and supervises caretakers, gets the strange calls at all hours, puts up with the angry outbursts of frustration, deals with the crisis of the day (like misplaced eyeglasses or hearing aids), and goes home exhausted. My sister's husband is a kind and soft-spoken physician who carefully watches over his mother-in-law with just as much love as though she didn't have those last two hyphenated words. My sister and brother-in-law deal with the paranoia, personality changes, and depression that can be a daily occurrence. My father died when he and my mother were only fifty-five. Twenty years later, my mother married Sam, a wonderful but quiet man. At eighty-five and ninety, they live in their own house and sleep together in their own bed. Caretakers spend the day with them cooking meals, doing laundry, and making sure pills are taken. Mother and Sam resent the intrusion; but in the back of their minds, they know what the alternative is.

Traveling to Montenegro was a trip Mother and I always wanted to take together. After Dad died, she took what little money was left and spent it on trips to Europe, Japan, and the Holy Lands. She finally was able to see some of the world she always told me to go see. She constantly talked about the two of us going to Montenegro, but the timing never was right. I didn't have either the money or time as I was working and going to graduate school while raising a family. When Mother finally saved up enough money so she could go by herself, the Yugoslav wars had begun. After hearing about the atrocities that were being committed on both sides, she was never very enthusiastic after that.

•

For being so conservative in their politics, my mother and father were quite liberal in their socio-cultural views. Growing up, they taught me to enjoy Mexican fiestas, German wurstfests, Czech May holidays, Greek food festivals, African-American Juneteenth celebrations, and especially Fourth of July parades. I was taught all of these cultures contributed to what made America—America, and, as we were all sons and daughters of immigrants, we should celebrate that. Mother and Dad did like to celebrate.

Appreciation of these peoples in the melting pot of our country only whetted my appetite to see them first hand. I wanted to experience the exuberance of other lives and see the origins of these significant contributions to my own life as well as the American cultural landscape. My paternal grandfather, who had spent his entire life in west Texas, mightily influenced my initial outlook on travel. Once he set me on his knee and told me to go see the world. He said he himself had once traveled as far east as a man could—yep, Corpus Christi.[4]

---

4 When I announced we were going to Montenegro, my family told everyone that we were going to live in *Yurrop*.

From that conversation forward, I have always had an antsy butt. I like traveling and experiencing new scenery, foreign food, and meeting interesting people. I get a thrill when my plane touches down for the first time in a new country. I get sensory overload when the taxi takes me downtown and I am bombarded by signage in a language I do not understand, viewing unfamiliar architecture, and the sights, sounds, and aromas of life lived in an entirely different way than mine. I get home from one trip and begin mentally planning the next one.[5] Knowing the next trip is on the horizon gets me through many of life's tedious trivialities. However, I have discovered spending a few days or even a week in another country allows you to see the tourist sites and taste the food but not much else. I wanted an extended experience in another country and culture for a sufficient length of time where I would actually have to unpack.

I was fairly along in life before all the stars aligned so I could have such an opportunity. Caught in an academic job that did not provide for a lot of growth, it was time to do consider other options. After a long period of investigation, I came back to something I thought was always just beyond my grasp—the Fulbright Scholarship Program. This international educational program is sponsored by the U.S. Department of State. It was created in 1946 by Sen. William Fulbright from Arkansas, who proposed that some of the money other countries were paying back to the U.S. after World War II be designated for international exchange. He saw that peace during the Cold War needed to be achieved at the personal level and believed what John Steinbeck had said, "Tourists are very useful to the modern world; it is very difficult to hate the people one knows." Coincidently, Steinbeck was also a Fulbright Scholar. The Fulbright program has placed over 121,000 students, scholars, teachers, scientists, artists, and professionals from the U.S. in over 155 countries and cultures throughout the world. At the same time, it has brought 190,000 highly qualified people to America in order to experience life and learning in these United States. About 7,500 grants are awarded each year. Fulbright alums have become presidents, prime ministers, cabinet members, judges, ambassadors, CEO's, writers, artists, and even college professors. Fulbright Scholars include such diverse individuals as *Lion King* director Julie Taymor, diplomat Henry Kissinger, composer Aaron Copeland, actors John Lithgow and Dolph Lundgren, former Intel CEO Craig Barrett, chemist Linus Pauling, humanitarian Muhammad Yunus, DNA discoverer James Watson, soprano Renée Fleming,

---

5 It must be noted that the author suffers from PPS, Perpetual Peregrination Syndrome.

and former Secretary-General of the U.N. Boutros Boutros-Ghali. Forty-three "Fulbrighters" have won Nobel Prizes and seventy-eight won Pulitzer Prizes.

•

As a "Fulbrighter," I was charged by the State Department with meeting as many people as possible, speaking and writing about my experiences, participating in a broad range of social and community activities, pursuing academic and professional objectives, and to learn about the history and culture of my host country.[6]

While researching for this book, I diligently tried to filter through regional historical references attempting to substantiate facts from multiple sources knowing the inherent bias and revisionist nature of most people (and writers) in the region. Reading about the events of the Battle of Kosovo as conveyed by a Albanian historian writing in the Communistic era who intended to stir up nationalistic hearts is quite different than that of a Serbian historian who wrote during the World Wars with the purpose of revenging four-hundred years of Turkish rule. These two, of course, are in stark contrast to recent Muslim writers whose offerings are tempered with religious righteousness. It is not apparent that English-language translations have helped provide clarity as many of these are accompanied by equally biased and opinionated footnotes and marginalia. In addition, many of the references that were available to me in English may have been translated for the sole purpose of propaganda to a wider audience, notably Western intellectuals. Although American journalism at least gives lip service to unbiased reporting, that is more than a foreign concept there where all writing (including scientific research) must address the political environment or is an outlet for an overt or covert political agendae.

However, this is not an academic book.[7] It is merely an entertaining adventure with, hopefully, a few informative insights so you can claim to have

---

6 It was interesting to us how few people knew about the Fulbright Scholarship program and country of Montenegro. The Venn intersection of those two sets of people was exactly one. For the Fulbright, it was mostly baby boomers, academics, but no students, neighbors, and no one under thirty. The only person that had heard of both was the academic coach for our athletic teams, a well-read man who had basketball players from up and down the Dalmatian coast.

7 Please be forewarned. I am not apologizing for my extensive use of footnotes. As a scholar, I am actually under professional obligation to create and give them life. They help illuminate points of interest without disturbing the flow of the text. They provide brief asides that help clarify and provide deeper understanding to the reader. They also assist when one is being paid by the word.

gotten double your money's worth. Due to the book's intended nature, in the case where local legend cannot be unequivocally substantiated by facts (and might be in direct conflict with documented history), I have decided to tell whichever story is the most interesting. Writing about life is just like living life—mostly mundane and it is up to you to make it interesting.

•

I went to see my mother just before we left, and I told her how much I wanted her to go with me. She sighed, and said she just was not up to traveling anymore.

Squeezing my hand, she said, "You go and send me back an article good enough for *National Geographic*. Come back and tell me everything."

Therefore, the trip became another item on her bucket list she knew would never happen. This trip was as much for her as it was for me. For her, I had to capture all the sights, sounds, experiences, people, and culture, and bring them back so she could live it all vicariously through me. I knew I had to keep a detailed record of the entire experience, something I had never done before. My mother had been a professional journalist so there were expectations to be met. I knew I could not just take snapshots, either. I invested in a good camera, took photography lessons, and ended up taking 13,000 pictures—about twenty of which were any good, but enough for one quality narration for Mother. Every adventure, surprise, culinary delight, family discovery, and historical tidbit was documented so I could return home and provide her a link to the heritage she never knew. The process of which, would turn out to be a thrilling and life-changing experience for me.

•

The Montenegrins believe that when God did create His green earth, He started with Montenegro. He was so pleased with what he had done; the rest of the world was just an afterthought.

Filip Radović

"I left Montenegro because we had a very bad King."

Filip Radović was born in 1894 in a very large stone house that already held his parents, grandparents, and two older brothers. All of them were slowly starving to death. Their house was one of a few that made up the hamlet of Drobnići, which sat overlooking the Adriatic Sea. The home hugged the slope between the pristine beach three hundred yards below and the mountains, which rose vertically four thousand feet above. Drobnići was located in the southern most isolated tip of the Austro-Hungarian Empire frontier on the Montenegrin coast. It was a magical place where you could eat oranges off a tree on the beach while you gazed at snow-covered peaks above you.

The Radović family was land rich but cash poor from acres that had been acquired through several generations of inheritance. They had vast olive groves (and barrels of olive oil), fig trees, acres of oranges and pomegranates, apiaries for honey, and goats for cheese and meat. But, so did everybody else. There was no one with whom they could sell or barter these goods for cash or other staples. Every family along the Adriatic coast had to come to the same fateful decision. Not only was there no future for their children, but the next generation must be sent away from home in order for the entire family to survive. Filip was forced to leave as a young teenager. He and his parents also knew when he turned sixteen; he would be conscripted into the Austro-Hungarian army and have to fight fellow Serbs, friendly Italians, and beloved Russians for the mean Austro-Hungarian king, Franz Joseph I.[1]

---

1 By World War I, half of the Austro-Hungarian army soldiers were from the Balkans. This created a problem even with the two official languages of German and Hungarian. The army had to create a pidgin language, Army Slav, consisting of

If they had the money, the family would finance the oldest son so he might find his fortune and return. The other sons were expected to find work in order to pay for their own passage abroad. The youngest son was to stay in the house and take care of his parents. Filip was the youngest, yet, even he had to leave due to the desperate economic conditions and certain fate the family was facing.

The Montenegrin *diaspora* that emigrated between 1800 and 1920 made up almost a third of the adult male population. They left to pan for gold in Alaska, herd cattle in Argentina, and to work in the slaughterhouses in Chicago. Filip's oldest brother, Andrija, left home first and ventured to *Amerike*. He had heard of jobs to be had in the mines of the west. For some reason, he chose the copper mines in Arizona as the most promising spot. After arriving, he wrote home and told of the incredible wages he was receiving and how he could make even more money if he recruited additional workers for the company. Within two years, the middle son, Miloš (Milosh), also left for Arizona, followed a year later, by the youngest, Filip.

When he left home, Filip packed a leather sack with clothes and enough *kronen* to pay for his passage. His father, Tomo, bid him a stoic goodbye, but his mother, Kata, broke down and pounded on the floor for him not to leave. She yelled about her baby being taken from her and she yelled at her husband for not being a better provider and driving all her sons from the house. Filip left home in this emotional maelstrom, hearing his mother wailing in the doorway. He walked down the road to hitch a ride on a goat cart that was headed for Kotor, ten miles to the north. From there he would catch a steamer bound for Trieste, Italy. One week later, the steamer would pass right in front of his home giving him one last look at a house he would never see again. From Italy, he would sail to Constantinople, on to England, and, from there, on to America.

The trip from Southampton to New York on the S.S. St. Paul took thirty-one days or about half the time he had been traveling. He arrived at Ellis Island on a cool spring day on May 9, 1909, and was processed through as "Filip Radovich." He spoke no English and, although the manifest states he was seventeen years old, he was actually only fifteen, having left his family at the age of fourteen.

He had been traveling with three other boys from the Montenegrin coast, Nasso Paolović, sixteen; Stefan Tomo Srzentić, eighteen; Niko Gjuro Zenović, sixteen; and a man, Andrea Giakonović, thirty-nine. Perhaps Giakonović was the chaperon of the group. They were all following relatives who were already in the Arizona Territory. Traveling with the other Montenegrins made the trip a little bit easier as they had someone to talk to and help interpret the commands the

---

about 100 words and half that many gestures.

train conductor would bark at them. They passed the time trying to understand the strange signs in the Latin alphabet that they had only seen when Italians and Croats used it.

All were destined for the town of Bisbee, twenty miles from Tombstone and only eight miles from the Mexican border with its revolution that would begin the next year. There was great joy that reunion day for Miloš and Filip, but it was tempered by the news Andrija had saved up enough money and already left to return to Montenegro.[2] Miloš had a bed reserved for Filip in the boarding house where the older brother lived. The next day Filip was issued a pick and descended into the copper mine.

It did not take long for the two brothers to discover there were jobs to be had outside of the mine that paid almost as well but came with the added benefit that they did not have to go back into those dark depths ever again. After a year, they moved north to Miami, Arizona, where Miloš was pouring drinks in a saloon and Filip learned to cook. He slapped down hash browns and sausage in the morning, ladled out chili at noon, and fried up steaks for dinner. He lived in the kitchen and slept behind the counter at night. What money they saved, they sent back to their parents. After a year in Miami, they splurged and paid a photographer to take a portrait of them in new matching suits, ties, and stiff white collars. It was the only photograph their parents were to receive of the two brothers together.

Eventually, they decided to open up their own eatery, the Palace Café. The partnership did not last very long with Miloš soon leaving in a huff but being smart enough to leave arid Arizona for seductive San Diego. Miloš soon met and married Agnes Jahns, a girl of good German stock who produced a son and daughter, Elmer and Eva. Life was difficult during the depression and hard work was what kept a family together. Miloš had secured a job in an ice cream factory and finagled one for his son when he turned twelve years old. The son had the same stubborn streak that his father did; and, when he, too, was fourteen, he ran away from home first going south into the Sonoran desert, then retreating to the Southern Pacific train yard where he hopped on an eastbound freight and began life as a young hobo. Even though they had never met before, he

---

[2] Andrija returned to Drobnići, married, and stayed long enough to have four children. He then left his family again to work in the mines in Australia, and stayed there for over twenty years. After a debilitating kidney surgery, he sailed back to Montenegro so his wife, Evica, could take care of him. She, having raised all four children single-handedly while taking care of Andrija's elderly parents, promptly threw him out of the house. She then took him back in on the explicit condition that she would make his life a living hell for the rest of his years. According to all reports, she fulfilled her promise.

stopped to see his uncle Filip who, by then, had moved to west Texas. He stayed three weeks before moving on to ride the rails across the south, up the Atlantic seaboard, across the Ohio valley, back over the plains and mountains to southern California. He was gone almost two years. It was breakfast when he walked unannounced into the house. His mother fell to her knees, crying.

His father took one look at his son, wiped his mouth, and said, "The shift starts in fifteen minutes, grab your hat, and let's go."

Not long after, Elmer enlisted in the Marines. This decision was based on the fact that they gave you a physical examination for free. He ended up being posted in Shanghai ahead of the Japanese invasion.

•

In Arizona, Filip formed a business venture with another man from Montenegro, M. L. Kristovich. There is a newspaper advertisement from 1925 that shows Filip and M. L. standing on both sides of a mule scratching his ears. Perhaps the mule was a silent partner. The Palace Café moved with the prosperity of the mines. First it was located in Miami, then Superior, and finally Globe, Arizona, where the Old Dominion Copper Company mine was now in full production.

Once Filip left home, his parents, Tomo and Kata, were despondent, missing all of their sons. Miloš was the more sentimental of the boys; he wrote frequent letters and sent them packages of foodstuffs, clothes, and blankets. Filip also sent packages but with never more than a post card of correspondence accompanying them. Miloš's letters were full of news. He wrote about his life in California and how much the weather was so like Montenegro's. He wrote about his new family and included news about America. He would ask about everyone in the village. He was always worried about his parents. Did they have enough clothes? Were they warm enough at night? Did they have enough to eat? Probably knowing his brother Filip's terse nature, he was always kind enough to sign the letters "Miloš and Filip" although the two brothers lived a thousand miles from each other.[3]

One Sunday in 1925, Filip was cleaning dishes when in walked one of the few women in Globe at the time. She was a teacher on the Indian reservation and

---

[3] During one summer vacation when I was a small child, we drove (without air conditioning) across Texas, New Mexico, and Arizona to see great-uncle Miloš who was lying in a nursing home in San Diego. I remember two things about him. He was a very skinny man with no hair and, when I was presented to him, he sat up in bed, said something in Serbian, grinned from ear to ear, and shook my hand with such a powerful grip that it was sore through the rest of the fourth grade.

had decided to treat herself to a meal at the local diner, an extravagance on her meager salary.

•

Jessie Sisk was born in Dalton County, Kentucky in 1888, the oldest sister of five girls. Their two brothers were the youngest and oldest and were twenty years apart. The sisters were two years apart each and were very close their whole lives. The other girls were Bessie, Helen, Cotta, and Gooch.[4] The family left Kentucky soon after Jessie was born and headed west because a Baptist minister told them there was opportunity to be had in Texas. They traveled by train to Amarillo and then by stagecoach to a western cow-town that you could smell long before you ever saw it—Hereford.

The sisters did well in school, raised money for the Red Cross and, during World War I, served donuts and coffee to the soldiers on the troop trains when the steam engines would stop in town to take on water. Education was important to the family and, when each child finished their public schooling, their father sent them to West Texas Normal College thirty miles away in Canyon. Each sister received a Mistress of Arts degree in Education, Nursing, or Home Economics—the only majors open to women. Jessie wanted to teach and had a flair for art, so she majored in Education. Her last year at West Texas, she studied painting with a young iconoclast named Georgia O'Keefe who was on the art faculty and only a year older than her students. O'Keefe was a large influence in Jessie's life as she, too, became a painter and developed a sense of wanderlust that was hard to satisfy on the plains of the Panhandle.

After graduation, Jessie spent a decade teaching in schoolhouses across the top of Texas in the thriving metropolitan areas of Hereford, Dawn, Vega, Friona, and Happy. Even living a year in that last town did not help her disposition as she recognized she was slowly becoming a spinster school marm. When she reached the age of thirty-five, she realized life was passing her by, and, with no other prospects, coupled with a sense of adventure not shared by her sisters, she decided to leave Texas and went to teach on the San Carlos Apache Reservation in Arizona. She moved to Globe and began instructing students from ten different grades in a one-room, desert schoolhouse. She loved the red mesas, her job, her students, and, in fairly short order, an exotic foreigner named Filip.

---

4 Their mother used to call them to dinner by yelling, "Jess, Bess, Hel, Cot, Gooch!" If the girls were really in trouble, it was, "Jess, Bess, HELL, I CAUGHT YOU!"

Whether it was the striking allure of this deep accented Montenegrin or her own sense of a biological clock, she fell for Filip, now Phil; and nature eventually took its course. He was thirty-one and she was six years older. They honeymooned at the Grand Canyon, and, when they discovered she was pregnant, decided wild and woolly Arizona was not the place to raise their child. They returned to Hereford where their daughter was born. They named her Phyllis after her father and had no more children.

Fortunately, Jessie's father, Roland, had already died. As her returning from Arizona pregnant and presenting her Baptist deacon father with a strange, bald-headed foreigner as his new son-in-law would have killed him. All of the other sisters had already married and most had children of their own. The newlyweds bought her parents' house from her mother, a nine-room, two-story wooden house at the western edge of town on Catalpa Street.

Jessie's family was very large, and the acceptance of the foreigner varied from member to member. Phil tried hard to fit in, not only with the family, but the community. He joined the Masons, learned the secret handshake, and worked his way up to become a Shriner. He joined the Chamber of Commerce but could not attend any meetings because he was too busy working, doing commerce.

He opened a chocolate shop creatively called "The Chocolate Shoppe" which sold confectioneries, sandwiches, and fudge cut on a marble slab. The store was open from 7 a.m. until 10 p.m. Three years later, the country was plunged into the Great Depression. Worried about being able to keep the shop open in order to feed his family, he did the only thing he could do—he worked all day, every day. During particularly tough times, he would leave the Chocolate Shoppe in the hands of his clerks and travel to California for months at a time to work on cooperative farms led by fellow Serbs and Montenegrins.

Even on Sundays, Phil would get up and go to work. Jessie would dress and take Phyllis to church. If it was a special Sunday, Jessie would pack a basket of fried chicken they could eat during the Baptist All-Day-Singing-and-Dinner-on-the-Ground camp meetings. Phil was probably the only Serbian Orthodox adherent for a thousand miles. When times got tough and he felt it necessary to implore the Almighty, he would fold up his collar, pull down the brim of his hat, and sneak into the back of the Catholic Church. Even though they were the traditional enemy, they shared the same early saints; and he could at least get a feeling of ceremony, which he never could in the protestant church where his wife and all her family attended. There, they actually made you sing and recite scripture. That was work.

During World War II, his neighbors treated him empathetically; however, after Yugoslavia came under Tito's rule, there was just the slightest bit of suspicion. The fact he did not attend church with his wife probably did not help his cause any as that was one more piece of evidence that Phil might have been a godless Communist.

Phil and Jessie had a very strained relationship, and neither one of them would say life turned out the way they expected. At least Jessie had her daughter, Phyllis and the rest of her family around her. Phil had only his work. He rarely saw his family. My mother is convinced he died from overwork at the age of only fifty-three. It was difficult trying to scrape out a living in west Texas struggling in a disintegrating economy and watching the land and crops blow away in the great Dust Bowl. He had no choice but to work so hard that he never really knew his own daughter. On top of which, he felt so isolated from everything he knew as a child. He could remember the idyllic place on the sea overlooking the vast ocean that held a promise of adventures and a better life.

He never told my mother a single thing about his childhood. He never spoke or said anything in his native language. With his new family, he never cooked or shared food that he had known growing up. He never told stories of walking to school or playing on the beach. He never mentioned his parents, what they looked like, or how much he missed them. He never even told his daughter that she had cousins in a land across the ocean or an uncle in Australia. He never said a word about his childhood, family, or heritage. Part of my trip was to find out why.

Preparation

The Fulbright application procedure is an arduous process filled with federal forms, essays, letters of recommendations, proposals, and paper cuts. You must apply to work in a specific country and on a specific project. The first of August is the deadline for most Fulbright programs for the following academic year. This means most faculty members are applying for something that may or may not happen at least a year ahead of time. If they are like my wife and I who need to repeatedly discuss getting mentally prepared for such a life change, then there is probably a two-year event horizon prior to application. In many cases, the applicant doesn't find out until May that he or she needs to be in another country before the end of the summer.

After applications are submitted, several events occur. The Council for the International Exchange of Scholars (CIES) is the organization that administrates the Fulbright program for the State Department. They screen the applications and pass worthy submissions on to a panel of Fulbright alums that then provide another level of evaluation. If the application makes it through these two assessments, it is then passed on to the U.S. embassy in the specific country where the scholar requested to go. If there is a Bi-lateral Fulbright Commission in the country, then they make the final decision, otherwise it falls in the laps of the Public Affairs Officer (PAO) at the local embassy. The Commission or the PAO is looking for an individual (and their proposed project) that compliments what the U.S. foreign policy is trying to accomplish in a particular part of the world. In my case, I knew about the problems Montenegro was experiencing in their transition from a socialist economy to one that encouraged more private enterprise. I thought I could contribute in that area.

My Dean and departmental Chair both encouraged me to go and wrote thoughtful letters of recommendations. They were both supportive and compassionate men (and good administrators). When I met with them, they were helpful and accommodating. Each one spent several minutes explaining why they could not go on a Fulbright, but wished they could. The Chair had a son who was a senior in high school, and it just would not be fair to pull him out of school with all his friends with him having a chance to play varsity basketball this year. The Dean said that ever since he pulled his back, he worried about being caught in the hinterlands of Lower Slobbovia and needing medical care. He could just see himself getting up one morning, reaching down to tie his shoes, feel his back go out, and then have the rest of the trip bent over or in traction. Until now, these were similar to the reasons I had for not applying.

After I submitted the application, Beth Lynn, my wife, and I did not dare talk about what we hoped would happen lest we jinx the entire approval process. However, every now and then I would get on the Internet and sneak a look at pictures from various Montenegro travel web sites. I mean what could it hurt? I was just browsing, right? It is not as if I was going to get addicted or anything.

In late spring, the letter arrived congratulating me on receiving a Fulbright Scholarship. It was bittersweet as it arrived on a day we were dealing with job and family issues, and, given the problems at the time, we decided it would not be possible to accept the scholarship. This was compounded by the fact that, a few months after I applied, there was a changing of the guard at my university and the new Dean said he would not permit me to go.

Despondent, I talked to a colleague a few days later about my dilemma. After I stated every problem we were facing, he would answer, "Yeah, but you got a Fulbright."

I would respond with what I thought were overwhelming reasons I could not go and he would say, "Yeah, but you got a Fulbright." I told him I was probably not going to be allowed to go anyway, so it really was a moot issue.

He grabbed my lapels and said, "Listen, Dishman, these things only come along once in a lifetime. This is something everybody dreams of doing, and most professors don't even apply. The timing isn't right, they are worried about tenure or their next promotion, or maybe they are secretly scared to go. I don't know. But, you have one *in your hand.* Everybody's got problems, but you're an empty nester, you're healthy—you can go. You don't have to spend the rest of your life here at this institution. Let me ask you, in ten years do you want to be a grouchy, old man; or do you want to be a grouchy, old man with fascinating stories to tell?"

The next day I resigned. It turned out the university down the street was much more interested in having me as a Fulbright Scholar, so I started there the next semester. I returned my letter of acceptance to Washington, D.C., and we began making plans.

At the CIES office, I was assigned to staff member Jean McPeek, a helpful and soft-spoken woman about my age. She guided me through the shoals of understanding stipends and over the boulders of bureaucracy while providing introductions to previous Fulbrighters and relaying all sorts of helpful advice.[1] When we met, she took one look at me and told me to get a physical.

•

Although they tell you getting through the extensive multi-stage approval process is the key to receiving the Fulbright grant, everything actually hinges on the medical examination. The State Department does not want you getting sick while you are overseas and accidently vomiting into the lap of a foreign dignitary during a Presidential state dinner. That had already been done.

To save time, Beth Lynn, and I had our physical examinations during the same appointment. We are a close couple and after seventy years of marriage, there are very few surprises left.[2] Besides, observing your long-time partner being poked and prodded does provide a certain element of sadistic glee.

The exam was thorough—head to toe and all the orifices in between. We had to cough, lean, exhale, bend, spread, and open. For some reason, Beth Lynn had never seen me get a prostate or hernia exam. The first is very personal, but the second borders on the barbaric. She said she did not realize those things could disappear like that but what a brave little boy I was. From various swabbings, scrapings, and punctures we donated all of the four classic humors for lab tests. I think we left with five Band-Aids each but very little humor.

We have a very good relationship with our Primary Healthcare Provider (which is how our insurance plan fondly refers to him). Whenever he examines us, he always tells stories about some previous professional experience we must remind him of.

"Need physicals, eh?" he says as he scans through the official State Department multi-page form.

"Did I ever tell you about the time I was giving this guy a physical and he died in the middle of it? Right there on the table! I'm in the middle of examining

---

1 The best advice I received from a former Fulbrighter was, "Pack your suitcase and fill it with enthusiasm."

2 Thirty-five years for her and thirty-five for me. I say that because, when we try to remember things, it's apparent that it was not the same thirty-five years.

him. I've got the stethoscope on his chest, and I ask him to breathe deep and he *won't.* I look up and he's falling back on the table. I look at the nurse, and she looks at me. I jump up on the table and start pounding on this guy's chest, she calls 911, the paramedics come in, but he was gone. Only guy I've ever heard of dying from a physical."

At this point, I instinctively clinched up; and the doctor just about lost a finger.[3]

Since our last physical examinations a year earlier, somehow I had lost an inch in height. I don't know where it went, but, looking at my belly button, I had my suspicions. For some reason, Beth Lynn was recorded as having *gained* an inch, which delighted her to no end.

It turns out that, not only do you have to get physical examinations from your doctor, but a State Department physician also has to review your own doctor's findings. After three weeks the letter came with our medical clearance approved and we were declared 1-A. We could now officially go.

The PDO

Prior to leaving on a Fulbright you are required to attend a Pre-departure Orientation, or PDO in State Department parlance. They are held in the summer in Washington, D.C.

People in D.C. have their own way of speaking; and you need to crack the code if you are going to understand what they are saying, much less fit in. Everyone outside of Washington, D.C. calls it "Washington, D.C." People there call it "The District." This Metropolitan area is somewhat surrounded by "The Beltway." Those companies (and their employees) that are designated government contractors (Democrat designation) or feed at the government trough (Republican reference) are known as Beltway Bandits. If you are at an office in Arlington, Virginia and you say, "I have to go into the District today" this tells everyone you have something important to do with important people. However, for real officiousness, nothing can top, "I have to go up to the Hill today." This means you are heading to Capitol Hill, the seat of all power. To say it right, you lower your voice and say firmly, "I have to go up to the Hill later today" even if it just to pick up your spouse after work.[4]

---

3 The finger was not where you thought it was. I started thinking that the chances something like that would happen to the same doctor *twice* were so infinitesimally small that I relaxed and he got his finger back.

4 Everyone goes up to the Hill and down to Foggy Bottoms.

When you meet employees of the federal government, they will introduce themselves by saying "Hi! Jones with FSA" or "Welcome, I'm Robinson with WAP." It is not that they expect you to know what those acronyms mean; it is just they rarely socialize professionally with anyone outside of their own departments. If you ask what the initials mean, they are delighted to explain what they do. Usually, by the end of the explanation, they always apologize about how boring their job actually is.

There seems to be no rhyme or reason for the way federal employees refer to their own departments. The people that work for the Department of Justice work for the DOJ. The same goes for the Department of Transportation (DOT). The people that work for the United States Department of State[5] do not work for DOS; they work for "State." For those toiling in the Department of Agriculture, they do not refer to it as DOA nor is it "Agriculture" either. It is the *US*DA.[6]

At the PDO, we met people from all over the United States. There were about 200 scholars and students at the briefing. Our PDO was only one of three the State Department conducts every year. There is a session for those going to the Far East, one for Europe and Eurasia, and one for South America. We were surprised at the number of people who were "going home" on their Fulbright. Most of these people were natives from other countries like Bangalore, Pakistan, and Ghana. One was a surgeon who was going back to teach new facial reconstructive techniques. Others were teachers who wanted to improve elementary education levels in schools they had attended as children. They were all making small but significant contributions to those countries that were so dear to them with training they had received here in the U.S. It was very humbling and inspiring.

Our son and his family live in the D.C. area, so the PDO provided the additional benefit of visiting them and our one-and-only grandson, the scion of the Dishman family fortune.[7] The night before the PDO, we took everyone out for a late Chinese dinner. My fortune cookie read, "You are about to embark on a most delightful journey." I kept that little slip of paper with me the entire trip. I still carry it and re-read it occasionally just to remind me that there is an adventure right around the corner.

---

5 United States Department of State always sounds rather redundant to me. In this current climate of political extremism, maybe we ought to have a United States Department of United.

6 Who wants to be DOA?

7 The fortune consists of a mortgage, miscellaneous personal property, and a 401(k) in the red.

T Minus 168 Hours and Counting

Five months of strategic planning had now come down to seven days of sheer panic. As we got closer to our departure date, anxiety flared up on the domestic front. Beth Lynn got ulcers, I started grinding my teeth at night; and we became obsessed with lists (and lists of lists). We had the packing list, the shipping list, the how-to-take-care-of-the-house list, the gift list, the medicine list, and the legal list (otherwise known as the what-to-do-if-we-don't-make-it-back list). We updated our wills and executed a power of attorney should something, very unexpected happen. The trouble with having two kids who are attorneys is they had to review everything. I think they were going to rewrite several of the documents, but thought better of it. We typed up itineraries and sent them to parents, kids, neighbors, and bosses with strict instructions should something startling occur. The last few weeks of preparation happened just before the Christmas holidays, so packing early for the trip was a priority. Decorating the house consisted of putting up the tree, and throwing some ornaments in its general direction. We had to have a tree up as our grandchild was coming to spend his first Christmas with us. Our big present was seeing him crawl for the first time.[8]

Several people were supposed to live in our house while we were gone. One by one, they cancelled until it was too late for us to get anyone else. We had a friend, a retired police officer, who agreed to watch the house only on the condition he could play trains on the layout in the basement. He gave the house his professional once over and suggested some minor security improvements such as deadbolts, bars for the windows and sliding glass doors, and timers for lights and televisions. He came by periodically while we were gone and randomized the timers so they didn't come on at the same time every day. We cancelled the newspaper, cable television, and had the local postmistress hold the mail. We covered all the furniture with bed sheets to fend off the dust.

One Sunday morning, I slipped on my good shoes and one didn't feel quite right.

---

8 This prompted two observations. One is that our grandson did not have enough incentive to crawl toward anything until he met his grandfather. Two, considering that was the highlight of our holiday season, we are very easily entertained. This is also the difference between men and women. After the trip, when we ran into old friends and they asked what was new, I always led off with the Fulbright, but Beth Lynn told them about our new grandson, accompanied by a multi-media presentation on her smart phone.

I took it off and inside was a small note that read "2.1 lbs." I had been so busy trying to wrap things up at work I had not realized our home had become a plethora of Post-it notes placed on various objects. They read:

"Don't touch. This is for the trip."

"Eat this cereal up before starting on that one." (With a right arrow pointing at another box.)

"Keep this clean."

"Use this one, not that one."

"Put in safety deposit box."

"Send to kids."

"File with will and personal papers."

"Where does this go?"

As we were going to be gone from January through June, we had to pack clothes for three seasons and still keep it under the airline weight limit. The fact that we had to take clothes and shoes for winter, spring, and summer, made the planning all that more difficult. If we were going to Hawaii, I could have fit everything I needed in the pockets of my bathing suit and then just worn that. However, this trip was going to require a major planning effort. Fortunately, Beth Lynn was born with superior spatial intelligence; and she loves such challenges. I have seen her pack clothes for a family of four on a five-week, cross-country road trip into two small suitcases with enough room left over for snacks and one of the kids.

She declared that, because the packing was going to take a while, whatever I wanted to take on the trip needed to be in the laundry two weeks before our departure date. If I wore anything after that, she could not guarantee it would make the cut. Thus, I began a very close relationship with a worn-out pair of jeans and a single set of underwear.

We had heard through the Fulbright grapevine that there were no dry-cleaners in Montenegro.[9] This news flash prompted a diligent "drop everything else" weeklong search in stores and on-line to find me dress slacks that could be machine washed. We looked through various travel apparel web sites recommended by our globe-trotting friends. The sites did have such pants; but they looked as though you needed the boots, hat, and whip to finish out the complete Indiana Jones ensemble. I could not imagine myself going to work dressed like that. (Well, not every day.) Beth Lynn did manage to find several

9 It turns out this was not entirely true but dry cleaning was such a novelty that nobody used it except the foreign embassy personnel. That, and the fact that it cost about twelve dollars per shirt (on a hanger).

pair of machine washable slacks at a discount store near the house, most of which were in my size.

She had read that the domestic weight allowance on our airline was fifty pounds per bag, and that certain lofty frequent flyer status levels (such as Platinum, Titanium, or Einsteinium) could ship several bags without any fees. After looking at what we were going to be allowed to take, I believe my (in) frequent flying behavior had attained me the high rank of Rust. We had to limit ourselves to two suitcases and two carry-ons each. Given these parameters, Beth Lynn's approach was to identify clusters of clothes and sundries that could be packed, stacked, and folded into freezer bags that were then individually weighed and labeled. It turns out that not diamonds, but polyethylene bags are a girl's best friend. Each was individually labeled with such tags as:

"3 Winter Sweaters 2.1 lbs."

"Cosmetics 3.5 lbs."

"Four Dress shirts 3 lbs."

"Dresses 3 lbs."

"Long Sleeve Blouses and Misc. Sweaters 3.25 lbs."

"Shoes: Day-to-Day 4.5 lbs."

"Shoes: Special Occ. 2.75 lbs."

"Gifts to go 4.3 lbs. (Did we get everybody covered?)"

"Medicines, Topicals, Diarrhea Med. 2.5 lbs."

"Gum 1 lb."

Taking the suggestions of some *ex-pats*[10] we talked to, we agreed to take one comfort food item each.11 Each piece of luggage had a list of what was going to go in it (by weight). Thus, she had created a huge three-dimensional puzzle where pieces could be changed around depending on the space available and the total weight in each suitcase. However, for all of this to work she needed room—lots of room.

"Sweetheart, where are the little zipper bags for my shirts and ties?" I asked.

"They are in the closet in the other bedroom. But don't go in there. That is now Staging Area A. It is for all items that begin with A-M."

"What's all the stuff in the living room?"

"That is Staging Area B."

---

10 "Expat" is short for *ex-patriate*, a person who lives in a country or culture other than his or her own. (But, doesn't it sound like you are referring to someone who was previously Irish?)

11 About a month into our trip we unwillingly celebrated LAPD-Last American Product Day. This is when all the comfort consumables you have brought from home have been eaten or used up.

"N through Z, I assume?"

"Of course. Now don't go in there, either. If you need anything, ask me; and I will get it for you. And for heaven's sake, *do not* move or rearrange anything, even if it is not in those rooms." This last caveat was important as some of the planning was spilling out into the hallway and alphabetically down the stairs. In the middle of an empty space on the living room floor, there was a note that read, "Do not use this space. This is where the medicine goes. (Pick up on Tuesday)." I went and examined all the *matériel* that was sorted by weight in perfect rows on the furniture and floor of each room and noticed there weren't any of my things anywhere.

"Dear, where, pray tell, are my clothes?"

"Oh, I'm just throwing all your stuff in that little carry-on bag over there."

Every day she would pack the entire set of luggage. Every night I would come home from work and she would have me lift each bag three times from a hanging scale she had bought. If the average of the weighing was over forty-nine and a half pounds for any given bag, there would be under-the-breath cursing and she would open all the bags and spend the next day re-packing everything all over again. This went on for a fortnight. With a week to go before we left, it was apparent not all of our essential items could go. We had to have serious discussions about what we could jettison because we really did not need it or we could replace it once we got over there. I thought I was being very helpful pointing out how many things of hers fell into the "unnecessary" category. I am still somewhat hurt my suggestions were not taken more seriously.

By making judicious (and somewhat reluctant) decisions, and with her constant rearranging, repacking, and re-stuffing, each evening we watched as the weighing results went from fifty to forty-nine pounds for each bag. (She thought it best to have a little fudge factor should our hand scale not match up with the scales at the airline counter). She was very proud of her work and with good reason. She could not wait to see the "official" results on the ticket counter scales.

When we got to the airport, she had to personally lift each bag up and look at the scale results for herself.

"See, they are all under fifty pounds!" she said, triumphantly.

The ticket agent said, "That's not an issue, ma'am. Since you are travelling internationally, you get two bags up to seventy pounds each."

She was crushed.

•

Before leaving the country, we planned a layover in Washington, D.C. with our children, as we desperately needed a grandkid fix before we left the country for six months. After our son and daughter-in-law had left for work in the morning, we got to spend the day with our daughter, who was serving as a temporary nanny, and grandson. Beth Lynn spent the time repacking the laundry she had done and redistributing the weight load between the suitcases. The seven-month-old decided to help by crawling in the open luggage and burrowing under the new clean clothes. We tried to encourage the little stowaway, but our daughter thought his parents might miss him after a day or two. I know we did.[12]

The kids lived in a 1930s house that had not had any tender-loving care in many years. Because of that, I was worried it was very close to being just that—tinder. There were no grounded plugs in the house, it sagged toward the center of the foundation, and there was a large basement stacked with very old wooden furniture. The wallpaper was peeling and the roof leaked. I thought as long as the roof leaked, the basement storage was probably staying damp enough to be fireproof, but it had to be growing penicillin fuzz down there. Baseboards and door trim carpentry were coming unattached from the walls. If you opened the downstairs bathroom door without pulling to the left, the entire exterior wall paneling would fall off. It was an old house that had long outlived its initial beauty, but it was located in one of the most sought-after neighborhoods in Arlington, on George Washington Parkway, right off the Potomac. It sat across from a state park with deer, fox, raccoons, and opossums in the backyard. It was a great place to live, just a bad place to live in. However, now that the baby had arrived, it gave them more room than their previous expensive one-bedroom apartment.

While we were in D.C., I was able to get an appointment with the Montenegrin Ambassador to the U.S., His Excellency, Ambassador Miodrag Vlahović. He was kind enough to allow me to pay my respects and introduce myself. We met on a Saturday morning on what had to be one of his few days off. He was casually dressed and had left the front door of the embassy open for me. He is a tall, square-faced man with a serious countenance that indicated his important responsibilities that included preparing for a state visit from the Prime Minister later in the week. Vlahović generously spent over an hour briefing me on the political and economic situation in Montenegro. Trained as an attorney, he served in the transition government as Foreign Minister, among many other roles. He said he was proud of helping Montenegro become an independent

---

12 In the airport, I later saw a magnet that explained, "Grandchildren are spoiled because you can't spank grandparents."

state, and especially proud that there was no violence or "excitement" when it happened—even though the vote was very close. Montenegro had a limited Foreign Ministry budget, so Vlahović had to serve as the ambassador to both the U.S. and Canada.

To provide further insight into the unique history that is Montenegro's, on July 13, 1878, it became the 27th independent country in the world. Then, on May 21, 2006, it became the 192nd independent country in the world having been absorbed into other countries during the interim. During the 2006 election for independence, only 2,300 people made the difference between autonomy and the country remaining part of Serbia.

Montenegro was then politically independent showing the world that it was no longer part of the evil state of Serbia and or its criminal leader, Slobodan Milošević. The fact that all the leaders of the new country were all Milošević's protégés should not lead you to believe they had anything to do with him or his policies. However, they were at least politically astute enough to know when to get off that bus and hang their future on being a distinct country, perhaps as part of the European Union. The vote for independence was a miracle in itself. No one was killed, the larger country from which they were separating, acknowledged the vote without major dispute, and it was the first time in their history, the fate of Montenegro was decided by the Montenegrins rather than at a conference of Great Powers where they had no representation or influence whatsoever.[13]

•

Our first night in D.C., both our daughter and daughter-in-law came down with what turned out to be a twenty-four hour bug, which kept two of the three bathrooms busy most of the night. They felt better by Sunday when we had to leave, but we carefully stayed away from women who were ill because we didn't want to catch anything and have to postpone our departure. For our last meal with them, we drove to National Harbor in Maryland and dined looking at the lights of Alexandria reflecting on the Potomac. It was a wonderful evening.

The next morning we had to leave for the airport. As there was obviously something "going around," we avoided kissing. It was hard to keep that rule when we were saying goodbye for half a year. The taxi was fifteen minutes early creating a time crisis. (The driver was smart enough to start the meter when I

13 The history of Montenegro is so captivating and intriguing, I was tempted to include it all from about 1,300 B.C. to this very minute. Cooler heads prevailed.

said we would be out in five minutes.) This meant cramming clothes into places they were not planned for and very rushed goodbyes.

We had to grab some lunch at the airport before we got on the plane to Europe. Here was my absolutely last chance to have a truly American meal. What to choose? Panda Express? Taco Bell? Sbarro Pizza? I realized that group of fast food places said as much about the melting pot of America as anything. After a lengthy internal debate, I made my decision. I'm sorry, I couldn't help it. As much as people disparage the menu, my choice was instinctive. It was the most American thing I could think of. *And, it was good.* Because Beth Lynn was feeling a little depressed about leaving, I picked her up a Happy Meal, too.

It turns out I needn't have bothered eating at the airport. Ninety minutes into the flight, they served us hot Pasta Primavera. I unwrapped my napkin, arranged my utensils, carefully removed the plastic cover over the entrée, and promptly threw up all over my food. The next eight and a half hours of the flight was a vomitus blur with my regurge regulator going off every hour on the hour. I shivered from chills and moaned in stupor. If you have ever found yourself in this position on a plane, after you experience the first gastric displacement, you look up to find just how empty the plane really is as your fellow passengers who were seated directly around you have suddenly decided the reading light is better two rows over. The other embarrassing part of this experience is the "Dead Man Walking" trek to the back of the plane carrying the now full disposable bag and trying to pretend the huge wet spot on your chest is part of the shirt design.

When we landed in London, they had a wheelchair waiting for me at the gate. We were worried with the H1N1 virus scare that I would be whisked off to British quarantine like a cocker spaniel, but it turned out they did not even have a First Aid clinic at Gatwick Airport. It might also have had to do with the fact that the flight attendants (who could not have been kinder) somehow got the impression my illness was merely due to airsickness. Because of my weakened state, Beth Lynn had to lug four suitcases, four carry-ons, and one husband outside, on and off the shuttle bus, and all the way over to the next terminal for us to catch our connecting flight to Podgorica.

Livin' La Vida Local

First Day on The Ground

Four hours later, we landed at the new Podgorica, Montenegro airport and passed through Immigration with relative ease. In our first twenty-two and a half hours here, we had to find our apartment, catch some sleep (which neither of us got on the plane), get at least *some* groceries, and do some repacking. We then had to head back to the airport, in order to fly to Venice where I was to speak at an academic conference. We had departed Salt Lake City in the midst of its typical winter inversion and had left one dreary, cloud-covered, smoggy city and arrived in another. Montenegro's capital city lies in an expansive valley ringed by mountains on all sides except to the southwest where Lake Skadar, the largest freshwater lake in Europe, sits. At first glance, this Zeta plain appears to be a sunken caldera. As we landed, we were surprisingly struck by how similar the geography is to the Wasatch Front where we live—a large lake, fertile valleys, surrounded by tall, snow-capped mountains.

After clearing customs and our heads, we arranged for transportation into town. Parked in front of the airport terminal were ten new, shiny black Mercedes sedans that served as the taxis.[1] As nice as these Mercedes are, they had nothing larger. With our entire luggage ensemble, we had to take two separate cabs. We thought it best to split up in order to keep an eye on the bags, so I put Beth Lynn in the cab with the driver who spoke English, so she would feel a little less uncomfortable. She found out during the twenty-minute trip he would speak only to other males, and the concept of caravanning with another cab was lost on him. After a few minutes of sheer terror and visions of white slavery, much to her relief, both cabs arrived at the apartment building at the same time.

---

1 Only new cabs greet the arriving visitors at the airport; the old ones they keep in town.

Housing is the most difficult problem most Fulbrighters encounter.[2] Typically, they arrive in their host country and immediately check into an expensive hotel (because that is what Americans do). Some scholars then spend the next week living out of a suitcase, accumulating laundry, searching for an apartment, and becoming more and more discouraged until, out of desperation, they take housing arrangements they end up not really liking. There are signs all over the country, especially in the tourist areas, advertising an *Apartman.* After seeing such signs for the umpteenth time, we invented a super-hero whose powers included being faster than an apathetic elevator, more powerful than a 220-volt vacuum, and able to leap lengthy leases in a single bound.

We had been fortunate enough to have the previous Fulbright Scholar tell us about the place she had rented. She had sent pictures of the interior, and it seemed very nice. This was fortunate because otherwise I think after Beth Lynn took one look at the outside of the building, she might have gotten right back into the cab and returned to the airport on her own. Drab gray architecture from the Communist era fills Podgorica, and this building was no exception. Exteriors and common areas are tenement-like with scarred walls, faded paint, and the ever-present graffiti. However, the interior apartments are neat, clean, homey, hospitable, and cheerful. The architecture is much like the Montenegrin people—scarred, weather-beaten, and tough on the outside but warm and inviting inside.

We were to meet our landlady and her husband at the apartment, so they could let us in. As the two cabs drove off, we looked around at our new home and smiled cautiously at each other. This was definitely going to be an adventure. We immediately discovered apartment buildings in Montenegro do not have addresses but *staircases* do. We found the exterior door to our staircase and learned another little cultural tidbit—there were no individual apartment numbers.

From the front door, it was up half a flight of stairs to the "lobby" where there was an elevator the size of a phone booth. It was large enough for two people or one person and one suitcase, but it was obvious it was going to take about eight trips to get our luggage up to the apartment. How were we going to watch the luggage at both ends? According to the lease, the apartment was on the third floor. But, the previous tenant said it was on the fourth floor (the first floor being designated the "zeroth" floor). I took one suitcase and rode the lift to the third floor thinking there might be a door ajar indicating which apartment was ours. Every door on both of the floors was closed, and none had the name on the

2 We were determined to face our new life without Balkan.

door that we were looking for. So, being a brash American, I knocked at every apartment. Nobody answered. I did the same thing on the floor above and got the same results. This was not good. I went back down to report to Beth Lynn who was guarding the luggage on the first floor by laying on top of them with her eyes closed. I decided to go next door to the bakery and ask to use the phone. Just as I was opening the door to the aroma of freshly baked bread, I heard my name being called.

I turned around, and a very lovely, dark-haired woman was crossing the street to speak to me. I am not used to this from attractive women. It was one more indication that we were in a foreign country. She was tall with long black hair, a radiant complexion, and pixie smile. Jelena Jovanović and her family had been sitting in the Unico restaurant across the street watching for us to arrive. Her husband, Goran, followed her over, and we met the Jovanovići family in the middle of the street. They surprised us by giving the typical, warm Montenegrin greeting of three kisses on alternating cheeks. Jelena worked in the marketing department of a regional airline and Goran was an attorney who had played on the Montenegrin national basketball team.[3] It showed. He was as tall and handsome as she was beautiful. We thought they had to have been elected Homecoming king and queen when they attended ol' Montenegrin U. Goran shooed us up to the apartment while he carried all of our bags up the stairs, in one trip. She let us into the apartment; and, fortunately, it was just like the photographs we had been sent. After a briefing about which key went where and what buttons to push on the various appliances, we freshened up and joined their family across the street where we met their daughters, Ivanica and Dorica, ages eight and ten. The two little girls were wide-eyed at the American strangers but tried hard to practice the English they had been learning in school. As we responded with Montenegrin phrases, we proceeded to emphasize the wrong syl*lab*le in each word, much to the amusement of the girls. The more I looked at them, the more I was astounded at how much they reminded me of my American Radovich cousins when they were that age. It was a wonderful way to be welcomed to a strange country, and they made us feel very much at home.

•

The next morning for some reason, we woke up very refreshed at 2:00 a.m., which did not make any sense, as that was actually 8:00 p.m. body time. Nevertheless, we were alert and able to Skype with our children and tell them we

---

3 Because of his athletic experience, everybody in the country knew Goran.

made it to Montenegro. After a rejuvenating conversation, we reluctantly went back to bed and did not wake up until 10:00 a.m. feeling much groggier than we had at 2:00 a.m., obviously from the suboptimal somnambulism.

I could not wait to get out and explore our new world. Due to time constraints, this adventure had to be limited to walking down our block and getting preliminary provisions. It was late in the morning when I finally left our apartment with the small, but not inconsequential task, of rustling up some grub. I went armed with Beth Lynn's grocery list and my Serbian phrase book. I need not have worried as most of the products turned out to have some English on them, although it often was third or fourth on a list of eight different languages. I started walking and, within a block, I had passed a bakery, a meat market, two green grocers, and a tiny little grocery store named Mercator Mex. It was about the size of a small 7-11 and the aisles were very small. If you were standing there reading labels, and someone needed to get by, you had to turn, flatten your body up against the shelves, and become very intimate with certain canned goods.

Before I had left the apartment, Beth Lynn said, "Here take this. Europeans take their own shopping bags."

She handed me a loud pink zebra print bag with a shoulder strap. *O-kay.*

"Don't you have another one?" I asked.

"Yeah, but it's smaller. You'll need this large one to carry the paper towels and toilet paper."

I got a lot of strange looks carrying that bag down the street. By the way, if anyone asks, the stores there provided plastic grocery sacks, same as everywhere else. I bought the things we had to have and spent a lot of time examining snack foods and things we could eat without cooking. I ended up buying a lot more than one pink zebra-striped bag full. By the time I lugged everything all the way down the street and back upstairs to the apartment, I could see we would be restricting our diet by eliminating heavy groceries because I did not want to do that again. We immediately broke open the packaged chow. The next few minutes were an orgy of opening packages and sharing flavors. I did not know if we were so famished or the food was that good.

"Here, take a bit of this pastry—it's apple."

"Oh, my word—try this strawberry yogurt!"

"Oh, wow! Taste these shoestring potato chips. They're ketchup flavored."

The milk was from Serbia. The soap was from Croatia. The Kit-Kat candy bar was from Hungary. The orange juice was bottled in Slovenia. The bread was from downstairs.

If you go to maps.google.com and type in "14 Ivana Vujoševića, Podgorica, Montenegro" you will see our apartment building. We lived on the right hand corner of Ivana Vujoševića and Bulevar Revolucije. By changing to "Satellite" view and zooming in you will see a parking lot behind the building to the right. We lived on the third floor, and our balcony overlooked that parking lot. If you zoom in once more and look three balconies from the left, you might be able to see us sitting there, relishing our newfound fare, enjoying the view, but thinking about all the unpacking we had to do.

It would just have to wait.

Apartman!

"I dislike feeling at home when I am abroad."

—George Bernard Shaw

One of the most significant adjustments for us in our new life was simply the change from our almost bucolic lifestyle in Utah to living downtown in a large, noisy capital city. In the U.S., we live in a quiet house in a quiet neighborhood on the side of a quiet mountain with empty lots on all sides of us. Traffic jams are caused by deer in the street, and the only noise is from cheerful birds and light wind rustling the leaves. The only time we even hear another voice besides ours is during the summer when we sleep with our windows open and hear the occasional laughter or argument drifting in on the breeze.

Living in an apartment was something we had not done since we were first married, which did add a certain romantic aspect to it. However, it took some time and several sets of earplugs to finally get used to the voices and noises coming from all directions. The clamor started at six o'clock every morning, stayed fairly constant throughout the day, and ended sometime after eleven at night—all from the hustle and bustle of modern, metropolitan lives compressed together.

It turned out we were the third Fulbrighters to rent this apartment. Academics make good tenants. They pay on time, keep the places clean, and the loudest noise they make is the turning of a page in a book.[1] The apartment was a one-bedroom affair with a living room, kitchen and dinette, and a bathroom/ utility room totaling about four hundred square feet. The apartment had been our

---

1 However, my office is messy. I like to keep it that way and I am fairly anal retentive about that.

landlord's bachelor pad before he got married, and the new bride and groom had spent a few years there as a couple before their kids started arriving.

It was a great place to live. The location was very urban, but not in the very center of town. The building was located across the street from the *Agencija za Nacionalnu Bezbjednost*, the Montenegrin National Security Agency. This was not unusual for us. It had happened before in other countries when we had been booked into hotels as guests of the host government. It was also quite common that the respective country's national security agency was always conveniently located adjacent to the American Embassy.

As previously mentioned, the apartment building had a tiny elevator, which Beth Lynn and I could take together, but only because we were already married. To get it to operate, you had to open the exterior door which turned on the light. You then shut the exterior door (making sure it clicked) and closed the bi-fold interior door that turned off the light. At this point, you had to feel around in the dark for the button for your floor. If, during the trip, anyone accidently opened the exterior door on any of the other floors, the elevator would come to an abrupt halt trapping you in the darkness. The first native phrase we learned after "Good Morning" was how to yell, "Shut the door!" (*"Zatvori Vrata!"*) with a great deal of meaning. We only used the elevator if we had luggage that was too heavy to lug up or down the stairs. Otherwise, we lived in a fourth-floor walk-up.

The first time we entered the apartment, we noticed there were keys in all the interior doorknobs as well. I was worried that we not only had to lock the outside door, but for additional security, we had to lock our bedroom as well. Perhaps this is not as safe a place as we were told. I knew I had to approach this judicially with Jelena as I did not want her to think we are being overly critical the first ten seconds after arrival.

"I noticed the doors all have keys in them."

"Da?"

"Are they there for a reason?"

"Da."

I thought it best not to say anything at this point and just to look inquisitive.

"Da. Where would *you* keep the keys?" She gave me a shrug and a look like "what else would you do?"

As I was to receive that look from someone at least once a day during our entire visit, I started to refer to it as the "WEWYD look". It is characterized by the simultaneous tilting of the head, lowering of the eyebrows, and shrugging of the shoulders.

Jelena showed us that the front door and its frame were steel, and the lock had five deadbolts. To open the door, you had to turn the key five times. After that we both felt very safe.

The apartment was supposed to be a quiet one. The previous tenant attested to that. However, I think in the interim, new neighbors had moved in next door. Jelena now thought there was a business being run out of that apartment ("nothing illegal—don't worry"). During the morning hours, we heard many women's voices. As we did not speak the local language, it was difficult to tell if they were talking to one another or working a bank of phones. About noon, a man would come in and his voice could be heard over the women's, shouting orders at them. After lunch until just before bedtime, there was a lull in activity. Then, two nights a week there was a group of men having some sort of meeting. Sometimes they would carry on until 2:00 a.m. or later. We could not tell if it was a business conference, a political rally, sports on TV, or something more sinister, like a multi-level marketing opportunity meeting. Except for the business next door, the apartments were relatively quiet. Aromas in the halls were something else again. There were days when I would linger in the hallways sniffing and trying to get high from the wonderfully exotic cooking smells that made me salivate almost twenty-four hours a day.

The apartment interior was decorated in yellow-orange, including the furniture and the accents were a bright orange. It was like living inside a pumpkin.[2] But, a very nice pumpkin, as all the furniture was new and modern. Thin space heaters standing two feet tall along two walls of the living room warmed the apartment. Each one had an adjustment dial. Coming from the mountains, we sleep cold; but the previous tenant liked it warm. When we arrived, they were set at 30° C (86° F). There was an additional space heater in our bedroom that had a knob and three switches. None of them had any writing or symbols. We couldn't make heads or tails out of them or tell any difference when they were switched, singularly or in unison. When it got particularly cold, we simply plugged it in at night and unplugged it in the morning. The living room had an air conditioner unit mounted high on the wall. It was conveniently controlled by a remote we used on more than one occasion to try to turn on the TV.

The dishwasher was Russian, the refrigerator was Serbian, the hot water heater was Italian, and the microwave was in English. The refrigerator did not

---

2 Perhaps the owners knew that people who stayed here in the wintertime would need a color to brighten up their world. It certainly helped us.

have a freezer compartment.[3] Appliances that required a lot of electricity were rare. Thus, there was no clothes dryer either. The dishwasher held enough plates and dishes from two people eating two meals. There was also no disposal. We had to take our garbage out back to the dumpster. (Inexplicably, it was not the dumpster directly behind our building but the one behind the fish market in the next block.) The kitchen was completely stocked with pots, pans, dishes, spices, and, lots of booze. The bedroom contained a double bed and, beside it, a single bed because the previous tenants had been a woman and her son. There were two large built-in closets with plenty of storage room.

Only a few weeks into our stay we were awakened at 3:25 a.m. by what sounded like a large explosion followed by a whole lotta shakin' going on accompanied by the deep rumble of an earthquake. Our bed walked away from the wall while the entire building above us made ominous creaking noises. It turned out to be 4.3 on the Richter scale with the epicenter only 12 miles away on the shores of Lake Skadar. After the motion stopped, we could tell everyone else in the building was awake because we heard lots of talking, people examining personal items on shelves, neighbors checking on older neighbors, and lots of toilets flushing. Then, it was quiet again. I don't know if there was any actual structural damage, but after that morning my sliding closet door refused to stay shut. I would carefully close it and it would slowly roll back open as though somebody was hiding in the closet and didn't want the door to close.

In the bathroom, there was a toilet, sink, washing machine, a hot water heater above that, and the shower. I am a shower person and Beth Lynn is a bath person. She likes a long, quiet, hot soak at the end of the day while I prefer actually getting clean. Having only a small, quarter-round shower was a big sacrifice for her. However, with some contortion, she could take a bath in the well of the shower if she sat with her knees up under her chin and put one arm out the sliding glass door. The two spigots in the shower were either scalding or freezing. I learned to be very careful when bending over to wash my feet lest I accidently hit one of the taps sending the water temperature to *surprise!*

The apartment had small, individual hot water heaters, which don't store a lot of water. But, unlike our own house, you don't have to run the tap wide open for twenty minutes while you wait for the hot water to arrive from some geothermal-like feature 300 feet below the basement. The heater made about seven minutes of hot water, enough for a shower but not enough for two. We learned to time our cleaning rituals and never accidently turn off the third light

---

3 It took some getting used to the fact that, for the next six months there was not going to be any ice, ice baby.

switch from the left as that controlled the hot water heater. The bathroom was heated by an exposed thick electrical coil that glowed red-hot when switched on and was very dangerous, or it would have been if it wasn't seven feet off the ground.

There was a single twenty-watt light bulb over the sink. It put out just enough light so that, in the morning, you could recognize yourself in the mirror.[4] This was so much different from the floodlights we have at home where, when I am shaving, I can see each individual pore. With the lack of lighting in the bathroom, I did the best I could shaving and fixing my hair; but it was only an approximation. Details were lost. If I got distracted while I was shaving, I might forget an entire side of my face and leave the apartment looking like a walking before-and-after advertisement. I had thought seriously about growing a beard, but the one and only time I did was when I got an adult onset of measles and could not shave for three weeks. I thought I looked good in it, but Beth Lynn thought it fell under the You-Are-Scaring-the-Children category.

Upon first usage, I could not help but notice I did not fit on the toilet seat. We were not the same size. If I got one cheek situated where it felt comfortable, the other was perching precariously on the opposite inside rim. My entire balance was off. On closer inspection, I realized the toilet seat was rectangular, not oval, like the ones upon which I had been tenderly trained. Are Montenegrins built differently than Americans in that department? This is not something that had come to my attention thus far. However, based on the repeatedly uncomfortable position I found myself in, I promised to observe this anatomical issue more closely. If there was a difference between their derrieres and mine, it would go a long way in explaining this unique seat design.

The small washing machine in the bathroom could only hold a small amount of clothes. This was also true for the drying rack we set up in the living room (because it was constantly wet and rainy outside). Thus, Beth Lynn ended up doing laundry every day. We finally got used to the concept of living with our laundry and having it hanging from every place available. When the drying rack would get full, we would hang our wet clothes over the back of chairs and sofas, across the kitchen table, over the footboard on the bed, and in the shower stall. At least the apartment always smelled clean and "As Fresh as All Outdoors." I learned that if I was working at home on the couch and Beth Lynn was doing the laundry, it was advisable to keep moving lest a damp towel be thrown over me and my laptop.

---

[4] At my age, that requires glasses and no fear whatsoever.

Since the labels on the washing machine dials were in Serbian, Jelena had to show Beth Lynn how to operate it. There were three compartments, and Jelena poured two cups of laundry detergent into the first one, then another two cups in the second one, and a cup of softener in the third. She helped Beth Lynn put in our clothes, started the machine, smiled, and then left. Beth Lynn then pulled up a chair and watched the laundry through the glass portal thinking with all that detergent inserted, the soapsuds were going to end up all over the floor and would never come out of our clothes. She said she was going to have to wash that load at least three times with just plain water to remove the residue. The express cycle alone took ninety minutes. We never used the regular cycle, as we couldn't estimate how much soap it would need or how many days it would take to finish. It turned out the setting that Jelena showed us was the right one; our clothes came out cleaned and rinsed.

There is nothing in Montenegro that is packaged in an aerosol can—no hairspray, no cooking spray, and no spray starch. Due to this, it took a while for Beth Lynn to master the concept of how Montenegrins got wrinkles out of their clothes when ironing. Jelena said we had to purchase a starch that got mixed with water and then poured into the iron.

"Iz too hard to exchplain. Come. I just scho you at schtore."

Fortunately, the store was literally across the street. After fighting our way through the crowded store scanning every shelf, Jelena went to the checkout girl to inquire and came back to report.

"Sche does not carry schpray sczartch," she said, pointing to a gap on the shelf. "Djou must go to Delta City." (Making one more thing to put on the list for the gigantic grocery store we kept hearing about at the local mall.)

Each apartment had a twenty-four square foot exterior balcony. The balconies were as varied as the residents. Some areas had discarded appliances like old hot water heaters stacked in corners. Some had chairs for sitting and watching the people below. Still others had voluminous flowers that bloomed at the first sign of spring. Some of the drabbest balconies in the winter became completely enveloped in beautiful red blossoms overnight. A few of the balconies had been enclosed with shades or permanent windows to make sleeping porches out of them. Whatever the balcony was used for, the functionality of drying laundry had to be taken into consideration. All the balconies were filled with laundry drying on ropes and racks. Clotheslines had to be installed next to the ceiling and the chairs or plants had to be arranged so there could be a row of bed sheets hanging between them. The laundry was there whatever the weather. If the rain was blowing onto the balcony, the laundry was left until it was dry. On one balcony, we saw washing hung in the precipitation for twelve days straight. We wondered what the tenants were doing for clothes.

Walking up a hill overlooking Podgorica a few days later, we paused a moment to take in the cityscape. On the side of one of the newer apartment buildings was painted its name, "Normal Habitat." We realized this was going to be our own new habitat and way of living for the next six months.

In Communicado

Our living room had two comfortable sofas around a large flat-screen television with "Extra TV" cable service. By flipping through the channels, we found we received three Serbian channels, two Montenegrin government channels, two Croatian, two Hungarian, one Slovenian, one Italian, one Albania, one French, and Serbian MTV. The only channel that was always in English was BBC World, which, surprisingly, paid little attention to our hometown news.

It was interesting to hear *The Simpsons* argue in Croatian but only for about ten minutes. Indijana Džouns would occasionally be shown with accompanying cartoons of Džordže iz Džungle. Sometimes one of the channels would air an American show like CSI and have subtitles rather than voice dubbing. Because it was in English, we would watch it even if we had seen it several times before.

Television networks in Europe are a conglomeration of culture. During February, Beth Lynn watched the Canadian Olympics on Eurosport, a British division of a French broadcasting company, which had Croatian announcers speaking over the English commentators and was sponsored by commercials from Austria. One channel did run English-language programs occasionally. Its evening line-up might include shows such as "Foster's Home for Imaginary Friends," "Wife, Mom, Bounty Hunter," and "Sex Change Hospital." We ended up reading a lot.

The apartment already had a phone installed, and we found the local telephone system required training in advanced mathematics. If you were calling mobile-to-mobile, you just used the last six digits of the phone number. If you were calling locally to another landline, you added a zero in front of the last eight digits. When people gave you their number, you needed to know (0)20 XXX XXX meant a landline, (0)67 XXX XXX or (0)69 XXX XXX meant a mobile phone. Thus, our apartment landline phone number was +382 (0) 20 247 344. However, people calling from overseas didn't have to insert the additional zero.

If someone wanted to call from the States, he or she would dial 011 (international access), 382 (Montenegro country code), 20 (Podgorica city code), and 247 043 (without the zero). However, most of this turned out to be superfluous as everybody used a mobile phone within Montenegro since it was cheaper to call mobile-to-mobile than it was from landline to mobile or vice versa. The few times we used the landline was because Jelena had called us and said, "I kouldn't get djou on djour mobile. Now, hang up and call me back."

There was no voice mail on mobile phones in Montenegro, as the companies don't have the server bandwidth. Therefore, if you didn't get someone on the phone, you hung up and texted them a message. We lived there three months before it dawned on me I did not even know what the main emergency services number was. It turned out there is no master 911-like number. 122 dialed the police; the fire department was 123; and 124 got you an ambulance.

Email, Skype, and Vonage were our links home. Every morning we couldn't wait to open our email and get those nice notes from Barnes and Noble, Borders, Hertz, Avis, and American Express. They offered us books we could not buy, free day rentals we could not use, and tips on using credit cards that wouldn't work in the Balkans. Hilton offered me discounts on hotels, the closest of which was three thousand miles away. The crazy thing was we were so starved for English, we found ourselves reading all the junk email advertisements we would normally just click and delete.

My spam box filled up very fast. Some of it was not even spam. It was not good enough to even qualify as spam.[1] We used Gmail as our primary email, as it seemed to be the most reliable across multiple servers, borders, and various telecommunication agencies. I could receive email through my American university's email system, but I couldn't send with any degree of dependability. Important messages would not get sent, lingering somewhere until I would get an email back from someone asking where my reply was. Then, I had to go track the email down. I would see the messages in the Out box, just resting there, in no hurry to take my important epistles to my emissaries across the globe. No amount of coaxing could get them to move. Clicking on the "Send" button just seemed to irritate them. They would dig in their heels, and refuse to budge. The only way to overcome their reticence to fly through the ether to their intended destination was to copy the entire message and paste it into Gmail. Although this worked, I think they resented it. The Montenegrin university email system was just the opposite. Outbound email worked fine (within Montenegro), but I wouldn't hear back from students on important assignments.

---

1 What is next down the food chain? Tripe? Menudo? Haggis?

"But Professor Deeshman, I did send you back message with reeson I no do homework. And, in English I did, too. My friend much helped me."

Because we spent so much time on Gmail, we became quite familiar with its screen layout. I began to notice the one-line ads that appeared above the latest email arrivals. When I would send out anything related to my students or the university, I would get the following ad:

"Rent a Textbook—www.TextRentNow.com—Don't Buy! Save up to 90% on Textbook Rentals—Fast Shipping!" or:
"Ph.D. in a Day—Get a Doctorate with Life Experience. Operators standing by!"
If I was writing to a fellow photographer, up popped:
"Passion for Photography?—PhotoUonline.edu—Turn Your Passion into a Profession at Photography University Online!" or
"Masterpiece Models—Certified Croatian Models at Your Beck and Call!"
The best ones were when I had to clear out my Spam box. They read:
"Spam Quiche—Makes 4 servings."
"Vineyard Spam Salad—Combine grapes, spam, peapods and onions in large bowl."
"Ginger Spam Salad—Serves one, refrigerate overnight."
"Spam Primavera—Toss with linguini, serve immediately."
"Spam Imperial Tortilla Sandwiches—To serve, cut each roll in half."
"Spam Vegetable Strudel—Bake 20 minutes or until golden, serve with soy sauce."

When Montenegro was aligned with its former partner, Serbia, they shared the Internet country domain extension, .yu, for Yugoslavia. However, when Montenegro gained its independence, it was assigned two extensions, one in Montenegrin, .cg.yu, for Crna Gora and one in English, .me. Realizing the worldwide appeal for such the latter extension, the Montenegrin government decided not to keep .me just for the government use, but to sell it on the open market. These extensions have been selling at a premium price as in insure.me, sync.me, date.me, love.me, hug.me, book.me, repair.me, make.me, justfor.me, allabout.me, whatabout.me, youand.me, willshemarry.me, and the Universal Pictures film, despicable.me. By 2010, over 320,000 domain names with .me had been purchased making it the fastest-selling, top-level domain in history.

The Vonage-Trapped Family

Before we left the States, Beth Lynn had only requested one thing so she would feel just a little less isolated—Vonage phone service with our American home phone number. Utilizing Voice-over-Internet-Protocol (VOIP), it is just like having your home phone with you anywhere in the world. Beth Lynn's cousin, who lived in Guatemala, highly recommended the service, as your family is only a convenient local phone call away.

Getting phone service hooked up to tell everybody we arrived safely was a top priority. While Beth Lynn unpacked, I was given the simple task of getting the Vonage phone working. I ended up spending six-plus hours trying to get something to work that was advertised as "plug and play ready." At the end of that day, I was sure my neighbors were going hear what a plastic box sounded like when it was thrown off a fourth story balcony.

It worked just fine when I tested it before we left the States. I took it out of the box, plugged it into my router at home, got a signal, and was ready to make a call. However, I had forgotten we had been landlineless[2] for some time and, thus, did not have an actual phone with which to test it. A trip to Walmart and $9.95 later provided a new cordless phone. I called Beth Lynn's cell phone to show her that it worked. She carefully repacked the Vonage box, the new phone, and secured them in our luggage.

At our new apartment, I unpacked the phone, the Vonage box, and opened the manual. I followed the instructions just as I did at home and, *voila*; I got "Error [008]" which meant it needed a user name and password. At home, we have a cable modem, but Montenegro had a DSL system, which required such things. Jelena had already provided them to us, but accessing the Internet this way was new to me.

I flipped over the Vonage instructions and read the additional DSL directions. It said to hook my computer up to the box and program the username and password. I did and got the same error message. I dialed the help line for T-Com, the local Montenegrin service provider (out of Hungary) that was a subsidiary of T-Mobile in Germany. The greeting and "push for" choices were, of course, in Serbian. Now, I was dead in the water. It was late, I was tired, and I was probably just making a simple mistake. I decided to tackle this problem when I had time over the weekend. Beth Lynn was very disappointed and my manhood was silently being questioned.

Five days later I tried everything the manual said to do all over again. For some inexplicable reason, I got the same results. I needed help. Earlier in the

---

2 My new vocabulary word for the year.

day, while searching for an ATM, I noticed there was a T-Com office about four blocks away. I put on my hat and coat, walked to the store, and asked them if there was any way I could get help.

"Did you call the help number?" the clerk asked.

"Yes, but it is in Serbian and I'm afraid I don't speak Serbian." (*Ne* on the *Srpski.*)

"Did you listen to the greeting all the way through? Because, at the end, it also gives you choices in English. They can help you in English."

The walk back was long and cold.

Sure enough, on the other end of the help line, there was a woman who spoke English. I explained what I was trying to do. Everything was okay until I accidentally used the word "Vonage." This threw her for a loop as, up until that moment, her English confidence had been running pretty high. "Vonage" was obviously a word she had never heard before. Now, her English came out in little dribbles until I heard, "Moment please." Then, a male voice picked up the conversation. I again explained what I was trying to do; and he said, "Need password. I change. New password is 'adsl123.' Bye."

I tried the new password. No luck. I called back and got a new person with better English skills. He explained there was a username and password required for both the modem *and the router.* He gave me my assigned usernames and two new passwords. As I was writing them down, my pen stopped working, and the operator hung up rather abruptly. Trying to remember the passwords he gave me, I repeated them out loud while I searched for a new pen. By the time I had them down on paper, I couldn't remember which password went to which device. As there are only four combinations, I just kept trying them until something happened. On the fourth try, I didn't get "Error [008]" anymore. Success!

Now I got "Error [004]." I decided I was going to have to bite the bullet, spend some real money, and call Vonage service in the States via my new T-Com mobile phone. I got helpful "Steve." "Steve" was in Mumbai, and he wanted to walk me through all the steps I had already done. At this point, I was desperately willing to have someone double check me. We were on the phone together for close to an hour. I didn't want to think about how expensive this call was going to be to a phone number in the States which was routed to India in order for me to get cheap long distance rates in Montenegro.

After six attempts of various configurations, "Steve" conceded the problem was beyond his capability. I identified with him. He thought I had the wrong password. However, to his credit, he was not willing to concede defeat. He proposed a three-way conference call between himself, T-Com, and me. I gave him their customer service number while I stayed on the line. He couldn't get a completed call through to Montenegro. I thanked Steve, called it a day, unhooked the device, and hid it in a drawer where I wouldn't have to look at it.

Four days later, I met James. He was the new IT guy for the U.S. Embassy. He had just installed Vonage at his house, and he offered to help. While I was on the phone with him, he discovered he and I had two different types of Vonage boxes. Undaunted, he downloaded the manuals to my set top box, wireless router, and Vonage box. He loaded those onto his computer and started to give me orders over the phone.

"Hook the Vonage box to the router with the blue cable," he directed.

"I did."

"What happened?"

"I followed the instructions in the Vonage Easy Steps Guide and I got Error [004]."

"Not good."

"No."

"Okay, let's see what you have under the hood. Hook the yellow cable from the yellow connector on the Vonage box to your computer. Open up a browser and type in 192.168.15.1."

"Done."

"Whaddya get?"

"Nothing."

"Type in 192.168.5.250."

"Okay, I'm in!"

"Set the choice to DHCP and let it get an IP address."

"It didn't like it."

"I don't understand. If it doesn't like DHCP or the PPPoE access you tried, we'll have to hard code in a static IP address. Find the WAN protocol page. I want to know what the Primary DNS is."

This was worse than trying to understand *Srpski.*

Whatever we tried didn't work, and we tried a lot of things.

Finally, James said, "What I think is happening is the DSL modem is in the router, and the router is already set up for VOIP, therefore, it won't recognize another VOIP device. I'm sorry. If that is true, it's just not going to work."

Sighing, he asked, "I hate to bring it up; but do you know that you have a known good cable?"

"I do. I tested them all by hooking my laptop to the router."

"Do you know if the port on the back of the router is good?"

"What's the chance of that being broken?"

"Infinitesimally small," he said. "But, let's make sure."

I unplugged the Vonage cable from one connector and moved it over. The Vonage box came alive with all sorts of blinking icons and displayed, "Plug in your phone."

I was giddy. My hand was shaking as I plugged in the phone. I got a dial tone. It was working! I profusely thanked James. Beth Lynn and I were so excited to have our phone service working. We called our kids, our parents, and all our close friends in America. Everybody was either busy or not at home.

We hung up the phone, looked out the window, and decided to go exploring.

I, Pod

Podgorica[1] may be the only city in the world founded on the confluence of not two, not three, but *five* different rivers—the meandering Zeta, the mighty Morača, the snaky Cijevna (with its mini Niagara Falls), the Ribinica (meaning "fish"), and the trifling Sitnica (meaning "trifle"). Each river played its own part in the development of the region.

The town began life as Doclea, a remote Illyrian trading post occupied by two tribes, the Labeates and the Docleats.[2] It was a city of ten thousand people where a tired traveler could refresh, take a bath, and spend the evening listening to a troubadour singing Illyrian illyrics.[3] Doclea served as a convenient crossing for weary wanderers and had the added benefit of offering cold river water and hot springs. When the Greeks overran the Illyrians, they didn't give the place a second thought and it became a bucolic watering hole. After the Romans took over in the first century A.D., they gave the city a new name, *Birziminium*, and an extreme makeover. They constructed a large main street[4] with covered *agoras* and forums to facilitate trade. They built palaces, a Temple to Diana, and piped in water for sizeable thermal baths. Residents were given loans, Roman citizenship, and self-rule. The town flourished until a devastating earthquake occurred in the early sixth century A.D.[5] This was followed by the invasion of the Slavs and Avars in the eighth century who thought they could improve what the Romans built. So, they leveled the place.

It is hard to tell if the Slavs were particularly aggressive; or, by this time, the Romans were resting on their laurels.[6] It is believed the Slavs originally

---

1 Pronounced "Pod-gor-REETS-a". Kind of rhymes with "Pleased-ta-meet-cha".

2 Guess who won out.

3 Accompanying them with his illyre.

4 The main street was named *Via Principalis*, Latin for Main Street.

5 Montenegro's history is influenced both by the geo-political and the geo-thermal.

6 The same ones they used for Olympic awards.

came from somewhere near the Baltic Sea as there are numerous geographic designations in the Balkans which are also in Poland. The Slavs must have been perfectly happy there until, in anthropological phenomenology terms, *something happened.* At which time, they migrated south until they found another body of water, the Adriatic. It is speculated this migration could have been due to crop failure, a natural disaster, or a huge rent increase.

It did not take but a few years for the Slavs to push the Romans over the mountains or into the sea capturing the entire Balkan Peninsula. Some historians believe the Slavs actually followed along behind the bloodthirsty Avars and Bulgars and let them do most of the conquering dirty work including destroying Roman Doclea on their way to their being castrated at Constantinople in 626.

The Slavs became Serbs, and the ethnonym "Serbs" was first mentioned by Pliny the Elder around 80 A.D. and Ptolemy[7] 200 years later. The Slavic root word "serb" means "same." When Ptolemy documented the Serbs, he also mentioned a town in present Bosnia and Herzegovina that had been named *Serbium* during Greek and Roman times. The two historians both referred to a tribe of Sarmatians, called Serboi[8], which were a group of South Slavs who lived on the shore of the Black Sea at the mouth of the Volga River. The Slavs took over the most important Roman city inland from the Adriatic, Doclea, which was renamed *Duklja.*

Around 850, the kingdom of Duklja rose up under King Vlastimir taking in territory from Dubrovnik to Raška in northern Serbia to Skadar, Albania, threatening the other Slavic power, the Bulgars. To gain additional strength, Vlastimir pledged allegiance to the Byzantine Empire. This occurred just in time for the first round of bubonic plague, which wiped out half the population. In 1077, King Mihailo, Vlastimir's great-nephew, was acknowledged by Pope Gregory VII as the King of the Slavs.

Under the Byzantine Empire, the little state of Duklja was an independent entity. For almost 100 years it had its own kingdom of Zeta, the historical and legendary basis for the pride of Montenegro. The first real Serbian King was Stefan Nemanja, crowned in 1217. He ruled from Raška; and, over the next 150 years, expanded the Serbian territory to include modern day Serbia, Bosnia, Macedonia, Montenegro, Albania, and northern Greece. Zeta then became immersed in the Serbian dynasty of the Nemanjići—a kingdom that stretched from the Danube to the Adriatic and all the way down to Corinth in Greece.

---

7 The basis of all history: "Ptolemy, ptold me."

8 Or haplogroup "I2a-P37.2" as they are known by geneticists when they are hanging around the water cooler.

The ruins of Duklja sit northeast of Podgorica, unprotected behind a cattle gate and a short fence. Unlike ruins in Rome or Greece, they are not supervised or policed. There is a treasure trove of archeological opportunity buried there. You would think that this alone would be a significant tourist draw for the area, but that is not the case since there are approximately 2,500 similar Roman ruins throughout the Balkans, Europe, and North Africa.

After the Slavs were converted to Orthodox Christianity by the constant incursions of the Byzantines, they did not want to build a settlement on the ruins of the heathen Romans. The population moved south of the Roman site across the river (and through the woods) to the other side of a small hill (*gorica*). Then known as Ribinica, one of the buildings was a Christian church, dedicated to Sveti Đorđe[9] in the Twelfth century. It was built under the hill or *pod gorica* providing the city with its toponym. The church design had running water, which flowed via an underground aqueduct from the Morača two kilometers away. For centuries, the church served as the focal point for the growing town.

The church's ramparts, the stone wall around its grounds, and the smaller building are believed to be the original construction. A fresco depicting the life of St. George was added in the 15th and 16th century and the additional nave was dedicated in 1880. On our first visit there, the docent let us peek behind the gold-leafed iconostasis screen and into the altar area so we could view the entire faded fresco. The interior is only about 400 square feet, and the walls are covered with paintings of Serbian Orthodox saints.[10] As with many Orthodox churches and monasteries, to get to the front door, you must walk over the graves of the former priests. It is an active church facility. While we were there, people came to genuflect, kiss the icons, and leave coins on the picture frames of their family's patron saint. They prayed for health, spiritual assistance, loved ones, and financial help.

As with the rest of the Balkans, Podgorica was a small sub-division of the Byzantine Empire until the Ottomans subdued the population in 1474 on their centuries-long march toward Vienna. The name *Podgorica* first appeared in 1326 and was the municipal moniker until after World War II. The Ottomans, not wanting to build their town on the site of the infidel Christians, moved the town center about a kilometer southwest to the confluence of the Morača and the Ribinica rivers. Here they established a traditional Turkish town with a *plaža* for a bazaar, winding lanes, and mosques with minaret turrets within a

---

9 In English, it is Saint George, the same one of dragon fame.

10 One of my students exclaimed, after glancing at my cluttered laptop screen, "You've got more icons than a church!"

high-walled city. Realizing the value of a watering hole along a caravan route from Dubrovnik to the east, plus the added advantage of being able to charge a toll for crossing the wide Morača River, the settlement grew with various sultans in charge (who had a variety of administrative approaches) for the next 450 years. The initial converts to Islam were by the sword, but subsequent generations who proved more recalcitrant were persuaded, not by death, but by taxes. If you converted, you did not have to pay any. That seemed to mollify most of the rest of the population.

The ruins of Ribinica still stand across the street from the Montenegrin Parliament building. The old city's tall walls rise overlooking the flow of the two rivers on the edge of the Old Town, the Moslem quarter. These ancient Ottoman ruins are also in some guy's backyard. He leans his painting scaffolding up against these priceless monuments from antiquity.

During World War II, when the Nazis made their regional headquarters in Podgorica, the Allies carpet-bombed the town. The only part that was not completely leveled was the Muslim Quarter. Still standing from the Ottoman era are the square, a clock tower, and a Turkish bathhouse. The bathhouse is now a bookstore/café called Karver's (after the American author, Raymond Carver). Because of where it is located (under a central road bridge) it is the only bookstore where it never rains.

Podgorica was decimated by the bombings. Most of the town had to be rebuilt after the war with Soviet money using the uninspiring, utilitarian style of drab (and cheap) cement architecture. In his heart, Tito always had a soft spot for Montenegrins since his primary headquarters during the war was in the mountains above Žabljak, near the present Montenegrin-Serbian border. The mountain clans nurtured him and protected his *partizan* soldiers.[11] Due to his sentimentality, Tito made it a priority to rebuild Podgorica after the war. He invested in an aluminum processing plant, and had the citizens plant tobacco and vineyards.

In 1946, the first year of Tito's reign, there was a favorite son of Montenegro, Milovan Djilas, who had fought alongside Tito during World War II. He rose up the ranks of the Communist apparatus to become Marshall Tito's obvious heir apparent. Djilas was so beloved by Montenegrins that, at a state dinner in Podgorica, the applause Djilas received was much louder and longer than for Tito himself. This did not go unnoticed by Tito or Djilas's mother. She was quoted as saying, "It is not good they love my son more than Tito." Djilas, apparently a very quick thinker, rose to his feet, and announced that in honor of the great

---

11 Currently the name for most of the sports clubs in Beograd, Serbia.

Marshall, this town would now be known as Titograd. This endeared him to the great man for at least another few years.[12]

However, Montenegro could not have a town named for their country's President and not have it be the capital. Two years later the entire government was moved from the old capital of Cetinje twenty-three miles to Titograd. Some of the local die-hard communists still refer to Podgorica in the old manner. We were once lost on a backcountry road and asked the way back to Podgorica. The older men corrected us when they would point south and say, "Ne! Titograd!" After Tito's death, the leaders of the municipal government changed it back to Podgorica after they were sure all of Tito's old cronies were out of power and there was no one they had to curry favor with anymore.[13] (The airport is still designated as TGD.)

There are still more than a few "Yugostalgics" who yearn for the economic stability (and the accompanying totalitarian fear) the Communist era provided. There are some road signs telling you how many kilometers to Titograd, even though the capital has not been named that for 20 years.[14] Tito had been the despotic glue who held all of Yugoslavia together and checked others' political aspirations. Upon his death, the relationships between the republics were at a breaking point. The Slovenes and Croats wanted more independence. The Serbs wanted a Greater Serbia, which they believed they deserved after World War II. The Macedonians with their unique culture never felt a part of Yugoslavia, and the Montenegrins just wanted to continue to be the recipient of the unequal distribution of wealth within Yugoslavia. In 1992, Slovenia, Croatia, and Macedonia all separated from the crumbling larger Yugoslavia. Croatia sent 200,000 Serbs packing. The Muslim and Croat communities in Bosnia and Herzegovina wanted to secede, but the Serbs there did not. Because of their mutual heritage, Montenegro stayed aligned with Serbia during the 1990s.[15] It

---

12 Djilas was eventually expelled from the Communist Party and imprisoned for his anti-party writings. These were published in America by the son of a Montenegrin emigrant, William Jovanovich, who, for 36 years, was president of Harcourt, Brace, Jovanovich.

13 Montenegro always had a disproportionate amount of representatives in Tito's government. Because of this, the tiny republic would receive an uneven amount of programs and pork, much to the displeasure of the other republics. This would come back to bite them after the old man was gone.

14 On some, a helpful soul had spray-painted the name Podgorica over Titograd, so we couldn't read either one of them.

15 The last vestige of the former Socialist Federal Republic of Yugoslavia collapsed in 1992. It became the Federal Republic of Yugoslavia, which, in 2003, became the country of Serbia and Montenegro. This unbalanced unity lasted until Montenegro declared its independence from Serbia three years later.

was during this period that war atrocities and bloodshed created another black period in Balkan history.[16]

Today Podgorica is a thriving capital city of 160,000 with a third of the employable-aged residents working for the federal government.[17] There is Stara Varoš (the old city); the rebuilt downtown area around Republik Trg (square) known as Nova Varoš; and the Novi Grad section, growing north across the Morača with its mix of modern office buildings and cement apartments surrounding the drab University of Montenegro campus. Not noted for their creativity, some anonymous city planners retained the Communist era-like designations when naming the neighborhoods. There is *Blok 5* adjacent to *Blok 6* and so on, as the city grew north toward Danilovgrad, each *blok* has its progressively newer high-rises and higher rent.

We lived in the Kruševac neighborhood of the Novi Grad section, one of the nicer parts of town because it was near the lovely city park that was King Nikola's (1860 to 1910) summer palace. It was also very convenient for shopping and perfect for participating in the Montenegrin national sport of the evening promenade.

---

16 One new Montenegrin friend said, "Discovering our country is like peeling an onion as there is always another layer underneath. And, sometimes, you don't want to peel anymore because it just makes you cry."

17 I am at a loss to determine what the English collective noun is for residents of Podgorica. Podgoricans? Podgoricaites? Podgoricaers? Podgoricii?

The Seven Hills of Roam

It takes the most adverse weather conditions to prevent Montenegrins from strolling after dinner. They leisurely mosey until they run into friends, then cluster around one another, and chat standing on the curb or even in the middle of the street. Such an evening would be capped off by a visit to a *caffé* house where they would order their last cup of coffee for the day and nurse it while they watched the other strollers. The men socialized with men and the women with other women. It was rare to see two or more couples out socially. Several times in the evenings, we could see a family eating dinner at a restaurant. After, they were finished, the mother would take the children home and the father would go next door to the café house to socialize with his male friends.

Like most of Europe, Montenegro is a café culture. During recessionary times residents are willing to give up many things, but not café life. Strolling and chatting are the two main forms of entertainment in this city. The latter involves the liberal use of libations and both are just excuses for extended animated conversation. The Italian ambassador to Montenegro, His Excellency Sergio Barbanti, said that hectic, modern life is crushing the European practice of strolling and café life. However, it is still very much alive in Montenegro.

One staff member of the American Embassy said, "These people drink about ten cups of coffee a day, and it is very strong coffee, too. Every time we have a meeting with them, they serve you coffee. Americans can't drink like that. If you did, at the end of the day, you are so hyped up you are shaking, and you can't sleep at night. Everyone at the embassy has learned to drink tea during the day. Sometimes I drink as much as seven cups of tea during multiple 'get to know you' sessions." Beth Lynn and I quickly learned to do the same thing.

•

Our introduction to strolling came when two of my students, Tanja and Marina, took us on a walking tour of the neighborhood pointing out where we should and should not shop. (Tanja's father owned one of the neighborhood fast food restaurants, so she was an expert.) Since they were women in their early twenties, they were authorities on where to get one's hair done, where to buy the best fashion accessories, and what clubs had the best disc jockeys. Things I filed away for future reference should we ever need them. Like every other set of female BFFs in Montenegro, the two girls had known each other since birth. Their families lived in the same apartment building, and the girls attended the same schools together in the same class. They would remain friends for life, probably living in the same town. Some girls made sure their future husbands would not move them away from their family or their best friends.

Strolling in a large city provides exercise and people-watching opportunities at the same time. There were two great places for doing both. Our own street, Ivana Vujoševića, was well lit and had a lot of foot traffic day and night. At the end of that block, we would turn left on the major boulevard, Svetog Petra Centinjskog. This would take us across Moscovska Street and past Rimski Trg (Square) with its cafés and restaurant. We would turn left onto (ironically) Đorđa Vašingtona (George Washington), Podgorica's answer to Rodeo Drive with its upscale shops and boutiques. This went for another block to the traffic circus in front of the University of Montenegro campus where we would again turn left and walk in the relative shade along Bulevar Revolucjie or, sometimes, cutting through the grounds of the Maksim Gorki Elementary School. Here, we discovered school children are not so different from their American counterparts. We rounded a corner once near the school and ran into an entire herd of Harry Potters complete with capes and marker-pen lightning bolt scars on their foreheads.

If we had the entire day, we would walk the other way down Bulevar Revolucije, past the American Embassy, across the Morača River, and into the "Old Town" (Stara Varoš). From there we wandered through maze-like streets under the minarets eventually connecting with Kraja Nikole Street, which took us across the Ribinica River and the Mali park to downtown, and Republike Trg (Square). Once there, we would window-shop, dine, or enjoy a dessert. The walls of the older buildings were covered in graffiti with the frequent "Fucmut?," "ACAD," and the ever-present "VAVARI," which meant the "Barbarians," the fan club of the Podgorica football team.

While walking in the neighborhoods, we would see *nekrološki*, flyers relaying the sad news of obituaries. They would be tacked on utility poles and taped to lampposts. The city provided columnar stanchions in the parks just for this purpose. Those nekrološki with black borders indicated the deceased was Communist. Green designated Moslem and blue denoted Orthodox Christians.

If we were downtown, we had a choice of wandering past the football stadium to the Gorica and its massive park or taking Bulevar Ivana Crnajevica across the beautiful suspended Millennium Bridge and turning onto Svetozana Markovica until it became our own street. Wherever we walked in Podgorica, we always felt safe.

From our observational studies on these field trips, we discovered winter fashion was primarily designer jeans with sweaters, jackets, and boots. The men wore business casual clothes from nine to five and warm-ups after hours. If young men are on the prowl during an evening out, they might be wearing leather jackets and slacks. Otherwise, it was back to jeans or warm-ups. Many times, we saw fathers out with their little boys, and they would all be dressed in matching warm-up outfits.

After strolling the streets of Podgorica for a few months, we realized we had yet to see a real blonde. We had seen a few bottle blondes, but even they were a rare species. Redheaded women were a different matter. The color choice of many women (mostly post-menopausal females) was red—a bright cherry red. On one evening stroll we estimated that 10 percent of all females in that age bracket sported that color hair. When we asked our new friends about it, they said, "Red? Of course. Why not? It is the universal color."[1]

We also noticed very few bald men. Montenegrin males all have great heads of dark, black hair, whatever their age. This does not support the genetic theory I have been using all my life. I knew I got my thinning hair from my grandfather. He lost his hair very early on and wore a hat in every single picture we have of him. Knowing that, I was always prepared to be bald later in life; so it did not come as a shock or sudden disappointment to me. Not seeing any bald men in Montenegro did. The only men with even medium-length hair were foreigners. A Montenegrin man's hair is cut over their ears and collars. Having long hair is the Montenegrin equivalent of a "sissie-boy."[2]

During the day in late February, when the weather was nice, we took advantage of Park Petrovića, which were the grounds of the Palace of the Petrović and was just across Bulevar Revolucije from us. The main palace

---

1 This response would be accompanied by the WEWYD look.

2 This is in a country where very masculine men carry tote purses.

building has been converted to the Museum of Modern Art. The front of the palace has a grand curved staircase around a fountain that led up a hill to the entrance. Turning around, you were provided with a wonderful vista of Podgorica. Behind the museum was a small park with outdoor sculptures, a small church, and benches for more extended anthropological observation. This was where lovers held each other under shade trees, old ladies met and gossiped, and caretakers from the hospital next door took a respite from their work.

On one surprising day, Ra, the sun god, came back from his mid-winter tropical vacation. The clouds parted and, with only about an hour of daylight left, I grabbed my camera and headed out to the park.[3] There, I came across a group of eight young men, all members of the Mediterranean University photography club. Because of the long stretch of bad weather, it was the first day they had been able to get out since November. The young men were engrossed in the same deep, philosophical photography discussion that takes place in every country in the world. The Canon guys were teasing the Nikon guys and vice versa.

I introduced myself as being a visiting faculty member from another university. I was immediately asked by the loudest Canon guy to settle an argument as to which equipment was better. The fact that I was holding a new Canon camera in my hand may have also contributed to his invitation for me to arbitrate.

"See, the professor has a Canon. He is very smart, and he would choose the best camera."

"Forgive him, professor. He was damaged as a small child. He does not know any better."

"My friend must be excused for his choice of Canon. He was born blind, and it has only gotten worse."

"Sava's taste for cameras is as bad as his taste for beer. Nikon- phooey."

•

In one day, we witnessed not one, but two organized protests. One was a large gathering outside of the Parliament building. The police would not let us closer than within two blocks of the demonstration. The protestors were former employees of the aluminum plant demanding the government resurrect

3 Too many times, in the morning, the sun would be shining without a cloud to be seen but, yet by the time I grabbed my camera bag and walked down three flights of stairs, it was pouring rain out of dark skies. I learned my lesson about being teased by the sun. I was not going to be fooled a fourth time.

the complex and put it back it the way it used to be. This was when the rest of Yugoslavia was forced to buy the plant's output at inflated prices. The other protest was a smaller group of picketers walking in front of the cigarette factory. They were striking for higher wages.[4]

Spring arrived several weeks overdue. The rain slowly faded away and, we discovered grapevines climbing over back porch trellises, kiwi vines growing blossoms, and cafés sprouting green Beck Beer umbrellas over tables on the sidewalks. The café crowds that were always apparent indoors during the winter seemed to have doubled once the weather became nice enough to sit outside. During the afternoon and early evening, the cafés were full of (mostly) men chatting, doing business, or at least looking like they were doing business. It was perfectly acceptable to go to a café or restaurant, linger for hours after purchasing a single coffee, tea, or espresso, and then nurse it throughout the afternoon while one smoked, argued, laughed, and greeted friends. As one's friends came and went, the group who arrived at noon wasn't the same group at that table who departed four hours later. Beth Lynn and I normally lived in a no-smoking, non-alcohol, and no-caffeine culture. But in Podgorica, we were imbedded in a very hazy café and pub culture. Smoke was everywhere, and our respiration systems were just going to have to adapt.

Kiša, Kiša, Kiša (Rain, Rain, Rain)

Our own strolling achievements never reached the championship level, as we were very late in the season getting started with our training. Living there during the winter to spring transition was like Seattle—rain with occasional sun breaks. From the time we arrived in January until March, there were thirty days of consecutive rain, twenty of which covered the cityscape with constant and continuous precipitation (which was not the normal weather pattern). It rained, it drizzled, it trickled, it misted, and it poured.[5] The water oozed off our windowsills and down the gutter, which made for a constant arrhythmic tapping noise that added to our general ennui. During this time, the kitchen faucet also developed a leak; so now the sound had invaded the sanctity of our apartment. Living up on the fourth floor, I figured we were safe from flooding although we did consider bashing our brains out from the incessant water torture coming from the kitchen.

---

4 Must have been a lucky strike.

5 It drove us mad, I tell you, MAD! (Sometimes, years later, in the dark of night, I can still hear it drip, drip, dripping on my window pane.)

We described each day by what the rain obscured from view. It was either a Mountain day where we couldn't see the distant mountains on the horizon, a Hill day where we couldn't discern the *gorica* that was a kilometer away, a Building day because we couldn't see the building across the parking lot, or a "Geez, ya gotta see this" day.

In the morning, we would look out the window at the downpour and say ironic things like:

"You know, they say it might rain today."

"Those may be rain clouds."

"You're not going to believe this, but it's actually starting to rain."

"Tut-tut. It looks like rain, Piglet."

I don't know if it was the invariable rain or the constant gray cloudy skies that was more depressing. The locals even commented on it. When I had lunch with an academic colleague, he looked out the window, and said, "This is the longest we can remember it raining." He then glanced at the floor and said in a low voice, "This has to stop soon. People are doing crazy things." We changed the subject.

Here is what the weather forecast gave us week after week:

27th: 28th: 1st: 2nd: 3rd: 4th: 5th:

It reminded me of the poem I learned when I was but a wee little lad:

"Rain, rain, go away,
And stay the #@!* there."

•

In middle of all the rain, one day it calmed down to a fine mist, which gave us just enough reason to get out of out apartment. Instead of having a specific objective this time, we decided to just go "walkies" and see what we could discover.

We went out the back way, cutting between apartment buildings and through parking lots. Crossing the Morača River, we found three fellows worm fishing off an old bridge over the Ribinica River. Being a fisherman myself, the brotherhood beckoned; and I went to inquire about current conditions. One toothless man wanted to talk to us. He pointed to the Morača, shook his head, and said "Voda, voda, voda," meaning "water, water, water." The river was very high because of the rains, and it was actually flooding the stone patios and first floors of the closed cafés along its banks.

It was interesting when we found someone who wanted to talk to us. They would start speaking in *Crnagorski* (Montenegrin) and I would interrupt, saying "Molim, molim. Ja sam za učenje Crnagorski." ("Please, I am sorry. I am just learning Montenegrin.") They would smile, nod appreciatively, and keep taking in Crnagorski. This particular angler continued to tell me (if I understood him correctly) the Morača River was flooding, and they were worried about the banks; but it was good for the plants and flowers and farmers and children. That was where I lost him. I tried hard to translate the remainder of his narrative, but it came out something like this: "Last week I Octobered fast and then friends carried Desmond Tutu to run at the moon with Kentucky covered in the green sauce." Of course, I could be wrong about that, since I had only had two language lessons. Nevertheless, this conversation was not much different than others I had with Montenegrins. Here, talking is still the best form of entertainment. As it was still raining, Beth Lynn and I held our umbrellas high and walked on singing Gene Kelly and B.J. Thomas songs.

Sometime around the Ides of March, the local residents, tired of recoiling from all the rain, took their families out for the first sunny Saturday morning in almost three months. It is hard to describe the view that met us that morning—an entire landscape of laundry. People aired out their bedding and even used the trees on the sunny side of the main boulevard for their "high-heat cycle."

At a local restaurant, the owners were washing the dirt off their awnings and windows. Their elderly mother took the sprayer from her middle-aged son and showed him how *she* wanted it done. Shade tree mechanics were now open for business. People exchanged pleasantries even if it required shouting up from the street to a third floor balcony.

It was a very nice morning. Then, of course, it began to rain.

Stranger in a Strange Land

Beth Lynn prides herself on being an independent but refined female. She was raised in the south where manners mattered, respect for others was instilled at a young age, and graciousness was an admired female attribute. She also grew up at the same time as the Women's Liberation movement and watched how gender equality changed the way American males treated females.

Soon after we arrived, Beth Lynn came down with a terrible respiratory ailment. This meant that I had to do all the shopping. After a few weeks, she was finally well enough to get out of the apartment to come with me so I could show her where to buy all our necessities. Having met the shopkeepers and retailers running the errands, I had found that most of the grocery clerks were very eager to help the new stranger find the items they needed. It was the same with the produce vendors and at the bakery. As I took Beth Lynn around to the various stores, everyone I introduced her to was extremely friendly and helpful. However, when she later entered those premises alone, she was virtually ignored unless they helped just to get rid of her.

In Montenegro, she found herself in a very male-dominated world. She discovered the way she was treated was different depending upon whether she was by herself or with me. She noticed while walking along the sidewalk, men would almost knock her into the street. They expected her to go around them no matter what side they were walking on. It became a game for her to see how determined she could be to not move out of their way, while also trying to make them be a little courteous (by our American standards). Several times, she was nudged out of the way or given dirty looks. She even tried pretending she didn't see the men, but that didn't work very well as they were much bigger than she was. Often, when she entered doorways, out of nowhere a man would appear and wedge himself in front of her to get inside first. When she would venture out, it became a pedestrian jousting match between a southern steel magnolia and Montenegrin *muževnost* (machismo).

Once, when standing in line to pay a bill at the phone company, several men cut in line right in front of her. After two older, well-dressed men did this, she was determined not to let a third man behind her do the same thing. She found herself mentally choreographing how she could accidentally trip him and make it look like an accident. Backing away from that strategy, it turned out a single, dirty glance was sufficient to keep most men at bay.

Beth Lynn had led a life where gentlemen held doors open for her, seated her at dinner, doffed their hats upon entering her home, and verbally thanked her for whatever little favor she had bestowed upon them. She decided she was a spoiled American Princess and liked being part of that caste system. But, she wasn't in Kansas anymore.

Registering with the Policija

Our State department told us we had to register with the local police within 24 hours of our arrival. Otherwise, we would be illegal, but, more importantly, out of compliance. In the world of government regulations, there is nothing worse than being out of compliance.[6] On the day we arrived, we called the

---

[6] Except, of course, not having a regulation that people have to comply with in the

American Embassy as instructed and asked if there might be someone who could escort us to the police station to insure our continued stay in the country. They suggested it might be best if someone from the university where I was to teach, took us to register.[7] I called the school's Associate Dean for International Cooperation who told me not to worry about it until we got back from the conference I had to attend in Venice. She didn't believe that being unregistered was as big a deal as our State Department did.

When we returned, she said she would be glad to take us to the police; but she was going skiing for four days, and we could register when she returned. That took us to the following weekend. On Monday, I called her back. She said she had a cousin that could help and she would call me on Thursday.[8] By now, Beth Lynn was scared to leave the apartment thinking we would be snatched off the street by men in black suits and thin black ties, and thrown in the back of a black sedan, never to be heard from again.

I called the Dean back on Friday. Her assistant told me she had called the police station to find out what forms we needed, but couldn't get a straight answer. Therefore, we would need to go on Monday—the first day of class. This was perfect as I had to go to the university, and we could all leave together from there. I put Beth Lynn on readiness alert for Monday afternoon.

That day, while I was in my office, I was informed the administrator still didn't know what forms were needed; but we would definitely go on Tuesday afternoon after class. I called Beth Lynn and told her to stand down as the mission has been rescheduled for mañana. After class on Tuesday, I couldn't find the assistant or the man she said would take us to the station. I called Beth Lynn and told her we were postponing the launch one more day. When I got home that evening, there was a message from a man at the university stating he would pick us up the next day at 10:30 a.m. At 10:30 a.m. we got a phone call stating it would be more like 11 a.m.

We made sure we had all the required legal documents. We were told to have ready our passports, the Fulbright letter of invitation from the university, a letter of explanation from the State Department, a copy of our lease, our medical statements, as well as a copy of our landlady's (and lord's) identity cards. The man who took us to the police station was very pleasant but spoke little English. I was

---

first place.

7 The buck, evidently, does not stop at the embassy.

8 Everybody who assisted us always had a cousin that could help do something. "My cousin owns a business that can do that for you." "My cousin owns a restaurant. He knows the best place to eat." "Iz okay, I call my cousin. He know somebody." Amazing-one set of grandparents single-handedly populated the entire country.

not sure he was going to be much help interpreting if we got asked by the guys in the thin black ties to step in the back room.

The police station was a large gray, drab building right out of *1984*. Inside it was dark and dreary with threadbare carpet and holes in the drywall from fist punches. We went into a small office that had barely enough room for the three of us to stand while our university representative explained what we needed to do. It turned out we needed a special form, not a regular form. The form was not available at the police station—you had to go to the public library and purchase it. The library, it turned out, was right across the street from our apartment.

The form needed to be filled out and returned the next day with our passports. That night I got a call from the office manager at the university who asked me questions such as when we arrived and how long we were staying in the country, etc. The bureaucratic wheels were now turning.

On Thursday, we were to be picked up at 11 a.m, then noon, and then 1 p.m. That made us double booked as our new language tutor, Bojana, was arriving then as well. I called and bumped her to 1:30. At 1 p.m., Beth Lynn and I stood in the rain for 30 minutes until both of them showed up at the same time. I thought it couldn't hurt to have a SSL (Serbian as a Second Language) teacher with us this time, so we all hopped into the administrator's tiny car and headed to the police station.

It turned out the forms needed to be more complete than we had estimated, as our answers were not enough to satisfy the officials. In the station foyer, there were no tables, chairs, desk or counter, or, for that matter, very much light. I was glad we had brought reinforcements with us as neither one of the native Montenegrins could make out what the form was asking for either. The administrator and language tutor kept excusing themselves, and ducking into the tiny sergeant's office to ask what things meant. They finally deciphered the questions; we filled in a few blanks and were ushered into the inner sanctum. The burly and officious officer on duty asked for the forms and our passports. He compared our names on the two documents and signed the form. After a short lecture about the visa only being good for 90 days, he wished us a good day and we were on our way.

We now had a visa that meant, on or before the 89th day, we had to leave the country and return. I asked other Americans what they might suggest we do at that time.

"We take a bus across the border, stimulate the Albanian economy by having a cup of coffee and come home."

We were never asked for any of the forms that our government, the university, our doctor, and our landlady went to so much trouble to provide (they ran to 27 pages). I still have them. They are either going in our scrapbook or on Ebay.

Bojana thought that the process went very smoothly and took a moment to teach us the Serbian words for “police,” “application,” “jail”, and “lawyer.” Words we hoped we never needed to use.

Srpskiing Uphill

We decided to learn as much of the local language as we could while we were *in situ*. What better way to learn a language than emersion?[1] The official language of the former Yugoslavia was Serbo-Croatian—their version of South Slavic. In Montenegro, the language that is spoken is the Štokavian dialect, the same as in Serbia, Croatia, and Bosnia. Serbo-Croatian is hyphenated because the same language uses both Roman (Croatian) and Cyrillic (Serbian) character sets. After the breakup of Yugoslavia, the language became just Serbian for the new country of Serbia and Montenegro. When Montenegro separated from Serbia, the nationalists wanted a new official language called Montenegrin (*Crnagorski*) using the Roman character set.[2] However, if they did that, it would just be Croatian, and that, simply, would not do. In order to differentiate their new language from Croatian, the Montenegrin government formed a committee to decide on a new alphabet. After much thought and deliberation, the committee thought it best to add two new letters, Ś and Ź. Therefore, we wanted to take our lessons in the brand, spanking new language of Crnagorski. However, there are no learning materials written in the new language, so we ended up taking Serbian (Srpski) lessons.[3] Turns out, these are just like any other kind of ski lesson except you don't fall down as often.

---

1 Of course, this *is* the same way you drown.

2 Actually Montenegro is the only country of the former Yugoslavia to officially use *both* alphabets.

3 Did you think the word *Srpski* needed an "e" in there somewhere? Serbians are nothing if not efficient spellers. Some of my American colleagues refer to our residence as "In the Bowels of the Land of No Vowels." I found that when I started writing about the Balkans, not to bother with the spell-check feature on my word processor. When it saw a proper Serbian name like *Predrag*, it dutifully underlined it in red, tried to correct it in English, did not find a suggestion, and then just sat there and pouted until I rebooted.

All of our more worldly friends told us the same old joke: "What do you call someone who speaks two languages?"

"Bilingual."

"What do you call someone that speaks three languages?"

"Trilingual."

"What do you call someone that only speaks one language?"

"An American."

This was driven home during one airline flight where our fellow passengers thought nothing of scanning a copy of the German newspaper, *Der Spiegel*, being entertained by the latest scandal in Italy's *La Repubblica*, and then checking stock prices in the *Financial Times* from the U.K. I was so envious. What sets Americans back as on the global stage is not being forced to learn a second language for our livelihood. In Venice, I met a Bulgarian professor who had just completed her doctorate at an Italian university and was learning French because that was the only job she could get (and we were speaking in English). On the other hand, if Americans do learn another language, they don't have any convenient place to practice it. Secondary education teachers tell me high school children in the U.S. do not want to learn a language because they know they will never have to (or get to) use it.

At various times in my life I have tried learning another language.[4] First, it was Spanish in high school where I was *Pablo* for two years and sat with my friends *Tomas* Fulmer, *Carlos "Caliente"* Young, and *Jose* Fleishman listening to Senora Bell recite all the inflected forms of Spanish verbs.[5]

Due to the importance of my first trip to Asia, I made the mistake of trying to learn conversational phrases in both Chinese and Japanese at the same time. I bought the Berlitz CD's and, in the car on the way to and from work, I repeated phrases back to myself—much to the entertainment of other drivers. I created my own pocket-sized reference list of words and phrases that I carried with me. However, I was forever getting the two languages mixed up. A toast in Japanese is "Kanpai." In Chinese, it is "Ganbei." To my tin ear, they sound so similar phonetically that, in my exuberance, I would use the wrong word in the wrong country. Beth Lynn stated, occasionally, I even created new words like "Ganpai." That is when I learned the essential difference between the Japanese and Chinese. If I made a social gaffe (such as the above), the Japanese would smile slightly, nod, and look at the floor. The Chinese would be rolling around on it, laughing. I guess I cannot hear the nuances that are required to differentiate

---

[4] Just for the record, I am bilingual. I do speak English *and* Texan.

[5] We referred to those class periods as "conjugatal visits."

syllables, words, and phrases in another tongue (much less any other part of the body).[6]

Another American in Podgorica recommended his own Serbian tutor, a woman named Bojana. After the preliminary introductions over drinks, we settled in around the kitchen table for our first lesson with bright shiny faces, sharpened pencils, and new Big Chief tablets. (I think Bojana was very proud to be teaching Serbian to a university professor.) I wanted to learn the language so I could converse with fellow proletariat that I met every day. What I needed to acquire was a vocabulary that was heavy on business and education phrases. In a local bookshop, I found a large Balkan equivalent of Funk & Wagnalls that was an English-Srpski dictionary; but they wanted €75 for it. It still did not have some of the words or phrases I needed every day like "No mushrooms, please" or "Just a minute Mr. Bus Driver, I know I have another ten cents somewhere."

A few days before our first language lesson, on a whim and for a few cents, I purchased a poster of the Crnagorski alphabet, like one you would find in a kindergarten classroom. It had large upper and lower case letters with pictures of teddy bears, flowers, and cartoon animals. I taped it to the wall above our kitchen table. Bojana saw it her first time there and LOL'ed.

Since we had invested so much money in the poster, Bojana started the lesson there. Beth Lynn and I repeated after Bojana: "Ah . . . Be . . . Ts . . . Ch . . . ," etc. (C's make a "ts" sound as in the tail end of "cats."[7]) The vowels were all shifted—"e" was a long "a" for example. Letters with the ˇ symbol over them added an "h" to their sound such that č is a "ch," but, then, so is ć but with a lighter punch. It has to do with where you put your tongue when you pronounce the letter and, evidently, mine didn't want to go wherever it was supposed to. To practice our pronunciation we would sound out such words as Šišići (a village on the coast) or the surname of Šuškavčević.

Bojana provided us with Xeroxed copies of a textbook published by the Beograd Institute for Foreign Languages entitled *Serbian for Strangers*. The authors went out of their way to make you feel comfortable right from the beginning. On the first page was a picture of the American actor, Joe Mantegna, and his speech bubble said, "Zovem Pedro Rodriquez" (I am Pedro Rodriquez).

I looked it up. Mantegna is his real name.

---

6 If you want some fun, ask one of your Chinese friends to say "Forty-Four Stone Lions." It is a classic Mandarin tongue twister. Stand back, it can get a little damp.

7 Don't miss the pun.

•

Bojana said, "Repeat, please."[8]

"Zovem se Profesor Pol Dišman." (My name is Professor Paul Dishman.)

"Ovo je Beth Lynn." (This is Beth Lynn.)

"Kako ste?" (How are you?)

"Ja sam dobro." (I am good.)

Bojana started us with the vocabulary in the first chapter. These included really useful words like newspaper (*novine*, no-vee-neigh), frog (*žaba*, zha-ba), and sheep skin vest (*gunj*, gun-ye). After listening to us trying hard to understand what she was pronouncing, Bojana thought we should also learn the phrase *polako, polako* (slowly, slowly) so we could use it liberally whenever we could not understand what the other person was saying. Whenever I would pronounce a word for her, Bojana would say, "Ne, ne, ne" (No, no, no) then make me say it repeatedly. Thus, an intended hour lesson would easily stretch into two.

We learned that not only were there masculine and feminine words (like there are in romance languages) there were also *childrens'* words. Nouns ending in consonants were *muški* (male), those ending in "a" were *ženski* (female), and those ending in "o" or "e" were *srendnji* (kids). All adjectives had to change depending on the gender of the noun. On top of which, there were seven different cases: nominative, genitive, dative or locative, accusative, vocative, and instrumental. Therefore, any given adjective may have *42 different* forms (*velik, velika, veliko, velikog, velicog, velioj,* etc.) depending on the case, the gender, and if the noun was singular or plural. After much practice, I eventually got where some of the Serbian nouns began to just roll off my tongue. Words such as *taksi* (taxi), *tunel* (tunnel), *biznis* (business), *telefon* (telephone), *viza* (visa), and *hotel* (hotel).

We decided we could only really learn "the local language" if we spoke it between ourselves. Thus, our convoluted conversations in Montenegrin were much like the scene in *Casablanca,* where the older couple practiced their English before immigrating to America.

He asks, "What watch?"

She says, "Ten watch."

And he replies, "Such much?"

Then, the waiter remarks, "Oh, you two will get along beautifully in America."

We did get along beautifully in Montenegro. But, when it came to the language, it was due to the patience of its people.

---

8 When we first arrived and would hear these heavy Slavic accents speaking English, I couldn't help but think of "The virst ting ve do is take care of Moose und Skuirrel."

Snežana and Marina worked in the bakery downstairs where we bought our bread. I tried to practice my new language skills with them. They were very puzzled at first but came to realize what was going on. By the first month, I had asked them their names and had told them mine. I inquired about their health and the health of their parents. I stated obvious things like, "it is raining," and "this is my hat."

After our third language lesson, I popped downstairs to purchase some bread for dinner. As I entered, Snežana pulled out a pen and note pad. She was ready for me. I asked for one loaf of bread, please. ("Jedan heljelb, molim.")

"Ne," she replied. "Hljeb."

"Ha-leb?"

"Ne. Hljeb."

She wrote it out for me phonetically in Latin characters.

"H-ljeb," I read slowly.

"DA!" she said, smiling. I smiled back.

"Jedan? (One?)" she asked. "Šezdeset centi (sixty-cents)."

I then thought to ask for all the names of the baked goods in the glass display and wrote them down for future reference. The next day when I came in she had thoughtfully placed individual Post-It notes all over the glass case in front of the pastries to help me learn what was what. I have always relied upon the kindness of strangers.

The most useful phrase I learned was the one I used on the fisherman, "Žao mi je. Učim Crnagorski" (I am sorry. I am just learning Montenegrin.)

However, it had unintended consequences. I found if I met people and said that, I might get corrected. They would respond by saying, "Ne Crnagorski! To je Srpski!" (It is not Montenegrin! It is Serbian!)

Then I began saying "Učim Srpski."

After that I was told, "Ne Srpski. To je naš materinji jezik." (Not Serbian. It is our mother tongue).

The response I got was based on how the person voted for Montenegrin independence, half did and half did not. I thought I would try "Učim Crnagorski i Srpski." Nobody liked that.[9]

The tutoring in the "local language" started out well, but it did not take long for me to fall behind the rest of the class. After we finished the first lesson, I thought I saw Bojana glance at the wall and wonder if that kindergarten alphabet poster was maybe a little too advanced.

---

9 In order not to offend anyone, we noticed that invitations to official functions always referenced the "local language" not Srpski or Crnagorski specifically.

•

As in English, one little letter in Crnagorski could make all the difference. The entire week our children visited us, I continued to introduce our son, his wife, and our turkey (ćurka) instead of our daughter (ćerka).

We noticed that syntax slaughter and limited vocabulary worked both ways. When we would call a hotel, we would inquire as to what types of beds they had.

"Normal ones."

"What types of cars do you have to rent?"

"Normal cars."[10]

"What kind of meat is on menu today?"

"Normal kind. Good kind."

There was also an diner close by our apartment named "Very Normal People."

One afternoon, I told the university secretary we were leaving to have lunch with a visiting dignitary. She told me to make sure I got the recipes. As I was running out the door to the waiting *taksi*, I thought "Recipes? What recipes? Why does she want the recipes? I don't even know what I am going to order."

So, much to the chagrin of our host, and the consternation of the kitchen staff, I returned with the recipes for all the entrees that had been ordered.

She said, "No, I meant how much you spent on lunch."

She meant "receipt."

Traveling through the country we would find pubs with such names such as "Cock and Bull," "Cock and Bul," "Cock and Boll," "Cock and Bole," and "Bul and Bare" (in the financial district). The strangest one was entitled "Damage Beyond Paragraph" (maybe a writers' hangout?). There were also the entertaining translations like one well-guarded building that was clearly labeled the *Ministarstvo Odbrane* (Ministry of Defense). To us, it sounded more like the Ministry of Mad Scientists.

We realized that we had to learn to listen very carefully to what people really meant.

---

[10] There were really just two kinds of cars, "normal" (those that had automatic transmissions) and "the kind you have to work" (standard transmissions).

Rules of The Road

The night we moved into our apartment, Jelena told me how convenient it was to the nearby bus station and pointed down the block. The next day I went looking for it, so I could plan how to get to work at the university. I walked up and down the street and even through the park thinking she meant another block down, but could not find the bus station. How could I miss a large building surrounded by a whole bevy of busses? I was certain she had pointed north. Just in case I was wrong, I widened my search perimeter to three blocks in all directions, but I could still not find a bus station. The next time Jelena came over, I asked for her help again.

"No problem. I schjo djou. Come. We go."

We crossed the street, walked for fifty feet in the direction she previously pointed, and there was a Plexiglas-covered bus *stop*, a small kiosk covering a depressed dirt floor that, most of the time, was in three inches of water. Because of the large mud puddle, nobody took advantage of the bus stop even when it was raining. Everyone stood on the wet sidewalk. When the bus arrived, the waiting crowd would simultaneously take a giant step back; so as not to be splashed by the morning bus driver.[1] No one liked that driver; he was not pleasant like the afternoon driver.

In the mornings, I walked to the bus station and waited for the Number Eight bus. It ran from the old Aerodrom neighborhood, through downtown, and into the suburbs where my university was located. On the 7:40 a.m. bus there would be people getting off work from the night shift at the hospital, small children going to school, and most of the students in the class I was teaching at the university. These were the same students who may have rudely talked incessantly the day before (some of whom I had asked to leave class). Nevertheless, when I boarded the bus, they would all rise to offer me their seat.

---

1 That was, everyone except the visiting American.

The bus named SANOS was the newer older one. It ran a regular route in Bremen, Germany until the city leaders there thought it had outlived its usefulness and sold it to the city of Podgorica whose city leaders did not. On the bus window there was still a decal showing all the transportation routes in the greater Bremen metropolitan area. Not much help in Montenegro; but if you want to know what transfers would take you to the *Marktplatz* or the *Ratskeller*, you were good to go.

When I went to work, I took the bus. If we had to do business in town, we took a cab. Taxis were plentiful and inexpensive. Rides across town were typically under three dollars.

There were many cab companies in Podgorica. We were happy with the Metro Cab Company. They came with three recommendations. They had an English-speaking dispatcher, the cleanest cars, and, if they said they would be there in four minutes—they were. Metro had a €1.20 base, which some of the others didn't charge. If we took a cab, it was usually well over the minimum fare. The exceptions were when it would begin to storm or Beth Lynn wore certain shoes to dinner and it was too painful to walk back.

During the week, Metro's dispatcher was named Javic.

It got to the point that when I would call, I would say "*Dobar Dan,*" and he would automatically say, "Yes, Professor? Where to go today?"

Many times, we would be picked up by the same cab drivers who knew where to take us without being told. In the late spring, the university ran some Public Service Announcements on TV that featured Yours Truly. This was about the same time some speaking engagements I had made got some press as well. We were picked up one morning and were on our way to an appointment when the cab driver surprisingly handed me his radio microphone.

The dispatcher said, "Professor?"

"Da?"

"This is Javic."

"Yes, Javic. How are you? Is everything okay?"

"Professor, you are famous! This ride is on us!"

I was feeling good about my newfound renown until, when I was traveling by myself, a cabbie I did not know greeted me "Morning, Professor." Startled, I asked how he knew who I was.

He said, "Everyone know djou. Djou are the one with the pretty wife."

One Saturday morning it was pouring, we had errands to run, so I called reliable Metro Cab. We waited outside in the cold rain for ten minutes before calling them again. I spoke to three different dispatchers requesting someone who spoke *Engleski.*

The last one said, "I no understand. You call another cab company."

He hung up. Obviously, the "B" team worked on the weekends.

We didn't have a radio in the apartment, so the only time we heard broadcasted music was when we rode in cabs. We would get tickled when we would hear such things on their radios as Mason Williams' "Classical Gas" being played on ancient, stringed folk instruments.[2] Sometimes we would hear such incongruous tunes as the theme to the "Munsters" in a Serbian retro-mix or the *taksi* driver singing along to "The Woody Woodpecker Song."

•

If one was not doing business, one walked. Leaving the apartment always provided an adventure, but you did not want it to become an accident-filled escapade. Walking was wonderful entertainment, but crossing the street was another matter. The advice from the natives was to always cross *against* the light—because then you knew which direction the cars were coming from. They also recommended when driving in Montenegro, watch out with *all four eyes.* Speaking as surviving pedestrians, we believe the local Rules of the Road were as follows:

1. Pedestrians had the right of way if they were, in fact, within one meter of the vehicle and were *directly in front of the car.* If they were off to one side even slightly (as little as one degree off true) or were beyond the stated one-meter range, the above rule was superseded by rule two.
2. Vehicles had the right of way in all other pedestrian situations.

We learned not to expect cars to necessarily stop when we crossed the street although they would slow down in order to physically demonstrate rule number two. It was perfectly acceptable for a car to come within inches of you as long as they did not actually touch you or any loose apparel you may have about your body. Pedestrians were also expected to maintain a fixed direction vector and not

---

[2] The Montenegrin national instrument is the *gusle*, a mandolin-shaped instrument with only one string. Montenegrins joke they are so poor, they couldn't afford any more strings. The *gusle* usually accompanies an epic ballad that depicts Serbian suffering, fortitude, and resilience. You know you are truly Montenegrin when, during times of *ennui*, you can hear the sound of the instrument that has but one string.

to deviate from their rate of speed. Changes in either factor would result in the approaching driver not being able to estimate the smallest distance between you and their car, resulting in confusion, physical contact, or worse—stalled traffic.

In the city, Montenegrins drove causally and slow, as there were many rumble strips on every street. They were courteous and rarely honked their horn at another driver unless they were saying hello, greeting a relative (of which there are many), or reminding someone who owed them money. Even then, the horn was a soft little beep.

Out in the country, driving habits were a bit more diverse. Either Montenegrins drove the way they did in the city—at 20 miles per hour or they got on the highways (one-lane each direction) and drove in and out of traffic, passing every vehicle with little room to spare for on-coming traffic. It was not unusual for cars to pass us on blind curves when we were driving on cliff-side mountain roads.

We were hosted by one family whose father rarely got to drive (because he had no car, but their son did). Picking us up one evening, he got an opportunity to get behind the wheel and, in doing so, got to express his lost adolescence. He did quick, rabbit-start accelerations when the lights turned green. He liked riding the tire rims when turning corners. He tested the car's brake response as we came up on slower traffic. However, it was during his passing of other cars where we began to seriously question his depth perception.

At one point during the trip, Beth Lynn leaned over to me and very seriously said under her breath, "I love you and I will see you on the other side of the veil."

When we reached our dinner destination, he offered to drive us to Sarajevo the next time he went; but Beth Lynn said she had to wash her hair that night.

Most of the cars in Podgorica were German Volkswagens and Audis, Spanish Seats, Russian Ladas, sometimes a French Peugeot or Italian Lancia, and the odd Mercedes, or BMW. I thought cars parked in Podgorica would be more like the town of Verplanck, New York, from the movie *Drowning Mona* where every car was a YUGO, the very inexpensive car ($3,900) that was made in the former Yugoslavia and imported to the States. It was weeks after we arrived when I finally spotted one. You may remember the reputation the car acquired as the cheapest car in the world. I asked my new friends why there were so few on the road. They replied the joke was: "Oi! Yugo—Yugo fix it" or "First Yugo and then you don't." Production quality and reliability were always an issue.

Montenegrin license plates were designed on the European Union standard, so it will be easier to convert as Montenegro hopes to gain EU membership someday. Plate numbers all started with a two-letter code that designated the municipality where the car was registered.[3] PG stood for Podgorica, BV was Budva, DG was Danilovgrad, etc. Thus, it was easy to tell who was a local resident and who was just visiting.[4] If the first letter on the plate was a single P, then it was a police car. For some strange reason, even unmarked cop cars had a P on their license plates.

During the first month of living in our downtown apartment, we never heard a racing engine, only a few horn tootles, and but a single siren. At least I thought it was a siren; it was high pitched and almost lilting. Though, it could have been the mating call of a male Renault; it was that time of year. Traffic was very quiet, but car alarms were another matter. Everyone parked in the open, and all late model cars had a car alarm. They tended to go off starting at 7:30 a.m. as people were leaving for work, fumbling with their keys and coffee mugs, and, then, accidently bending over and bumping the car next to theirs. The next alarm period was after midnight, especially on weekends, when celebrations had ended, and people were returning home. Drivers would park their own cars, and then stumble into someone else's.

In the back of our apartment building was a coffeehouse named *Caffé Caffé.*[5] Twice a day the members of the Ancient and Fraternal Order of Taxi Drivers met there. During the mid-morning break, we counted as many as 17 cabs parked in front. Like other car owners in Montenegro, they parked very carefully on the street. However, if the street was too narrow, they parked on the sidewalk. If there was no room on either, they would park anywhere they could fit—on the crosswalk, the grass, or the even the median.

The first time I rented a car, I quickly learned that traffic lights are on the near side of the intersection, not the far side as they are in the U.S. Thus, if I pulled all the way up to the zebra stripes at the pedestrian crossing—I could not see the light. In Montenegro, if you were pulled over for speeding, you paid a €35 fine directly to the police officer. If you were caught running a red light, it was a whopping €1,000 fine. After the law was enacted, letters to the editors ran something like, "How am I going to afford to pay all those fines?"

For the first times in our adult lives we lived without a car. Almost everything we needed to get to was in walking distance of our apartment. We got spoiled as shopping was especially convenient and relaxing.

---

[3] These municipalities are like states in the Montenegrin representative government.

[4] If I had a car, I would have a personalized license plate honoring one of my favorite authors, PG WDHSE.

[5] The name was officially approved by the Ministry of Redundancy Ministry.

To Market, To Market

Shopping in Montenegro was the exact opposite of shopping in the States. When we shopped at home, we would go to one store and buy everything there. In Montenegro, you had to go to many places in order to purchase, perhaps, one item at each store. Since we had no freezer, at least one of us was shopping every day. This was quite different than the efficient once-a-week trip to Super Wally-World we were used to. However, we could do all our essential shopping within yards of our front porch. In the evening, we were exactly seventy-three steps from a thirty-cent, postprandial, chocolate gelato.

In our apartment building, there was a toy store, a stationery store, the national employment office, a bakery, a travel agency, and an electronic casino. Across the street was the Unico restaurant, a "Štampa" news stand kiosk, "Maestro's Pizza", an unnamed green grocer, a watch/clock repair store (which was never open), "Bar-Kod" cosmetics, "LM Shop" (women's apparel), "Mimi's" fast food, "Chic" (women's apparel), "Printemps" (women's apparel), and "Piranda" (also women's apparel). Beside those were "Martinovic Meats" (and market), "Tobacco Shop" newsstand, an *apoteka* (pharmacy), the Frizerski Salon (barber shop), "Delizia Dessert," "Be Happy Lingerie" (with an interesting fig leaf logo), and "Sonja's Poslastičarnica" (confections and desserts). This was followed by, "Mimoza" (another market), another tiny unnamed tobacco shop and newsstand, the "Mercator Mex" market, an unnamed newsstand, and the ПЕКАРА bakery—all in the space of 100 yards. Most stores on the block opened at 6 a.m. and closed at 10 p.m.

I learned to actually love last minute grocery errands. Some of these stores were so small the proprietor had just enough room for a place to sit, but had to come out of their store onto the sidewalk so a serious customer could browse inside.

All shopping was strictly on a cash basis. Credit cards were unheard of except at hotels. Therefore, we had to visit the ATM frequently and carry around a lot of cash. It was typical for us to have upward of €500 on us at any given time. Anyone in Montenegro had change for a €100 note; but in the U.S., no one can break a twenty-dollar bill.[1]

Early on in our marriage, Beth Lynn learned not to send me to the grocery store without a very specific (and limited) shopping list with explicit instructions not to buy anything that was not on the list. I once brought home a new can of dog food just because I thought the brand name was clever. At the time, we didn't even have a dog. Therefore, The List has become a major communication mechanism in our marriage. Strict adherence to it contributes to marital bliss. As Beth Lynn was initially ill when we arrived, I was fetching all the groceries. Therefore, I knew the new brands and products we preferred. When she got better, I handed the shopping duties (and the list) over to her. It also included the names of the specific brands, where to buy them, and any other important notes about the products.

I came home one day and she frustratingly said, "I did all the shopping, but I couldn't find the eyeglasses cleaner you wanted. I went to five different markets and spent *all day* looking for this one item! No one had any eyeglasses cleaner spray, much less the 'S or L' brand. Where do you buy it?"

I reviewed the list I had written down. It read, "Orange juice (Next), Snack foods (Chipsy's or Čips), Cookies (Eurocreme), Eyeglass cleaner spray (S or L)."

(S or L) meant buy it "sooner or later."

•

As a student of marketing, I am fascinated by grocery stores. Where else can you see so many promotional messages and creative appeals in one place? To have entire stores of new products I have never seen before is thrilling. (However, it didn't take long to realize all the little markets on our block carried virtually the same products.[2])

---

1 Each euro denomination bill is designed to be very distinguishable in color and size from another. However, one-euro coins are about the size of American quarters. The physicality of this created a unique psychology for the first couple of weeks as I found myself spending Euro coins as if they were two bits until it dawned on me that they were worth $1.50.

2 When shopping in this new country, I noticed that I felt the same sensation as I did in my local grocery store back home. Is that because I feel at home wherever I am or because I always feel isolated and emotionally detached? I decided that it was the former, as the

Grocery buying tasks are the same no matter where you are in the world, but we did have to think beyond what we were used to looking for and expecting to see on the shelves. In the Balkans, we learned we could not depend on brands we knew from America even being the same product much less how it should be packaged or labeled. Tomato paste came in a large tube, like toothpaste, as did mayonnaise. Butter (hard to find in the neighborhood) came in little foil wrapped squares, about the size of three pats, but margarine was packaged in huge plastic containers. *Snickers* were wrapped like *Tootsie Rolls*, *Kleenex* was the brand of (strawberry scented) toilet paper, a *Mars* candy bar was an American *Milky Way*, and a *Milky Way* was closer to a *Three Musketeers* bar. *Vanish* was not a toilet bowl cleaner but a spot remover like *Shout*.

After our initial retail excursions, we realized we needed help interpreting the language as well as with some specific product recommendations. Jelena was delighted to come over and lead us on a store tour. From previous shopping trips, we learned *Fairy* was the most popular laundry soap brand if shelf facings were anything to go by. (The fairy on the package waves her magical wand, and all your clothes come out sparkling clean.) However, on advice of Jelena, we became *Ariel* purchasers as she said it was the best. That, and her kids liked the mermaid on the box. *Calming* was the brand of clothes' softener guaranteed to get out your wrinkles because it calmed your clothes.

Beth Lynn was excited to find a box of *Special K* cereal. It was manufactured in Germany. Like most of the consumer-packaged goods, it had separate compliance labels for sales in Bosnia and Herzegovina, Bulgaria, Croatia, the Czech Republic, Estonia, Hungary, Latvia, Lithuania, Macedonia, Romania, Russia, Serbia and Montenegro, and Slovenia. Thirteen different countries in eastern Europe—yet the front of the box was printed entirely in English.[3]

There were also new shopping rules and etiquette to learn. I found this out the first day after reaching for an apple and getting reprimanded by the clerk. Customers did not touch the fruit or vegetables. You told the clerk (or, in our case, just pointed to) what you wanted and indicated the quantity you desired. She picked out whichever ones she chose and placed them in a bag.[4] We noticed as we became regular patrons and friendly with the clerks, that we did not get the older, bruised produce anymore.

---

second one would require extensive therapy.

3 The fact that the box listed Serbia and Montenegro as one country showed that Kellogg's had not changed their box design in over four years.

4 It was always a she.

Produce choices were quite limited. There were not a lot of varieties. For example, there was only one type of lettuce, and it had a rather bitter taste. With enough other ingredients in a salad (like powerful green olives), you could mostly cover up the bitterness. Green bell peppers were not the deep green we were used to—they were the color of celery. We saw something that looked like celery, but the stalks were two to three feet high, more like rhubarb. Some produce stands also had bins of shelled nuts, walnuts, almonds, peanuts (*kikiriki*), and pistachios.[5] These were cheap, like three pounds for a dollar. There are also all kinds of dried beans, which we bought a lot of because they made a delicious soup. During our first month, that was one of the few things Beth Lynn felt confident enough to cook. Looking for something new to eat, we discovered a new produce stand two blocks over that was open twenty-fours a day. Beth Lynn got excited because it was rumored to carry cilantro and basil. It turned out they were neither.

There were few choices among the canned goods—some fruits, a small shelf of vegetables, and no prepared soups at all. One store stocked only canned corn, canned peas, and canned peas with corn. We bought them all.[6] There were, however, plenty of tinned tuna, sardines, salmon, and, caviar. They did have different kinds of tomato sauces in glass jars. We learned the Bolognese spaghetti meat-sauce was made with ground ham not hamburger.

The yogurts, on the other hand, were to die for with their creamy textures and fruit that melted in your mouth. There was a wide variety of fruit juices. *Real* fruit juices—apple, strawberry, and pear, not cartons of corn syrup with a few drops of gratuitous processed dead fruit. Here, the fruit juice content ranged from fifty to one hundred percent pure fruit. We couldn't drink enough of them.

Being in the Mediterranean, there were many different kinds of olives (*maseline*), balsamic vinegars, and olive oils. Each one we tried was superb. To be eaten with the olives were two categories of cheese (*sir*). There were imported cheeses (all from Holland) and the local contribution that came as either new cheese or aged cheese, all from very white goats.

The breads in the bakeries were, of course, fresh every day, and they seemed to stay fresher longer than in the U.S. There were little loaves of pre-sliced bread in the markets, but they had no taste and were very expensive. We came to

5 We bought a lot of *kikiriki* because it was just so fun to say.

6 The only thing we did not have in the apartment, as it turned out, was a can opener. None of the neighborhood markets sold any. However, on one of our evening strolls, I headed up the block to a previously undiscovered shopping area where there was the *B-Market,* a grocery store on the bottom floor and a housewares/toy store/pool hall on the second floor. Next to the pool cue rack was a shelf of can openers.

prefer the large baguettes from the bakery downstairs. Early in the morning, the appealing aroma of baking goods would drift up to our apartment signaling that breakfast was ready and to bring money.

In order to get personal products, (or even aspirin), you went to the *Apoteka* (apothecary/pharmacy). The selections were slim, and we were glad we took the advice of previous ex-pats and brought our own Sinutab, Mucinex, and Tylenol with us. During cold season, it would have been very difficult finding anything comparable.[7]

•

In the lobby of our apartment building were tenant mailboxes. Made of thin metal, they were old, rusted, and most of their covers had been torn off long ago. We did not get any mail the entire time we were there. Other tenants did, just not us. Water, electricity, and garbage bills did not come in the mail; once a month they were stuck in our front door. The phone company saved even more money on postage. Once a month, we had to collect our phone bill from their city office.

After the bills arrived, we stood in line at the ATM to get the necessary cash and, then stood in line at the post office to pay the bills. Around the first of the month, there was a woman who came to collect €3.00 for keeping the apartment building clean. The ground floor was always full of litter, trash, and debris. We could not figure out what she did exactly as we never saw her except when she came to collect. We were told by Jelena just to pay her every month.

•

I am one-quarter Montenegrin but must not be the quarter that is on the outside. I spent the better part of two weekends trying to buy one long-sleeve dress shirt. The shirts I found in the local shops came in S-M-L-XL sizes and, thus, did not fit, as I was clearly an L-and-a-half in their sizing system. If I went to Marks & Spencer, the U.K. clothier, I did find shirts sized in inches rather than centimeters. However, all the shirts were standardized to one collar size equals one specific sleeve length. Therefore, if you have a 16"/40.5 cm collar, your arm has to be exactly 35"/89 cm long. The assumption is that if you are not built that way, there must be something wrong with *you*. I am a very normally

[7] It tells you something that the U.S. State Department considers Montenegro a hardship assignment because of the lack of western standards of medicines and medical services.

constructed man. I wear a 16" collar and have a 32" arm. My dimensional ratios are quite average but, not in Montenegro. I either needed to have a smaller neck or grow longer arms. Other men came into the stores, tried on shirts, and they fit great. After this shopping experience, I began to notice a large number of men who never wore ties. Now I knew why.

Fleeced

Four weeks in, I was looking a bit scruffy and could not put off getting a haircut any longer. I had an important appointment coming up, so I dropped into the neighborhood clip joint for a trim. My new barber was Moslem. His business partner was Orthodox. You could tell by their names and the various pictures and postcards stuck around their respective mirrors. One had pictures of the Moslem Quarter, its Glavatovići mosque, and the clock tower there. His partner had pictures of Sveti Džorđže and the Madonna. They must have been close friends as they talked to one another the entire time I was there. They had five barber chairs, three were empty, and they chose to use the chairs right next to one another. Customers and friends would drop by for conversations and help themselves to the combs, mirrors, hair tonic, and aftershave. The shop was open from 8 a.m. to 8 p.m. I noticed from our walks after dinner, it was always crowded, but there was a lot more fat-chewing than hair cutting getting done. They had an apprentice barber, a young man of 18 who sat in the waiting chairs texting until he was handed a comb to clean or a razor to sterilize.

For the investment of €4.00, I got my ears lowered, my scalp examined, and my neck scraped. The haircut really took me back to my childhood. Ibrahim used a pair of scissors and a straight razor. He would shred balled cotton and place it in the tines of the comb when he straightened my hair, and I have no idea why. I got "whitewalls," over my ears, a rub of hair tonic, and he finished me off with a whisk of talcum powder. I have not had those things done to me in a very long time. The only things missing were the Barbasol and the Dubble-Bubble gum. I won't say he cut my hair short; but for some reason it dawned on me I was a lot closer to the shores of Tripoli than I was to the halls of Montezuma. There was always a dog asleep in the back corner of the shop. He was also sporting a buzz cut. I mentally named him *Semper Fi*do.

When I got to the apartment, Beth Lynn didn't recognize me and wouldn't let me back in until I showed her my passport picture through the peephole.

I Tell Ya, I Was Framed!

At some point in an extended trip, you are going to have a health-care crisis. Mine was not a burst appendix or something that required an infectious disease specialist, but was far worse. I broke my glasses.

I was cleaning them one morning in anticipation of needing to see that day and—snap, off came the right nosepiece. I called to Beth Lynn who looked at my glasses then closely examined my large Montenegrin nose.

She said, "It's probably a stress fracture."

During our around-town wanderings, I had been smart enough to note where the eyeglass retailers were. I had already discovered none of them sold lens cleaner except for a very fancy store near the football stadium named "Luxottica," which tended to describe the girls who worked there and sold every eyeglass brand but that one. There they had a generic lens cleaner without label for €7.50. I suspected it was poured out of a larger Windex bottle in the backroom into a tiny spray bottle and then sold to me. However, this was the only store that stocked such items.

My eyeglasses are trifocals (for typing, reading, and driving), with non-glare coating (for bright classroom lights) and progressive lenses (for vanity). They are great glasses but set me back about the price of a mortgage payment. I was at least smart enough to bring my older pair with me on the trip. When I put that pair on, the only thing that was clear to me is why I bought the new, replacement pair. The close-up lens is so low in the glass I have to hold my head back, in order to see stairs descending before me.

I do not know if this happens to other eyeglass wearers, but for the first day or so after getting a new pair of multi-focal glasses, my eyes, brain, and equilibrium have to get used to the new visual stimulus signals. This usually results in a slight headache and the tendency to step really high onto curbs and dodge things that are, say, a hundred feet away. One of the things you do not do is go drag racing around town, as your inner ear does not catch up with the glasses change for several days after.

But that is what I ended up doing in the taxi I called to take me to the football stadium. The driver spoke no English and evidently didn't know *palako, palako* either, or just didn't want to slow down. It was a record-setting trip in which I closed my eyes and waited for the taxi to stop completely along with the rest of my spinning world. We landed at the stadium but at the wrong end.[8]

---

8 The stadium is where the hometown football team, the *Podgorica Buducnost* (the "Futures") plays and, in typical European space-saving fashion, the inside of the structure is the stadium and, under the stands, are corporate offices, retail establishments, and even university classrooms.

A wet and very careful walk around the structure took me to the optical store where there was a woman[9] who didn't look up from her fashion magazine when I came in.

"*Dobar dan*," I said.

She looked up.

"*Da li govorite Engliski?*" I asked.

"*Ne*," she replied.

This is going to be tougher than I thought. I took a moment to flip through the Serbian phrase book I carried with me. There were phrases declaring an appendicitis or infectious disease (social diseases were given a lot of coverage) but nothing about eyeglasses.[10] I did find the phrase for "I need help with . . ." and I pointed to my glasses. She nodded in agreement, went to a shelf, and returned to offer me a pair of frames that Elton John wouldn't even be caught dead in.

I shook my head and showed her my broken pair of glasses. In sympathy she nodded which became shaking meaning they did not repair glasses there. However, she wrote down an address and drew a cryptic map for me. She pointed to her own glasses, then walked to the supply closet door, and pointed to her glasses, then at the door, her glasses, and the door again. She cocked her head to one side, indicating the international inquiry of "Are you smart enough to get this?" Wherever I was going next, I was to look for glasses on a door. I got it.

She smiled at me with the "Will there be anything else?" smile. I bought another bottle of overpriced lens cleaner, and she was kind enough to call me a taxi.

This ride took me to a residential area I had never been to where there was a dark, ominous cement apartment building. There were no stores or signs on the ground floor. I showed the cab driver the map. He pointed to the building and then pointed up. I got out, paid the man, entered the building, and ventured up an unlit staircase. On the second floor, I examined all the doors. The last one in the corner has a miniscule pencil drawing of a pair of eyeglasses on the faded paint. Dis mus' be da place.

I knocked on the door. There was no answer, and I was about to leave when the door was opened by a stooped, white-haired woman who glared at me.

"*Dobar dan,*" I said, smiling at her.

---

9 This is just being Politically Correct. The female was in her early twenties and wore jeans, leather boots, a loud, tie-dyed t-shirt and green nail polish. But it was the purple glasses frames that set off her pink tinted hair in a subtle way that, somehow, made her look *much* younger.

10 Surely, some of the writers and editors of these books wear glasses?

She nodded, knowing I was not from around these parts and wondering what a stranger was doing in her building. I pointed to my glasses.

Without changing expression, she turned, leaving the door open and began yelling. A middle-aged man appeared who nodded, pointed behind him at the woman who was no longer there, and then pointed to his ear. *(Please excuse her as she is hard of hearing.)*

"*Dobar dan,*" I said, using my new Srpski Phrase-of-the-Day.

"*Dobar dan,*" he replied.

"*Da li govorite Engliski?*" I inquired.

"*Ne,*" he said, smiling.

("Rats," I replied, mentally.)

He motioned me into his apartment where we stood in the hallway next to a tiny table that served as his service counter. I poured my broken glasses out of the case onto a piece of old felt.

"Ah," he said while he thoughtfully examined both parts through a magnifying glass.

"*Da? Ne?*" I asked. (Yes? No? Can you fix them?)

"*Veomajeteškodapopravinaočareodnajlon,*" he said rather rapidly.

He repeated the word *najlon* (nylon) and pointed to the bottom of the lenses. I took it that he did not like the nylon cords that held the lenses on, as they tended to melt when he tried to solder the frames.

"*Veomajeteškoraditisatitanijumokvirimaoninećedržativarkaoštoječelik,*" he said, slowly shaking his head.

I also understood titanium frames (which I paid extra for) were not his preference as didn't hold a weld very well.

"Žao mi je. Učim Crnagorski," I said feebly. ("I am sorry, I am just learning Montenegrin.")[11]

He nodded, picked up my glasses, put them back in the case, and wrote down his phone number. He motioned for me to do the same. He proceeded to motion with his hands making big arching gestures I interpreted that he would try his best, but he wasn't guaranteeing he could fix them. I gave him my best WEWYD look and left my $450 glasses with this stranger who might return them to me in more pieces than they were when I gave them to him.

Two days later, I got a phone call.

"Paolo?" (For some reason, he used the Italian form of my name.)

"Sì?" (For some reason, I now knew Italian.)

"Glasses. Ready."

[11] A great phrase to know. Learn it. Use it. Live it.

Then he hung up. I was sure he had to look up these English words but did not want to press his luck with any more conversation. I immediately took a taxi to his place.

He was so excited when he greeted me. He had to explain how difficult it was to work around the nylon monofilament because he couldn't get any replacement for it in Montenegro. He had to mime how he had to hold the glasses frame, the nosepiece, the soldering iron (and his mouth) just right in order to get it to all come together at that perfect moment of heat and meld.

Now I am smart enough to know when I am being set up. This is the same spiel my dentist uses when he is working his way up to the final bill and explaining why it is going to be all worth it. I let the man finish talking and motioned by rubbing my thumb and finger together. *How much*? He wrote down a figure and I did not even quibble or try to negotiate. He had my glasses in his hand and me over a barrel. I just paid, thanked him, and left.

Two taxi rides: €2.75.
Lens cleaner: €7.50.
Getting your glasses repaired (and polished): €5.00.
Getting your whole world back to normal: Priceless.

•

The first time we entered the Martinović Meat Market across the street, the visual and olfactory sensations were completely overwhelming. We had to immediately back out, breathe fresh air, and reenter. Red and brown dried cuts of beef, lamb, pork, and sausage hung from overhead and covered every wall. Slabs of old meat, mixed with the current day's fresher offerings behind the glass display case, produced an odoriferous combination that made it hard for us to even concentrate on what we were looking at. Beth Lynn stood in the middle of the store and examined everything. Nothing looked familiar except several large hams hanging over the door to the back room. This was the comestible of which Montenegro is most proud—Njeguški pršut. When dried, it looks like thin slices of bacon that appear to have been left out on the counter all day. Cuts will be about half meat and half fat (because fat is good for you). It is salty and quite savory.

None of the countless cuts of beef looked like any we had ever seen before. We tried to mentally reassemble them to see if we could figure out from whence they came. The coiled sausage was somewhat recognizable. From its color, we could not tell if it represented the last vestiges of bovine, ovine, or porcine. When chicken breasts were available, they cost ten dollars apiece. So much for transplanting our normal American diet here to Montenegro. After a few weeks, we learned from new friends that most of what we were examining in the shop was lamb. Initially, Beth Lynn was very leery of purchasing any meat. She did not believe that it was up to USDABL standards, and she did not know what the heck she was buying. She knew she was eventually going to have to break down as it was going to be a tough task to convince two displaced Texans to become vegetarians for six months.

Her first purchase was processed deli meat for my sack lunches. It was a large loaf of bologna imbedded with chunks of white cheese. It turned out not to be cheese, but I found if I just poked out the white stuff, it was quite edible—sort of a Swiss Bologna. Martinović just sold meat. If you wanted fish, you had to walk across the street.

During our first few weeks, we only shopped in the neighborhood and could only find simple packaged goods like what you would find in an American convenience store. We thought that was all the retailing choices there were. We like salads and, because we could only locate olive oil and balsamic vinegar initially, we had our choice of three salad dressings: mostly olive oil with a little balsamic vinegar, half and half (rare), or mostly balsamic vinegar with just a drop of olive oil. The mixture you got depended on how steady your hand was at the time. Once we discovered the larger grocery stores at the mall and elsewhere, our culinary choices expanded considerably.

There were two shopping malls in Podgorica; each had its own unique characteristics. Delta Center was the Podgorica version of its big sister mall in the capital of Serbia. It was a contemporary upscale mall with apparel, entertainment, and an immense modern Mercator Mex grocery store. It became our primary provision provider; but it was just a bit too far to walk and carry back heavy bags of groceries. It became a special trip where grocery and window-shopping provided our date night for the week.

The other shopping center was the Mall of Montenegro known locally as the Big Market (*Velike Plača*). This doesn't refer to its size, but to the green market that is attached to it. This mall was built on the site of an existing farmers' market, so the developers were required to provide a permanent cover for this traditional market. The Mall itself only had a grocery store and coffee house on the first floor but, due to the poor economy, no other tenants. The farmers' market was a large open area with vegetables, fruit, nuts, hand-dipped candles, and local honey. On the first floor, there were separate rooms for fresh fish (*riba*), eggs (*jajas*)[12], and cheese. Browsing the booths, you were accosted by vendors yelling, hoping to convert their greens into green. Once we figured out how to shop for groceries, the next step was to master cooking the local cuisine.

12 Hence the phrase in English, "Look at the *jajas* on that chick."

Balkan Up

Montenegrin cuisine consists primarily of food.

Someone once asked a Montenegrin for the country's most valuable contribution to humanity.

"That's easy," he said. "Sour cream, onions, grilled mincemeat . . ."

If you dined inland the fare was a farrago of foreign influences including Venetian, Italian, Turkish, Arab, Serbian, and Hungarian. On the coast, it was heavily influenced by Mediterranean food with fresh fish dominating the menu. All of it was characterized by the generous use of spices, aromatic herbs, vegetables, and, most significantly, olive oil.

It is impossible to overstate the importance of olives and olive oil to Montenegrins.[1] What is true for Montenegro is true for all the Mediterranean cultures. In Montenegro there are estimated to be over one million cultivated olive trees or about two per person. In the 19th century, after each battle, Prince Nikola told every army volunteer to go home and plant an olive tree. Most of the larger groves were situated around Bar and Ulcinj on the coast. This was another reason for pirates to covet the area, as olive oil was the liquid gold of its day. In the Middle-Ages, Montenegrin olive oil was shipped to Venice, Rome, Cairo, and Constantinople.

•

We could not wait to experience the local cuisine, but, when we first arrived, we thought it best not to venture into the world of Balkan food without some guidance. We decided pizza was safe enough, and we ventured over to *Maestro's*, a pizza joint directly across the street from our apartment. The previous

---

1 They are just popeyed for olive oil.

Fulbrighter said was her favorite place to eat.[2] The menu items were in Italian, and the explanations were in Srpski. The friendly waiter spoke a little English so as we would point to the various pizzas, he would say "meat" or "weg-atable."

"What kind of meat?" we would ask.

"Iz good meat."

"I'm sure it is. What *type* of meat?"

"Normal meat. Djou want beg or lettle pizza?"

Not willing to take our chances on the mystery meat the first night, we settled on *Quattro Formaggi*, a four-cheese pizza. When it arrived, each quarter slice had a different cheese on it. Not what we were expecting, but it was a circular smorgasbord of zesty flavor. Just before we took our first bite, the waiter leaned over and politely squirted ketchup all over the pizza. He smiled at us and left the bottle on the table. We looked at the pizza, at each other, and glanced around to notice everyone else's pizza was covered in ketchup, too. Cultural dining lesson number one.

•

The most popular fast food in Montenegro is a filled filo pastry called *burek*. Another remnant of the Ottoman era, it could be baked or fried and comes full of either meat (*meso*) or cheese. If you wanted a choice besides the cheese, you had to get to the bakery early. Most burek were baked in large round pans and then cut into slices. They were offered on the "salty" side of the bakery counter. We learned that "salty" items, those with meat and cheese (lunch and dinner items) were kept on a separate shelf from the sweet items (those for breakfast and dessert). Most of the pastries looked alike except for the ones that were dusted with powdered sugar. If there weren't white pastries behind the glass to guide you, you might get a surprise whatever meal you were buying them for.

Ćevapi is one of the national dishes and is popular throughout the entire Balkans. Ćevapi is the Persian word for kebab.[3] It is a ground mixture of meats like a sausage and is grilled as links or in a patty. It was explained to us thusly:

"It has meat *bif*, swine, lamb, and, how you say, small cow."

"Calf?"

"No."

"Veal?

---

2 Granted, she did have her teen-aged son with her and you know what picky eaters they can be.

3 Which is odd, as *kebab* is the Persian word for *kebab*.

"Da, weal. It has weal. Thirty-percent weal."

"Ćevapi iz tradizinal Montenegrin dish. But, we do not eat it. It is not healthy. You do not know what is in it. All children like it, but we do not let them eat it very often. It is like Coca-Cola. We do not let them drink that. We only let children eat healthy things."

What turned out to be healthy was anything made from milk (*mlijeko*), cream (*krema*), cheese, or fat (*debeo*). It was especially healthy if it came from Montenegro and particularly good for you if it was raised anywhere near the village of Njeguš, at the base of revered Mt. Lovćen. Dairy or anything else with fat was considered beneficial to the system, as it was natural and organic. This category also included eggs and butter (especially the "Burro" brand).[4] Yogurt was questionable, as the fermentation process introduced a mysterious bacterium that created suspicion. Sodas were okay as long as they were fruit-based like *naranča* (Fanta Orange) or *limun* (Schweppes Bitter).

"But Coca-Cola, that brown juice it is made from—where does that come from?"

During one of our walks when rumbling was heard overhead in the clouds as well as internally in our stomachs, we decided to try Montenegrin fast food for the first time. This is harder to do than it sounds. In the entire country, there are no McDonalds, Burger Kings, Taco Bells, or Starbucks.[5] In fact there are no American or European fast-food chains of any kind.[6] However, we had heard hamburgers are readily available, made with the local ćevapi; and they were most generous with their portions. Near the football stadium we found a fast food restaurant called, surprisingly, "Fast Food." On the menu were a *Gurmanska Pljeskavica* (Gourmet Burger), *Domaća Pljeskavica* (Homemade Burger), *Ražnjici* (Kebabs), and *Vješalica* (dry pork loin hung above the fire). At the bottom was Hamburger—the plain version. They grilled a ćevapi patty and toasted the bun over an open wooden barbeque pit. It cooked fast, and we were given the choice of accouterment: dill pickles sliced long ways, three different selections of prepared cabbage, pickled carrots, and a roasted red pepper and eggplant pate. Observing the other patrons, it appeared mayonnaise was the preferred lubricant of choice although mustard was available. They served the food on a short, wooden bar with four stools under an old awning. This place

---

4 That is not the animal from where we get our butter back home.

5 This is a true statement with one tiny exception. We discovered there was a McDonalds *kiosk* that was open in Budva, but only during the summer.

6 There is not a single golf course in all of Montenegro, either.

became one of our favorite hang-outs because we could eat outside and watch the world go by no matter what the weather was doing.

•

After we had settled into our apartment, Beth Lynn was anxious to begin cooking. She started by serving meals she knew how to cook using the ingredients she could recognize at the store—pasta, salads, and soups. After those became routine, she decided to mix things up a bit. When we initially took stock of the kitchen, there were some spice jars in the pantry. None of the labels on the jars were in any of the four Serbian or Croatian-English dictionaries we had purchased. However, Beth Lynn could tell what most were by their aroma. The first whiff of cinnamon made her sneeze, and the curry brought tears to her eyes and a demand for an open window. The spices were so potent you only needed to use about a fourth of the portion you would use in American recipes. Most of the spices came in containers that ground the contents—nice for potency but hard to measure. The first few meals of hers that used those spices emptied the milk carton pretty quick.

As adventurous as we believed ourselves to be, it did not take long for us to miss certain American foods we never would have considered essential to our survival. Along about mid-February, I was suddenly overcome by a ravenous desire for something I could not have—an Oreo cookie. As a rule, I don't even eat Oreos. But, *I had to have one.*

An ex-pat we met who had lived and thrived in several countries, pontificated that it was not only psychologically reassuring but probably necessary to find local foods that could provide you at least a modicum of comfort either as a substitute or a distraction from the food you missed from home. No local grocery will have the brand of cereal that gets you started in the morning, but they probably have something that you will like and makes noise in your milk. If the neighborhood wine merchant does not carry your preferred vintage, discover the local favorite. Find little treats that give you something to look forward to weekly, if not daily. Finding these little delights in the local stores will go a long way to postponing the inevitable languor that comes sooner or later.

Nosing around in the grocery store one day, I discovered *Eurovafel* wafer cookies (filled with *Eurocrem*). They are sweet, light, and oh so good. I usually bought all the packages that were on the shelf. It was hard not to consume an entire package after dinner and be completely filled with *Eurovafel* wafer cookies (filled with *Eurocrem*). Here was my Oreo substitute. And, they were good.[7]

Most meals we ate at home as that was our middle-aged habit, and restaurants were so filled with cigarette smoke, it was hard to see who your dinner partner was, much less breathe. However, we enjoy epicurean exploration and found that if we ate out at the time we normally did in the States (5 p.m. to 7 p.m.) and not when the locals did (which was much later), we might have the restaurant almost to ourselves with a minimum of atmospheric contamination. Some restaurants had a separate no-smoking section that meant little as the ashtrays and matchboxes were stacked underneath the No Smoking sign on the wall above the serviette. Every café and restaurant would be filled with smoke save one. *Bratstva i Jedinstva* ("Brotherhood and Unity")[8], was a restaurant on Njegoševa Street, one of Podgorica's pub-crawl avenues. Owned by the Serbian Orthodox Church, it served an inexpensive lunch of soup or goulash with homemade pomegranate juice. There were eight hand-carved picnic-like tables with hard benches draped with woolen shawls for padding. Next-door was a large gift shop with CD's of spiritual chants, icons, and saint medallions.

After exploring many of the featured restaurants in Podgorica, we discovered that, at least in our price range, 80 percent of those restaurant menus were the same: pizza, pasta, Greek salad, *pom frites*, soups, olives, and cheese. We could not decide if this was due to a lack of broader knowledge on the part of the chefs/cooks/owners or if it was a case of giving people what they wanted, Montenegrins basically being "meat and potato" people.

Some chefs attempted to be very creative with their cuisine offerings. We dined several times at the only Chinese restaurant in town. We ordered the same entrée on three different occasions and got three completely different dishes. We also noticed no matter what dish was ordered, we received the same diced-chicken and vegetables, merely with different sauces.

We also learned what was advertised as exotic gastronomy in the Balkans, wasn't necessarily so. Wandering around the Lapad neighborhood in Dubrovnik, Croatia one evening, we stumbled upon a Mexican restaurant. Not one to pass up a chance to chow down on a chimichanga in Croatia, we paid our money and took our chances. The menu was labeled Mexican food, but it was all made

---

7 I shared *Eurovafels* with every friend and family member that came to visit. They all ended up taking several boxes home to America. The five packages I brought home provided me a month of bliss, followed by a period of mourning in which my sorrows were drowned by Oreos in milk.

8 "Brotherhood and Unity" was also Tito's motto in unifying all the separate countries and cultures into Yugoslavia following World War II.

out of Italian ingredients. The burrito was ground beef rolled in pizza dough smothered in ketchup and the tortilla chips were served with marinara sauce. It was full of tourists from the EU, but not a place any transplanted Texan would go twice.

Fresh food was the rule, not the exception. Many times, we would enter a restaurant, place our order, and watch while an employee went out the front door to fetch the raw ingredients for our meal—an example of Just-in-Time Inventory control for small businesses. On the island of Hvar off the Croatian coast, we were strolling on the promenade in front of its quaint harbor, which ran in back of the hotels and their *al fresco* dining facilities (which provided wonderfully tranquil views of the boats and bay). A small pea-row boat pulled up, and the owner threw a 25-pound tuna onto the walkway. He proceeded to gut and filet the fish in full view of the dining customers. Upon completion of this task, he picked up the guts, tossed them to the waiting cats, and took the fileted fish into the nearest restaurant, dripping blood all the way up the steps. There he stood in the doorway holding the fish while he negotiated a price with the chef. I think urgency was on his side.

In Podgorica, the *Carine* restaurant was the diner of choice for Americans as it had a tri-lingual menu (Serbian, Italian, and English), and the prices were quite reasonable. *Carine* had a bar, a casual pizzeria, an extensive dessert menu, and, in the basement, a *nacionalni restoran* for those special occasions when you wanted to dine on traditional Montenegrin fare. Besides all that, it had free Wi-Fi. As such, it was the *de facto* employee cafeteria for the American Embassy personnel.[9] Waiters loved new Americans to arrive in town, as they would continue to tip 15 percent until told by colleagues you only tipped fifty cents or, at most, a Euro, no matter what the bill was.

A typical Montenegrin meal might begin with an appetizer plate with pršut,[10] *stari sir* (aged cheese)[11], *masline* (olives), and *suhe smokve* (dried figs). This would be followed by a thick soup (*čorba*) of onions, potatoes, vegetables, or cheese. *Kačamak*, a warm porridge of wheat or cornmeal, might then be served with cheese or yogurt. The main entrée would be a choice of veal, beef, or lamb prepared "under the bell" or "under the ashes" in which the meat was

---

9 Ask for Igor or Zoren. Tell them Professor Paul sent you.

10 As mentioned, the pride of the country was pršut, cured ham that had been salted for at least fifteen days then smoked from December to June using beechwood. When the entire yard smelled of ham, everyone knew that July had arrived. If you ordered a small serving of pršut you learned not to be surprised when they brought the entire ham, hoof and all, to the table in order to slice off a piece.

11 There is also *Njeguški sir,* cheese aged in olive oil.

slow cooked Dutch-oven style covered in glowing embers making it succulent and tender. The entrée would be accompanied by *raštan*, a green cabbage cooked with mutton. If it was a very special occasion, you might be served lamb in milk with spices and potatoes. A more casual evening might produce *popečci*, a crunchy, fried chicken Cordon Bleu.

It was said the fish in Montenegro swim three times. First, they swim in the sea, the second time in oil, and the third in the local wine. At any seaside resort, fish choices might include European sea bass, gilthead sea bream, red mullet, amberjack, grey mullet, horse mackerel, European pilchard, wrasse, spiny lobster, shrimp, squid, and the ubiquitous octopus. Other domestic delicacies include carp from Lake Skadar prepared with plums and black risotto—rice cooked in cuttlefish ink.

Like most of Europe, a Montenegrin meal lasted as long as the conversation could. There was no rush and customers do not have any sense of obligation to the patrons who might be waiting for a table. The fact was no one was really waiting. This allowed time for more conversation, an aperitif, or dessert, which might include baklava or tulumba, a pastry, shaped like a *churro*, which was soaked in sweet honey syrup.[12] After the last course arrived, we were always left alone for as long as we liked until we finally asked for the check.

•

As the time approached for us to return home, dinner invitations started arriving. These were always special occasions in the homes of families we had grown to love. Through these opportunities, we were able to experience typical Montenegrin family life while enjoying wonderful homemade Montenegrin cuisine. We learned to expect and enjoy the inevitable pršut, aged cheese, and olives at every meal. If the woman of the house was a good cook and loved to indulge in national delicacies, she would have cooked all day and proudly displayed the food on the table when we arrived. This gastronomic gallery might include a pot of *pasulj,* a savory Serbian soup of pork and beans. Next to it would be a platter of Montenegrin veal cut into thin slices of *schnitzel.* This would be beside a pan of Croatian *struklje*, a pastry made from ricotta cheese, sour cream,

---

[12] Honey and its fermented derivative, *medovina*, were also a specialty of Montenegro. The locals would tell you that good medovina takes over a year to ferment properly. This is what produces the entire vitamin B complex, it having a positive effect on fertility. Thus, honeymooning couples are encouraged only to drink medovina the first month of marriage. There is a Honey Fair held every September in Podgorica. It is not reported what effect it has on the local birth rate.

and light dough.[13] There would be a deep dish of Bosnian *sogan dolma*, sweet onions stuffed with meat and rice (a specialty of region around Mostar). The largest pan would hold a tray of *goveđa pržulica*, beef ribs soaked in olive oil and milk and *začin* spice. The *pièce de résistance* would be a Serbian seven-layer banana cake surrounded by *priganica*, fried dough balls smothered in honey. The beverage would be a passionate purple-colored juice made from a mixture of *sok od šipka* (pomegranate syrup) and *sok od grožđa* (grape syrup). Consuming such a meal would take hours; digesting it—days. We gained fifteen pounds during our stay, fourteen of them during the last two weeks.[14]

•

After dinner, the conversation would invariably converge upon a certain subject, that of the Montenegrin persona. One trait they would all agree on is that Montenegrins pride themselves on their lack of love for physical labor. Known for centuries as the sloths of the Slavic family, they take great pride in their reputation for laziness.[15] A few of the Ten Commandments of Montenegrin Life are:

- *In shade is salvation.*
- *Love thy bed as you love thyself.*
- *Man has trouble being born and should spend the rest of his life relaxing.*
- *If you see other men working, excuse yourself and do not trouble them.*
- *If you see a man napping, help him.*

Their reputation in the Balkans has created tribute jokes to their sluggishness which are told in the other former Yugoslav republics.

Montenegrins are too lazy to even finish a sentence.

---

13 Which everyone says Sophia Loren used to cook for Tito. No, really.

14 I now know a secret as to how to lose weight. Have you tried the *E. coli* diet? You eat a meal of, say, salad that has not been washed properly and, within two weeks, you will have shed twenty pounds. They just melt away! And, if you act now, we will send you a free coupon to wait in a socialized medicine clinic to be examined by a nurse who you can't possibly understand. You only pay shipping and handling. *But wait, there's more.!*

15 Ask any Montenegrin woman and she will supply you with a plethora of anecdotal evidence to support this contention about Montenegrin *men.*

Do you know what the Montenegrin world record is in the 100 meters race? Seventy-four meters.

Montenegrins are so lazy; they have to marry pregnant women.

Why does the Montenegrin have two rocks beside his bed? One is to turn out the light and the other to see if the window is closed.

A Montenegrin was lying down in the grass and yells at his wife, "Woman, hurry and bring me serum for a snake bite!"

Running to him, his wife asked "My darling, did you get bit?"

"No," he replied, "but it is moving my way."

A Montenegrin came to the police station and brought a pillow.

"How can I help you, sir," asks the officer on duty.

"I heard some people mentioning 'sleeping policemen' (speed bumps), so I decided to come and apply."

We heard the following story repeatedly about a couple who entered a tavern and ordered two beers. The proprietor was watching a national football match on television and served them without taking his eyes off the screen. When it was time to leave, they asked for the check. Without looking up, he waved them out the door, because it was too much trouble for him to get up and collect the tab. It never happened to the people that told us the story; it was always someone else those people knew. It never happened to us either. We always had to pay.

If Montenegrins were lazy, they never let on to it. Due to the current economic conditions, almost all of the people we met may have held down two jobs, rented out rooms or a second car, and tended a very large garden.

•

Every culture has to have its inferiors to look down upon, and Montenegrins are no exception. For this purpose, they believe, God provided the Bosnian.[16] This is best expressed in the jokes that are told at the Bosnians' expense. (Although you will note the Montenegrin laziness does not escape from inclusion in many of the anecdotes.)

---

[16] There are Serbs, sub-Serbs, and those that are just sub-serbient.

A Slovene, a Bosnian, and a Montenegrin run a 100-meter race. The Slovene wins. Why? The Montenegrin gave up and the Bosnian lost his way.

Haso and Mujo are the Bosnian equivalent of Pat and Mike or Ole and Lena.

Mujo went to Germany to find a job that paid real money. The employer begins the interview.

"So, where are you from?"

"I come from Bosnia."

"I'm sorry, but you people from Bosnia cannot work in our company because you are so lazy!"

"No, no, no! We are not lazy! People from Montenegro are lazy. We are the dumb ones. So, do I get the job?"

A Montenegrin, a Serb, and a Bosnian come to the railway station. Once they arrive, they realize the train is leaving. They start running. The Montenegrin gives up immediately, and the Serb runs but misses the train. Only the Bosnian manages to hop on the train and depart. The Montenegrin and the Serb return looking somewhat discontented.

A person who observed it all asks them, "How is it the Bosnian got on, and you didn't?"

"Oh, that guy? The fool was only supposed to take us to the train station."

A Bosnian television station was shooting a documentary intended for children. In this episode, they visited Mujo, who was working on his farm.

"How do you start your day?" asked the reporter.

Mujo responds, "Well, when I get up, I drink one shot of rakija [plum brandy]."

"Wait a second," said the reporter. "This is a show for children! We want you to say something that is good for them. For example, when I get up, I read a book."

Mujo thinks a moment and says, "OK, I get it. When I get up, I read a book. Then when I go to work on the farm, I read another one. When I get back from the work, I read two books. A little later, Suljo and I go to the library and there we read five to six books. When the librarian kicks us out before closing, we go see Haso, because he owns a publishing house."

We found if you wanted to get a conversation moving with a new acquaintance, it paid to have a few Chuck Norris jokes in your repertoire, as Montenegrins love Chuck Norris. They are appreciated not so much for their humor but for the machismo represented in them, allowing a bit of self-projection of the Montenegrin manhood to be conveyed.

Chuck Norris has a bear rug in his bedroom. The bear isn't dead, he's just afraid to move.

Did you know Chuck Norris has the lead role in Star Wars? He was the Force.

Superman and Chuck Norris had a bet on who would win if they were to fight. The loser had to wear his underwear on the outside of his clothes.

I found that memorizing a few of these always helped when I was introduced to new Montenegrin friends.

Portrait of An Artist

One evening, some new photography buddies, Branislav, Dejan, and Saša invited me for a night out. Branislav is Serbia's most accomplished landscape photographer. His aerial photos of Serbia and Montenegro are on every calendar, on many of the two countries' travel posters, and his books are for sale in almost every store. Branislav is of the natural school of nature photography. As an American, I was the focus of his tirade against *National Geographic* magazine. He claimed their art directors were brightening the ordinary and sometimes dull colors that appear normally in landscapes. He bemoaned the fact that this was setting the standard for such photography and ruining it for those that wanted photography to remain pure and unadorned. He wanted me to take that message back to the NatGeo offices and tell them to change their policy. I promised I would do it next time I was there.

Dejan was the president of the Podgorica photography club and was hosting Branislav for a visit and exhibition in town. Saša was chair of the Finance Department at the University of Montenegro. He was also a fellow Fulbrighter (having studied at Columbia on a post-doctoral fellowship), a fly fisherman, and photographer. We hit it off immediately.

The outing was to visit the studio of an artist they said was Montenegro's premier landscape painter, Dragan Karadžić.[1] As chair of the Art Department at the University of Montenegro, he has been inducted into the Montenegrin Academy of Science and Art, and is considered to be a national treasure.

We drove out to a secluded summer home that Dragan had built himself. The cabin was a small affair, just a few rooms, but it provided the artist inspiration by being situated on a bluff overlooking the slow moving Morača River north of Podgorica. Upon arriving, we were greeted by a man whose expansive intellect

---

[1] Another cultural lesson to us was common Serbian male names might be Dragan, Srđan (pronounced "surgeon"), and Božo.

barely fit into his large body. In his late fifties with thinning grey hair, Dragan had sad, but wonder-filled brown eyes. He was dressed in loose pants and a very casual plaid shirt giving the impression that he was most at ease with the world when he was painting.

He ushered us into a kitchen that smelled of paint, turpentine, and sawdust. Friendly, dirty dogs welcomed us, accepted a few pats on the head, and went back outside. Dragan had not only built the studio, but had made all the furniture as well. He joked that because he was so big, he had to make the chairs with six legs. He offered us drinks and strawberries before sitting down and pontificating on the poetry of Paul Valery. Saša, the only other English speaker, was kind enough to translate for me. This was one of many times on the trip where I was surrounded by intellectual people speaking in a strange language that I did not understand.[2] As Saša and I were from business and not the art world, there were more than a few vocabulary words that had to be looked up.

From poetry, the conversation drifted to a discussion of Kenneth White, the geo-poetical essayist, and from there, the future of Montenegro. They all agreed that the people of the country wanted to be part of something greater, not just *Crna Gora*, but a combined Balkans, or a united Europe.

Dragan eventually asked if we would like to see his studio and paintings. After what I had been told about him by Saša and Branislav, I was very much looking forward to seeing his landscapes of his country. Montenegrins refer to their country as having wild beauty and some of it is breathtaking to the point of requiring resuscitation. I was anticipating something along the lines of the Hudson River school or perhaps Winslow Homer.

Upon entering his studio, I discovered that all of his works were *abstracts*. He referred to his work as landscapes, but they were more conceptual representations of what he saw and felt when he was outdoors. There were watercolors, acrylics, and mixed media. Most canvases had layers upon layers of paint in vivid, cursive-like strokes of bright colors. Some paintings were like multicolored feathers conveying both the organic and inorganic parts of nature. He said he came from the school of the "not yet three dimensional," a combination of cubist, futurist, and expressionist. The choice of color seemed to be an afterthought second to the dynamics of his lines and range of space. The only thing I recognized as landscapes in the paintings were flat lines just hinting of a horizon. Titles of his paintings included: "Breakable Notes," "The Poetics of Space," "Moment of Condensation," and "Evergreen and Nevergreen."

---

2 In that regard, such conversations were not much different than most university faculty meetings I've attended.

He sat on a daybed, took a deep breath, and, in a low voice, told us about his life and his art. He said he didn't play games in his childhood but was always a very serious little boy. He got in trouble for drawing things in school instead of paying attention. He spoke about how his art had changed when he got a chance to leave Yugoslavia in 1981 and discover the artistic freedom of the Paris art scene. Then, having to adjust again when he returned back to witness the disintegration of Yugoslavia, the terrible years of Milošević, and the separation of Montenegro from Serbia. He told us about his daughter, Jovana, who had died in a car accident in 2005 at the age of nineteen, and how it had affected his life and work for so long. Even with all those troubles, he seriously worried that his artistic spirit wasn't as strong as some of his colleagues who had suffered more than he.

Rummaging through his portfolio, he provided us a private and personal retrospective of his life's work. He had begun as a realist and had kept some of his classic portrait and line drawing studies from when he was a student in the 1970s. I asked him why he had gravitated to abstracts.

He lowered his voice and said, "That was the only way I could paint and [the Communists] not know what I was really thinking."

The other three nodded in quiet understanding.

He discussed negativity, negative space, and negative attitudes toward art. We jointly commiserated about the common problems of aging academics despite the differences in our respective disciplines and cultures.

Branislav and Dragan would occasionally get into very passionate conversations just between the two of them. Here was a realist photographer and an abstract painter emphatically disagreeing on approaches to art. However, once the subject of art critics arose, they immediately bonded together.

Dragan exploded, saying, "Critics! All they want to do is deconstruct art and in doing so destroy its essence."

"Who understands their philosophy?" Branislav spat out.

When we got to the end of the evening, Dragan offered me one of his watercolors. It was a blue and orange conglomeration of geometric shapes that depicted the unique shaped twin hills north of Lake Skadar under large cubic clouds. Dragan explained when his father was a boy, the Nazis invaded Montenegro and he got separated from his family. His father's younger sister would sit on a hill overlooking the lake and send her lost brother her love in the clouds. After two years, the brother miraculously returned to the family home. Dragan never forgot the story of steadfast hope during a tragic time. When I got back to Utah, I had the picture framed and hung where it would always serve as a reminder of the love, hope, and faith expressed by so many people in Montenegro—including my own family.

•

Toward the end of our stay in Montenegro, we were invited to our landlord's home for a farewell dinner. Their apartment was very contemporary, decorated in Scandinavian modern, and the walls were hung with original oil paintings and water colors. I spent some time examining the artwork and complementing Jelena on their collection. I got to the last one, which was obviously the centerpiece of the room.

"Ah, a Karadžić!" I exclaimed.

She shrugged and said, "Of course."

"Gee, I thought you'd be impressed that I could recognize a Karadžić," I said.

"Everyone knows a Karadžić," she replied.

(Not where I come from.)

She glanced admiringly at the painting and said, "Iz a pity you don't have great artists like Dragan Karadžić in Amerike."

She had me there.

Doing Biznis

In most capital cities across the globe, U.S. ex-pats have at least two links to America—the American Corner and the American Chamber of Commerce (the AmCham). Both are sponsored by the U.S. State Department. In Podgorica, the American Corner was an outreach, library, and seminar center that the embassy rents in a community theater building behind the national football stadium. It was stocked with American literature, magazines, and educational reference books. A warm woman named Anica oversaw the operation. The Corner served as a gathering place for not only Americans but also anyone who wants to practice his or her English.[1] It hosted weekly lectures, coffee-klatches, discussion groups, and activities that are open to the public and were well publicized. The Podgorica AmCham chapter has 40 corporate members. It was a meeting for American ex-pats to get together, schmooze, exchange business opportunities, and provide stimulating conversation in hopes of doing the same for the local economy.

The P.M. in the p.m.

In late February, I had lunch with the Prime Minister of Montenegro. I was invited to the AmCham monthly meeting at the Hotel Crna Gora where His Excellency was the guest speaker. The Executive Director of the Chamber had invited me as his guest. The next day his secretary sent me an invoice. I called him back and told him that, as I was not a member, I would be happy to pay for my own lunch—hinting at the oversight on the part of the secretary. He gushed and said, "Thanks! Money is a little tight right now."

---

1 It was there I met three very nice college students all who had spent their high school junior year as exchange students in the U.S. One was sporting a purple Florence, Texas High School varsity letter jacket with her name on it. She was very proud of it as it she had lettered in Journalism there and had won an award. She also liked the fact that it was the only jacket of its kind in the entire Balkans.

Because the Prime Minister was the headliner, there was a crowd of about 200 people when I arrived. There was a mix-and-mingle in the foyer of the hotel where I chatted with friends from the American Embassy and met some local business professionals. As the Prime Minister entered, a hush fell over the room, since he was a highly respected man. I could not actually see him as, not being a full-blood Montenegrin; I was the shortest person in the room. We quietly followed him and the U.S. Ambassador into the banquet room. Lunch was a mix of wilted lettuce and stilted English. I sat next to an Albanian petrol retailer, a Montenegrin furniture manufacturer, and a Greek banker.

As the Prime Minister rose to deliver his speech, the press descended en mass to the front of the room and they set up 17 video cameras on tripods between his podium and the dinner tables. This did not include the 11 photographers who were wandering between tables taking flash photos of the crowd. This human blockade prevented anyone except the dais from being able to see the Prime Minister while he spoke. When the cameramen would occasionally aim backwards to get shots of the audience, you would see everyone sit up straight and look very attentive. Local business leaders attended the luncheons so they could tell their clients back in their hometowns they had just had lunch with the Prime Minister and could be seen on national TV doing so. ("How you say, 'Iz goot PR!'")

The P.M. spoke in Serbian, but the organizers were thoughtful enough to provide an interpreter for the three of us there who could only understand English. In my headset I could hear a female whispering a translation of the speech. Because it was what businesspeople are always interested in, the Prime Minister took 20 minutes to explain the current economic situation in Montenegro.

"GDP is down, but we're not as bad off as Albania or Bosnia."[2]

He also set down his specific plan for dealing with the current economic crisis—"We need to build a bridge to the future."

"We must work harder for the glory of our people."

It was not a lot different from the rhetoric that was heard during the last American presidential election.

After the luncheon, I quickly tried to be the first one outside because I wanted to see the Prime Minister as he entered his limousine. The crowd that had gathered along the street was too large to even get close. I walked down

[2] Montenegro's Gross Domestic Product (GDP) is just under that of Provo, Utah if Provo was its own country. The GDP per person is about one-fourth that of the U.S. ranking it just between South Africa and Brazil.

to the corner to get a view of him as the car passed by, but all the windows of his car were tinted. The motorcade, consisting of a lead security car, the Prime Minister's car, an aft security car, and one for his staff, roared out from under the hotel portico, zoomed across the intersection, and immediately parked. The hotel was only a block from the P.M.'s Parliament office.

The luncheon cost me $61.20. It was the most I have ever paid not to see a Prime Minister. I told this story to a new Montenegrin friend, who, unbeknownst to me, was a member of the opposition party. He said he would pay even more.

•

Montenegro's economy has been the victim of a triple whammy, some of it self-inflicted. Since Montenegro was aligned with Serbia during and after the Yugoslavian war, it suffered through the associated trade embargo, which created one of the worst hyperinflation periods in history. Since 1993, Montenegro has changed its currency four times. In 1998, Montenegro went to a two-currency system, the Yugoslavian dinar and the German Deutschmark, the latter of which became its official currency a year later. When Germany converted to the Euro in 2002 so did Montenegro—illegally as the country was not a member of the Euro Zone. The country's economy was so small the EU simply ignored it. The country's estimated total Gross Domestic Product is $4 billion or the same as Blockbuster's annual revenue, the last company on the Fortune 500 (and equally as in trouble).

To get through the bleak period of economic sanctions in the 1990s, the leaders of Montenegro resorted to illegal activities just to keep cash and goods flowing into the country. Today there are few new jobs, and a flat economy; thus no new ventures are being created. Unemployment runs 15 percent, and up to 30 percent in the rural mountain areas. Spread out across the country stand multi-story steel frames of large office buildings and hotels whose construction has simply stopped due to the recession.

On the street where our apartment was, there were two full-service travel agencies. When we first arrived, each of the many desks was occupied. By May, there was only one agent minding the store in one of the offices. The other had a sign asking customers to go to their downtown location. One faculty colleague stated, "Montenegro's largest import is managers, and its largest export are university graduates."

Almost all products in the country were imported. Most of the factories were closed. The largest plant in the country, the bauxite facility, was so outdated it cost more to produce aluminum than the price they could sell it for. The government wanted to privatize the plant to get rid of the onerous subsidy at the same time the Russians their primary customers, started buying aluminum on the spot market to save money. Thus, the government had fired about half of the workforce, which had prompted almost continuous demonstrations by workers not understanding the economics of the situation. They demanded the government keep the plant open with full employment even though there were no customers for its products.

This scenario was played out all through the country when, beginning in 2006, the government needed to raise cash. It began selling equity positions in their government-owned companies, which has only been partially successful. Many of the industrial plants are so dated that no profitable company wants to invest in them. In the uncertain economic environment, it was difficult to understand how the government was keeping the currency stable and the country functioning. One U.S. State Department official said, "You've seen the big recreational vehicle traveling slowly in front of you? Remember the bumper sticker that read, 'We're spending our children's inheritance as fast as we can.'? That's Montenegro. All they know how to do is borrow."

The citizens joke about their dire economic situation. One business woman said, "Our new tourism slogan should be, 'If your finances are a disaster, come to Montenegro. You will feel right at home!'"

Transitioning to a private enterprise-based economy after being communistic for decades was charging ahead at a snail's pace. Many business leaders told me, "We don't need new business knowledge. We just need to change the economic climate back to when it was good." In private they would say, "It used to be that the government would take care of you. Now you must take care of yourself. It is very hard."

I didn't know how much help the new government could provide Montenegrin businesses in terms of real market data. When I interviewed a high-ranking government official in the Ministry of Tourism, I asked him how much tourism contributed to the Montenegrin economy. He said he did not know the exact figure, but he could look it up online at the CIA World Factbook site if I really wanted to know.

•

When we were surrounded by advertisements in Serbian, English names and brands jumped out at us. Many retail stores liked using English as it was considered sophisticated; although some of it may not have had the intended appeal when translated literally. There was a small store selling laptops named,

"God Computers." A do-it-yourself store sold "Police Car Laminated Cabinets." There was the red "BUM Taxi Service." (They didn't use the obvious logo I assumed they would.) The restaurant chain of "FATI Fast Food"[3] used the slogan "Best Prices, not the Lowest Prices." A language school a few blocks from our apartment was entitled, "The Institute for Strange Languages."

The liberal acquisition of American trademarks and copyrights was also widespread. There was "Snoopy Transportation" in Tivat and a "Dizney" toy store in Podgorica. The comic strip character, *Hagar the Horrible*, by Dik Browne, was the mascot for the supporters of the Podgorica Barbarians football team.

During a consultation with one of the national mobile telephone companies, I was sworn to secrecy as they were about to launch a new major advertising campaign.

The vice-president lowered his voice and whispered, "Ho-kay. Djou no tell anyone about theese."

He leaned back with a self-satisfied smile and said, "To be in our adz, we got da guy from the movie, *National Treažure*."

"You got Nicolas Cage to be your spokesperson?" I exclaimed.

"Not him," he said dismissively "we got the *handsome* guy."

It turned out to be Justin Bartha, Cage's sidekick. They were going to put him on every billboard in the country. When I saw the artwork for the campaign, I wasn't sure Bartha had ever posed for these particular photographs, much less contracted for this advertisement campaign.

This phone company segmented its market on two criteria: income and employment. High income was above €500 per month (or $8,000 per year). They further divided the market by those that were employed and unemployed. As the "Low Income"-"Unemployed" quadrant was so large; the company had specific pre-paid products for that segment.

Marketing and promotion were things that had not come easy to a culture that equates any messaging with propaganda. At every downtown intersection, there was at least one cement kiosk that sold newspapers, magazines, cigarettes, and candy. The same company owned almost all of the kiosks. The female attendant (usually an older woman) sat in her booth all day long, from 6 a.m. to 10 p.m., six days a week. When you made a purchase, it was through a window not much larger than her face. There were 230 of these magazine stands across

---

3 Fati is "fate" in Albania. But, either way . . . Albania is also the home of a chain of gas stations named *Kastrati*. I just could not bring myself to stop there. It turns out *Kastrati* means cranberries (translation double entendre?).

Montenegro. Competitors were now opening up in higher traffic locations and, sometimes, right next to the other company's locations. Yet, the company does not do any advertising. The reason? "Everybody already knows where we are."

In America, congruency in promotional messaging is essential so as to create consistency in the mind of the potential customer. Thus, the brand, *Victoria's Secret*, hints at mysterious sexuality which the basis for their products—feminine lingerie. Its primary color mark is a very alluring pink, which it also uses as the name of one of its product lines. All three elements, the name, the color, and the product are purposefully integrated to communicate the essential nature of the brand. In Montenegro, message congruency was not necessarily apparent. This may have been because Balkan companies were in their early growth years, and their marketing was neither sophisticated nor strategic. An example was the company BAR-KOD. The logo didn't even use a bar-code. The company put its name in a type font as though it had been punched out of a Dynamo label maker. Their signage made us think of office supplies. Yet they sold cosmetics and fragrances.

•

At one of the American Corner functions, we met the CEO of the Montenegrin Stock Exchange; and she invited me to take a tour. It was in a new office complex only a few blocks from our apartment. We were buzzed up to the second floor where we met her, and she introduced us to the Managing Director.

There has been a stock exchange in Podgorica since 1863. In their office, proudly displayed on the wall, was the first stock certificate ever issued. I thought the operation would be more like Wall Street with lots of people running around on a trading floor, yelling. Since all trades are electronic now, it was completely run by five very quiet employees.[4] The exchange oversaw the trading of 400 stocks with an annual volume of about $1.72M. Every public company in Montenegro was required to be listed on the exchange. Of these 400 stocks, only about 40 of them are traded on a daily basis. Investors could only buy Montenegrin stocks through brokers who were physically located in Montenegro. There was a stock index, the Montex; but you couldn't trade it; it was only for tracking.

---

4 In true government fashion, the Montenegrin Securities and Exchange Commission that oversees them has a staff of eight.

As we were leaving the office, the CEO and Managing Director told us they were married. I don't know that this is the only mom-and-pop stock exchange in the world, but it's the first one I ever toured.

•

The Young Inventors' Program (YIP) was an effort to create a sense of enterprise among the future contributors to Montenegro's economy—its high school students. YIP was the brainchild of John Tabor. John was a "retired" projects guy who had worked in Pakistan, Moldova, Indonesia, and Montenegro. I put the word retired in quotes as I suspect he was working as hard as a volunteer as he ever did on a payroll. His formal training was in political science with a doctorate in Public Administration, but he has spent his life helping create and administer USAID programs throughout the world. After traveling extensively, both on the job and off, he chose to retire in Montenegro, first in Budva, then in Podgorica.

In May, he brought 25 students from various high schools in Montenegro together for a one-day workshop. It was sponsored by the U.S., German, and Montenegrin government and was held in the Engineering Faculty (College) of the University of Montenegro. The program was like Junior Achievement; but instead of the emphasis being on the business side, this was about the creation, design, and engineering of a prototype that could be transformed into a marketable product. At the workshop, students were able to see innovations in various fields of electronics, mechanics, civil engineering, computer science, metallurgy, and environmental protection in order to inspire them and provide ideas for incubation. This workshop was the first phase of the project. There is a deep entrepreneurial yearning among young people in Montenegro and John was smart enough to tap into and encourage that energy. When we left, he had 200 students signed up for the next workshop.

•

Because the Montenegrin government is desperate for an infusion of cash, it has created a task force whose sole purpose is to appeal to the successful Montenegrin diaspora (most of whom are in the United States) and encourage them to make investments in the country. They are asking Montenegrin families to provide the names of such persons. As can be imagined from the massive emigration that occurred at the first part of the 20th century, the diaspora is relatively large. The task force refers to Montenegro as a *bijelo polje* (white field) that is ready to be colored with investments.

There was just one little issue that was making outsiders a bit hesitant to invest in the Montenegro economy.

Bribes and Corruption

In downtown Podgorica, there was a large billboard that shouted, “Korupcija, Ne Smije Biti Izlaz” (“Corruption, There is a Way Out.”) It was by no coincidence that the sign was directly across the street from Parliament.

One of the questions Montenegrin citizenry philosophically asked themselves was, “Does the government run the mafia or the mafia run the country?” Corruption was such a common joke that, when a group of my male students took me to lunch once, one of them took a photograph, posted it on Facebook, and entitled it, “Bribes and Corruption!” With the prolific auto theft rings in the region, others suggested the tourist slogan for the country should be, “Come to Montenegro. Your car is here already!”

During the recent Yugoslavian Wars, Montenegro, as it was then part of Serbia, was under siege, politically, economically, and militarily. In order to get around the economic sanctions forced on it by NATO (and to provide no small amount of graft to political allies), Slobodan Milošević’s Yugoslavian government encouraged smuggling operations across the still-Serbian controlled part of the crumbling republic and on a grand scale. It has been stated the entire Serbian government became criminalized in one form or another. Everything from heroin to humans were smuggled across the Balkans and, then, across the Adriatic to Italy, the easy, illicit gateway to the European Union. The most convenient drop off point for that was Serbia’s small cousin, Montenegro.

Tito might have been a Communist when he ran Yugoslavia, but he was a strict monetarist and financed his 35 year deficit budget with bailouts from other countries and by printing money. Between 1946 and his death in 1980, annual inflation averaged 20 percent. This meant every four or so years, the currency devalued by half. During the recent war beginning in 1992, the Yugoslavian government went through all of its hard currency reserves. It then froze private citizens' bank accounts and used their money. Fuel was in incredibly short supply. The government refused to turn on heat in apartment buildings during the winter. Fire trucks and ambulances could not be dispatched for emergencies. One man, who publicized he would set himself on fire as a protest in front of a government building, showed up with a can of gasoline and was immediately arrested. Everyone wanted to know what happened to the can of gas.

The government mandated price controls, which created shortages of food and meat and created a huge black market with its accompanying smuggling, which still exists today. This governmental policy created the worst hyperinflation up to that time. Some economists estimate that between the fall of 1993 and the beginning of 1995 (just fifteen months) prices increased a staggering 15,000,000,000,000 percent. In October 1993, the Yugoslavia government printed new currency. One "new" dinar was worth one million old dinars. In January of 1994, the government issued another, "super" dinar, which was worth ten million of the just printed "new" dinars. During this period, personal checks were outlawed, as people would write checks knowing that, by the time they were cashed, inflation would wipe out 90 percent of the value of the check.

The government reprinted the money seven times before the recent war was over. The war period began with inflation at two percent per month and peaked at two percent per *hour*.[1] (In comparison, U.S. inflation ranged from 1.5 percent to 4.5 percent per year during the same time.) Yugoslavian government workers and pensions were not paid. The wives of the mostly male workers would meet their husbands when they got their paychecks and then race to the store to buy up any groceries they could find. Food lines were so long, the price of some items rose from the time customers took them off the shelves until they eventually arrived at the cash register. This hyperinflation also worked to President Slobodan Milošević's favor. Although he was starving the population, he was forcing them to purchase more and more from the black market, which he and his henchmen controlled. Unfortunately, many of those survival and opportunistic behaviors are still very much a part of Montenegro's economic landscape.

•

With the graft and corruption that was pervasive throughout the country, living as we did, we were able to completely avoid it. That is, until the very last day we were there.

---

[1] Even today, Serbian inflation is 10 percent a year.

We had packed our suitcases with everything we brought and bought. Beth Lynn had somehow managed to find nooks and crannies in the luggage for all the gifts from our new friends and family—books, dolls, photographs, objects d'art, seashells, lavender, and a whole shelf of spices she had fallen in love with.[2] She had even managed (very impressively I might add) to get two large oil paintings (framed) of the island of Sveti Stefan to fit inside one of the to-be checked bags. As before, she knew the exact weight of each piece of our luggage. Because of that, we knew we were going to be overweight on the small airplane taking us to London and would have to pay a fee.

When we took the bags to the airline service counter, we showed the attendant our passports and e-tickets and lifted the bags up onto the scales. We noticed each bag was about five pounds heavier than they were when we left the apartment.

"Iz problem. Overweight. Must pay," she said.

I nodded and reached for my wallet.

"Four hundred euros, plez," she stated with a deadpan expression.

"What?!?" I exclaimed. This was higher than the actual airfare.

"Iz four bags. Iz four hundred euros," she explained.

"Wait a minute. That's not right," I said, whipping out my printout of the airline's website. I showed her what the stated charges were for each bag.

"I get shoopervisor," she said, getting off her stool and disappearing into the back room.

That's more like it, I thought.

Instead of a well-dressed manager, out came a very large baggage handler. He was wearing a day-glow orange safety vest, his noise reduction earmuffs, and was covered in dirt and grime from his job.

He moved our bags off the scales, stepped over them, and motioned me to follow him. By now, there was a long line behind us at the counter. He walked me to the windows that overlooked the parking lot but in full view of everyone at the airport where we could have a private discussion.

"Sorry. You are overweight," he said. (I assume he didn't mean me personally.)

"I understand that, but your own rules state that . . . ," I said, beginning to quote him his company's overweight tariff rules.

He corrected me by interrupting, "Those were old rules. Now new rules."

(As of this morning, I suspected.)

---

2 I was worried about the spices. I could see some well-meaning, but uninformed, Customs canine, smelling our luggage, and setting off Def-Con Three.

"Fee is four hundred euros. But, for three-fifty I can solve this problem for djou," he said sympathetically.

Ah, ha. I saw I could be held up by the blasé woman at the counter for four hundred euros or extorted by this nice gentleman for three-fifty. A clear savings either way you looked at it. I glanced around and noticed that not only were we being watched by the woman at the counter, there was also a policeman not 30 feet away. Then it dawned on me, the baggage guy was only the front man.

"I don't have 350 euros," I stated defiantly.

"Iz hokay, we have ATM's," he replied, smiling, and nodding toward the wall.

I boldly retorted, "I am a distinguished scholar who has been teaching and *writing* about Montenegro. An incident like this would be very bad publicity for Montenegro."

He thought for a moment and said, "Djou're right. Tree hundred euros."

I then threw out some names of the most important people I had been working with, or knew, or even had heard about. Some impressed him, others, I thought, not so much.

"Hokay, hokay. Two fifty."

I said I had been working out of the United States Embassy. Did he want the full weight of the United States government investigating this sort of thing?

He scowled and said, "Three hundred."

So much for our foreign aid investments.

I looked at him and asked, "Where are you from?"

This took him back for a moment, but he said Petrovac.

"Petrovac! I am Montenegrin! I am a Radović. My family is from Drobnići!

"No!" he exclaimed. "I know Radovići! That is different! Only two hundred for djou."

Not the complete waiver I was hoping for, but it was good for something. We settled on 150 euros, which was what the official published tariff was to begin with. I doubt my contribution ever made it onto the company's daily receipts. I paid him in plain sight of the cop who was, rather intently, examining the shine on his shoes.

I said, "For this kind of personal service, our bags better arrive in London in perfect condition."

"But, of course," he said, somewhat offended, as he put the money in his shirt pocket and gave me the WEWYD look.

He then ticketed us, tagged our bags, and placed them on the conveyor belt. After we got through security into the waiting area, we noticed him again. He was buying several bottles of imported whiskey at the duty-free shop. He must have been very thirsty from all his hard work.

As we boarded the plane, I saw him loading our luggage and giving it special attention so it would be the first bags off when we arrived in London. I thought about having just spent a semester teaching students about the value of private enterprise to the Montenegrin economy. It appeared that, for the final lesson, I was the pupil.

Town and Gown

There are three universities in Podgorica. One is public, the *Univerzitet Crna Gora,* (The University of Montenegro) known locally as "State," and only part of it is in the capital as its main campus is in Nikšić, the brewing center of the country.[1] There are also two private ones, *Mediterran Univerzitet* and the *Univerzitet Donja Gorica* (UDG). These last two are also for-profit ventures. Until 2007, the Montenegrin government spent more annually on its National Theater than it did on all of higher education. That is the U.S. equivalent of Congress allocating less money for higher education than they might for the Kennedy Center. Faculty salaries in Montenegro averaged about $680 a month. Many of the faculty members had to hold down a second (in many cases, full-time) job just to make ends meet, so they could be able to teach.

For my Fulbright teaching responsibilities, I was very excited I had been assigned to UDG. This unique institution exists because of the dream of one man who believed the future of Montenegro was best vested in a free-market economy. Prof. Veselin Vukotić is the founder, President, and Dean of UDG. He had been chair of the economics faculty at the University of Montenegro and was one of the few economists in the former Yugoslavia that advocated a free-market economy. This was when even the most avant-garde of them promoted socialism. UDG is the first university in all of the former Yugoslavia dedicated to training students in the principles and advantages of private enterprise. The university was founded in 2006 and construction on the building was completed in 2007.[2] Prof. Vukotić was kind of like the Milton Friedman of Montenegro. That is if

---

1 Where would you want to attend college?

2 As incentive for the construction workers to complete the building on time, the university gave free scholarships to all their children.

Friedman had also served as Secretary of the Treasury and founded Stanford University. Vukotić is so revered that when he held class, the entire school shut down; and even all the staff went to hear him lecture.

The UDG facility was a very modern, single six-story building of 175,000 square feet located out in the country about five miles from Podgorica. About a third of the building was yet unfinished. It had four large lecture halls that sat 200 students and 12 smaller, tabletop classrooms. The school boasted five Faculties (colleges): International Business, Legal Science, Information Systems and Technology, Humanities, and Art. (They also had a think tank, the "Institute for Strategic Studies and Prognosis" which provided consulting services and additional income to the university.) UDG also offered five languages: English, German, Italian, Albanian, and Arabic. All of this was conducted with only 20 full-time faculty members (but dozens of adjuncts).

In the basement of the building was the student lounge with its loud décor *a la* 1960s Austin Powers—perfect for animated conversation and forging lasting friendships. Next to it was the library that had desks for 200 students complete with wireless connections. But, the library had more chairs than books. Only a few of the shelves had any tomes on them. One creative librarian had taken 50 copies of a free magazine and had placed them face up in order to fill the bare shelves. I donated over 40 books on marketing and management from my personal library and it increased the library holdings by 20 percent.

There were about 1,100 students at UDG. All of the students were full-time and took exactly 12 hours a semester. The curriculum was very structured, so all students in a given class (First Year, Second Year, etc.) took the same classes together. There were only three years of study required for a 72 credit hour undergraduate degree. Such a program had no general education requirements as students began courses in their major field their first semester. For the most part, the students did not work. This was because they were expected to study in the afternoon and evenings. (In addition to which, there were no jobs.)

Prof. Vukotić had chosen orange as the school color because Netherlands used it in the 17th century, and, for over 100 years, they were the most powerful capitalistic nation in the world. The school motto was *Budite Dio Istorije Budućnosti!* or "Be part of the History of the Future!"

The entire business faculty had doctorates in economics—even if they taught finance or management. That was because the only doctoral programs in Eastern Europe (until fairly recently) were in economics. Therefore, a great deal of theory was taught but not a lot of actual business skills (as the faculty had no real business experience).

Almost every business in Montenegro is a family business and UDG was no exception. Vukotić's daughter, Milica, is the Vice Rector. Besides being qualified by blood, she also has an M.B.A. and a Ph.D. and, more importantly, the respect of her students. With her there, UDG will have strong leadership for many years to come.

•

When I first arrived in January, I went to the university; but none of the faculty or administration was there as it was between semesters as well as being ski season (just like here in Utah). I was met by the university's Business Manager and shown to my office—a very large room on the third floor next to Dean Vukotić. From my window, the surrounding landscape was a bucolic valley with green farmland surrounded by high hills and snow-capped mountains beyond.

My class was held in a large lecture hall that was very modern, and it had state-of-the-art audio-visual equipment. To help with my class, I had two teaching assistants. That is, I had one teaching assistant; and he had a teaching assistant. My TA was Nikola Perović who had two master's degrees (one was an M.B.A. from Brandeis) and was completing his doctoral thesis in economics at "State."[3] His real job was Director of International Business Development at *Plantaže* (Plantation), the local winery. His assistant was Nina Radonović who had a Ph.D. in economics and two small children, so she was part-part time.

Toward the end of the semester, I found my office in disarray, my desk a complete mess, and a strange man sitting in my chair. It was as though he had gone out of his way to live up to the stereotypical college professor look. His longish hair was combed over a balding pate, and his eyebrows were only slightly bushier than the grey van-dyke that lent itself nicely for stroking while in deep contemplation, which was the state he was in when I introduced myself. He came out of his reverie and shook my hand. He told me he was a visiting professor from Serbia there to teach a condensed course in advanced economics. We started to talk shop, and I asked how long he was teaching his class every day.

The professor wailed, "Four hours a day, I am teaching. It is terrible. They are dying. I am dying. Everybody is dead."

---

3 Nikolai's favorite English expression was "šure . . . šure". Whatever I asked of him, the response was "šure . . . šure," and it always got done.

He had a habit of leaving a trail of wadded up notepaper, lunch litter, and other rubbish around the office that we were now evidently sharing. I dubbed him Oskar Madisonović.

•

Before I left the states, I was told I would be teaching an advanced Marketing class for a few students who had good English skills. To that end, I identified an appropriate textbook and the publisher, Cengage, was generous enough to donate 40 copies. A few days before the term began, I was told there was a change; and I would need to teach International Marketing. They had had a marketing professor there in the fall, but evidently things did not work out. Thus, they needed someone to cover the basic class for all the business students. Dean Vukotić told me I would have the honor of teaching the first required class at the university ever to be taught in English.[4] When he announced that the first day of class, the entire room of 120 students collectively gasped. The next day there were only 40 students in attendance.

I had second year students in my lectures. The classes were not scheduled MWF or TTh as they are in America, but were held on Mondays and Tuesdays from 10:15 a.m.-11:45 a.m. There was also a Marketing Lab for exercises on Mondays from 12:15 p.m.-1:45 p.m. that Nikola proctored. I quickly learned what the accompanying Marketing Lab was really for—reviewing all the concepts I had lectured on, but in a language the students could understand.

American university administrators always want to plan their academic calendar as far in advance as possible. No one knows why, but it is a fact of life in academe. Therefore, it is not uncommon to have to schedule classes 12 to 18 months in advance. The advantage to this is that students can then know when their classes will be offered and can make satisfactory progress toward graduation. Additionally, everyone knows exactly what day classes start every semester. (This also allows faculty to stretch their own vacations out to the very last possible minute.) This was not the planning scheme in Montenegro. It was not until the end of each semester that the university Rector decided when the next semester's classes would begin.[5] By January 15, the school had not quite decided if the first day of spring term classes would be February 1 or February 8.

4 Required courses were known as "forced exam" classes, electives were "free exam".

5 One colleague who taught at another university and liked to pun in English explained that, when things were not running smoothly, they referred to him as the Wrecktor.

Once classes started you did know when the last day of classes were, but finals were another matter. Finals might require an additional *six weeks* to administer. Under the Bologna Agreement protocol (an articulation agreement to standardize curriculum throughout universities in Europe) undergraduate degrees require three years of study. In addition, there are also many "traditions" associated with this standardization that included an interesting application of the final exam.

A typical semester class might go like this. Students enroll for a class in, say, *History of the Balkans.*[6] The class would meet twice a week during which the professor would lecture by reading out of the textbook, sometimes for hours on end. I once asked a colleague why the professors didn't just record themselves reading the textbook and then have the TA play it back during class.

Facetiously, I inquired, "Wouldn't it save a lot of time? You wouldn't even have to be in class."

The new colleague raised his eyebrows in horror and said, "That would not work. The government would find out, and we would all be replaced with tape recorders."

Each class has a TA, which is a "professor in training" in order to answer questions for the students and to administer exams. There is no class discussion and a student does not ask the professor any questions—they are all directed to the TA. Throughout the semester in many cases, there is no homework or assignments, with only one exam at the end of the semester. But, there is a pressure relief valve. If students take the final exam and don't like their grade, they are given two additional opportunities to re-take the exam. If they didn't like their grade the second time, they could take it a third time. But that's it. Any other chances to pass the exam would just be ridiculous.

Some students don't even take the exam the first time it is offered but get the test questions from their friends and take it during the second and/or third administration. Many students don't even attend class at all during the term as the lectures do not provide any additional illumination beyond reading the textbook. The students just show up for the final exam. When I would call upon certain students in class or gave a homework assignment, they complained, "But we are not supposed to know this material until the end of the semester!"

Attendance was such a problem, the university administration was experimenting with a policy where students had to attend 80 percent of the class sessions in order to pass the course. Most students didn't want to go to their classes, as they considered them boring and not as interesting as hanging out

---

[6] This, in itself, is problematic as the version of history you get taught is greatly dependent upon the background and ethnicity of the professor.

with their friends at a café. Additionally, most of them were smart enough to pass their courses without attending class. To enforce this rule, faculty would pass around a sign-in sheet. No matter how few students were actually in attendance, at the end of class, there were always 120 unique signatures on the sheet.

As per American standards, I had learning objectives, PowerPoint slides to present during the lecture, videos to show, case studies for discussion[7], in-class exercises, and multiple exams administered throughout the semester. For many students, coming to my class was overwhelming as they were so used to a passive learning environment.[8] Moreover, I shortly discovered some students had never been called on in class. The first time I called on a young man to answer a question, all the students became deer-in-the-headlights, beamed-aboard-a-UFO terrified.

Dean Vukotić was trying to change the university's pedagogy. For professional development, he had invited the younger faculty to sit in on my class to learn the "new and progressive" way of teaching. When they came and saw how much trouble it was to create class material and provide actual examples of business situations, they did not return.

It was university policy to limit each exam to 50 questions. Additionally, no single assignment or exam could be more than 40 percent of the course grade. I decided the class would have three exams with the last two having some questions from the previous material. Considering the shock the students got about the class being taught in English, I wanted to be fair but also challenge them just a bit.

The administration of the exams was always a trying time for the faculty, much less the students. We would spread out the students so there was at least one seat between each of them. Nikola and I decided students could take the exams in Serbian, or they could take it in English and get an additional ten points. That meant two versions in each language. Each version then had to be distributed in such a way so that no two students sitting near one another received the same version. The room was large and the administration thought four staff members ought to be present during the exam to prevent cheating. During the exam, the proctors would see lips moving and yell out "*Bez Priče!* (No talking)."[9] The plan was more of a containment strategy as passing answers

---

7 Or Dishcussion.

8 The state that is just above that of unconsciousness.

9 It sounds like "Bez Preachy" which is probably what the students wanted less of from me, too.

was rampant and constant. When I saw my star student slipping a note to the woman behind her, I called her out of the room and asked her why she was helping another student cheat.

She replied, "She is my friend! Why would I not help her?" This was followed by the WEWYD expression. I lowered her grade, but she took it more as a comment to dedication and friendship than the message I was evidently unsuccessful in conveying.

The class might have been just a series of lectures to the students—whereas it was a life lesson for me.

•

There were days when the learning and the teaching became reversed and I became the student. For an in-class exercise, I had students decide on possible market segments for a retail paint store. This usually results in discussions about commercial versus consumer buying and the different customer needs that must be met by the retailer. The UDG students did not see it that way at all. They suggested having a separate section for the various shades of green paint. Puzzled, I asked why just *green* paint. I was told that was because green was the color Muslims painted their houses.

To facilitate additional cultural exchange, I would invite six different students to my office every Tuesday after class for a noon brown bag lunch discussion. I wanted to learn about the students, their lives, and aspirations. The first thing I learned was they did not know what a brown bag was, as plastic was what the local grocery stores sent you home with. I tried to explain it, and they were very patient about my description. I think my answer went down in the "Humor-Him-He's-Our-Professor" column. The second thing I learned was that noon was not when they ate lunch. Montenegrins did not eat breakfast *per se* when they got up in the morning—they drank just a little juice or had a small bun. Breakfast was eaten much later in the morning when they would eat a sandwich or burek. Thus, none of the students joined me in my noon noshing as they had just eaten breakfast. Lunch was the big meal of the day when everyone came home from work at four or five o'clock. Dinner was a light salad, cheese, or fruit just before you went to bed.[10] During these noon meetings, I would sit at my desk while the students chatted and watched me eat.

---

10 Note to readers contemplating doing business in Montenegro: If you offer to take someone to lunch understand that it will be late in the day and it will be the most expensive meal. Learn from my experience.

After one such discussion group, some young men took pity on me because I had to bring my lunch to work in a "leftover bag." Therefore, they conspired to take me to a place that served a real Montenegrin meal, *Pod Volat* ("Under the Arch"), which was in the Moslem Quarter. When we arrived, I noticed that there were no females in the entire restaurant. A real lunch to these young men consisted of a large bowl of goulash, followed by two charbroiled beefsteaks each, and all the French fries they could eat. I scanned the middle-aged males at the other tables and saw what they were all eating. I doubt any patron in the place had an LDL cholesterol count lower than 650.

•

Tuition at the state school cost about $150 per term, but private universities charged approximately $750. Most of the students' tuition was paid for by their parents who sacrificed enormously for their children's future.[11] Aida was a female Muslim student from the western mountains near Kosovo. Her father was a logger. During the summer, she took him his lunch and drove his logging truck as she had done since she was 12 years old. Her father did not want her to go to the big city to become corrupted, but her mother argued they had sent her two older brothers to college, and it was not fair for daughters not to get an education, too. She told her husband the old ways did not work anymore. The preparatory education she had received in her village school had left Aida ill equipped to handle college-level work, but her cheery disposition and willingness to work hard was endearing to this professor. Her mother had a vision for her family and the fortitude to see it through. Aida and her progeny would reap the rewards.

At the end of the semester, I wanted the students to have the experience of listening to a professional in the field of international marketing, and who better than my own TA? He not only agreed but also arranged for a tour of the winery, a visit to the vineyard, and then provided a tasting for the students. He ended the tour by delivering a lecture 90 feet underground in the wine cellar.

The *Plantaže* winery was the largest agricultural exporter in Montenegro. They shipped to 75 other countries via distributors, brokers, and agents. Most of the export was to Russia and countries that were part of the former Yugoslavia.[12] The company grew 25 different species of grapes, but it was mostly *vranac*, a

---

11 As one student said, "At my house we have no TV, no mobile phone, and no money—only the good life."

12 *Plantaže* is so significant to the Montenegrin economy that just a few years ago, it represented 30% of the entire trading volume on the country's stock exchange.

large and deeply colored red variety, which produced a dry, red wine.[13] Our first stop was the winery where we viewed the processing machinery. From there the tour took us to the vineyard. We stood on the roof of a three story building in the middle of fields and surveyed 2,500 acres of planted vines, each having hundreds of tiny green beads that were beginning to fruit. *Plantaže* claims to have the largest single contiguous vineyard in Europe.

The company had taken one of the bunkers that had hidden Serbian jets during the last war (and was bombed) and converted it into a posh cellar that was designed for future wine tourism visitors. Plans had been drawn up for the recreation of a typical Montenegrin village (complete with a church) on the top of the hill. We asked if they rented out the cellar for entertainment groups. Saša, the wine master, replied, "Yes, but we have to be very careful. The wine does not like loud music."[14] After the tasting and informative lecture, we all went outside for a class picture. Ending the semester's efforts with students having purple lips from a field trip was not something that would ever happen in Utah.

---

13 The word, "vranac" means black stallion, implying strength and stamina.

14 This was confirmed by the oenologist who said that reverberating bass sound disturbs the fermentation process and sours the wine. Californians are right-wine is best with New Age music.

Innocents Abroad

Men are from Mars, Women are from Venice

Beth Lynn is a Martino. As such, she has always loved Italy. She is fond of the history, the people, the architecture, getting lost in its meandering streets, creeping through castle towers, and moseying through museums. We had visited Rome and Milan but had not been to one of the most unusual cities on the planet, Venice—which is both old world and otherworldly.

I had to attend a conference there immediately after we first arrived in Podgorica. There had been a blizzard during our layover in Vienna and it was very cold, dark, and late when we eventually arrived in Venice. After the taxi ride from the airport to *Pizzale Roma* (where cars can go no further) we still had to take a waterbus ride along the *canali* to the hotel. Being an island, everything within the city is transported by water. There are boats filled with groceries, building materials, furniture, office supplies, and humans—alive and otherwise. Fast cruisers serve as ambulances, slow boats as hearses.[1]

It was late when I paid off the cab and we walked down a very long, unlit pier to catch the last waterbus operating for the night. I was thinking all that has to happen was for a big Italian ruffian to rush out of one of those dark doorways, push me in the canal, and somebody else would be enjoying my laptop, camera, and clean underwear.[2]

---

1 The mourning party trailed behind in their own boats in a black bedecked (pardon the pun) wake.

2 Upon my return to the States, I got into an argument with my budget officer that I could not have had to take a taxi *and* a waterbus to get to my hotel. Thus, the waterbus had to have been for sightseeing; therefore, it was disallowed. I got the impression that he had never been out of town.

We were hungry, as we had missed dinner stranded on the tarmac in Vienna. It was already 11 p.m. and the restaurants we passed were closed. (We got to two just as they were sweeping the cigarette butts out the door.) Arriving at our hotel, we went to bed without eating. At midnight, the bells from the nearby church rang out the end of the day. We knew they were Italian, as they sounded distinctly like *fig-GAR-ro, fig-GAR-ro.* As we lay there, it dawned on us that we had been in five different countries in less than 48 hours and had traveled approximately 6,241.37 miles. Maybe this is not in the same league as the famous Venetian, Marco Polo[3], but, so far, it was our Personal Best.

During this intense travel, our body clocks had been so out of kilter that our circadian rhythms were doing the bossa nova. We awoke at 1 a.m. and could not go back to sleep until about 4 a.m. when the Sandman would nudge us gently into slumber land, where we would get another two hours of sleep. We might as well have been feeding a baby. During the early morning period, I would work; and Beth Lynn would read. She was wading wide-eyed through a true-life crime thriller, and that meant she would stay up saying, "just to the end of the chapter, Dear."[4] Because of our sleep patterns, I knew we probably were not achieving our REM period and could not possibly be getting any really deep, recharging rest. This was evident the next day when we were the only people at four o'clock in the afternoon on the waterbus snoring, making more noise than the outboard motor did.

Venice in January is just like Venice in August but with an average seasonal temperature differential of minus 68 degrees. It has far fewer tourists, fewer pigeons, and most of the gondolas have migrated south for the winter.[5] And, the locals say, it smells a whole lot better. After the conference was over on the first day, we hopped on a waterbus and leisurely floated down the Grand Canal to Piazza San Marcos. We quickly toured the Basilica and marveled at the gold tile, the plaza, and the tower. We also took a tour of the Doges' Palace and walked across the Bridge of Sighs. There, in the "Council of the Ten" room, they had portraits of all the Venetian Doges, the previous rulers of the Republic. This led me to ask the tour guide, "How much is that Doge in the window?" She huffed and said it was not for sale. The "Council of Ten" was not stupid; they set

---

3 Who was actually from present day Croatia.

4 There she was, in bed in a dingy Venetian hotel under a dim light completely engrossed in a book about a serial killer in Italy. I pretended I was asleep and then grabbed her really fast. We still wonder what the Germans in the next room thought.

5 I have been told that, at one time, the New Orleans City Council wanted to introduce gondolas in the river in front of the French Quarter. One councilman was concerned about the cost and asked why didn't they just buy two and let nature take its course?

themselves up as the real power in the Republic with the Doge as the head of a puppet government.[6]

As we had previously discovered on our travels, whatever national landmark we wanted to see was always under reconstruction and *restauro*. Such was the case in Venice. San Marcos Basilica had scaffolding over it, and the Bridge of Sighs was completely surrounded by plastic wrap, which served as a billboard advertising the corporate sponsors of the current restoration project.

Every town has its tourist trap, and we fell into one the next day. I met Beth Lynn during a lunch break, and we decided to eat at a true Venetian *trattoria*. As we walked to it, we marveled at how packed all the sandwich shops were. It was standing room only and not a centimeter to spare. The sandwiches on display looked okay, but they were not *that* appealing. Maybe it was the temperature; maybe it was just a European thing. Finding the recommended restaurant, we perused the English version of the menu, which included such things as, "Starter of Fish with Tipical Venetian Things." Not willing to find out what the "Things" were, we settled on some recognizable pasta dishes and ordered some water. The place was humble but the prices were not. (The cost of our bottled water equaled one of the entrees.) Every restaurant in Venice added a service charge for the privilege of sitting down as well as a 12 percent gratuity. After all was said and done, a brief respite of lunch consisting of Caprese salad, two small plates of pasta, and water ran us $81. After that, we decided to eat pizza and spaghetti standing up like everybody else. For three days we had basically nothing but carbs, carbs, and carbonara. We left Venice feeling very bloated—every place except in my wallet.

•

If you look at Venice from the sky, you will see this city-on-the-sea looks like a big fish facing the mainland. The city is actually an archipelago of many islands, each one having its own personality. On Saturday, we decided to celebrate the emerging sun by shuttling past the island cemetery of San Michele north to the islands of Murano, Burano, and Torcello.

Thanks to advice from a close friend, we ventured farther afield from Venice than we otherwise would have. We would have been perfectly content to stay in Venice proper and, by doing so, would have missed one of the highlights of the trip, Burano—a sleepy village of houses on canals painted in lovely and soothing pastels. As it is now an art colony, you would think they had started

---

6 Known, in Italian, as the *Puppi Doge*.

with the exteriors of the buildings. We walked around marveling at the colors of the homes and stores. The landmark of Burano is its own leaning tower. It is just out of kilter, and no one knows why. I thought, considering Beth Lynn's family, it was perfectly named the tower of San *Martino.*

Another short island hop took us to the tiny island of Torcello, which was absolutely pastoral. It was the original home of Venetians until the 12th century when the valuable salt marshes turned to swamp and malaria forced the occupants to move south to present day Venice. Torcello had aligned itself with Constantinople and had a Byzantine cathedral in the town square, which served the current population of 20. This was the island where Attila the Hun was halted in his quest to capture and destroy the Venetians who, having boats, could escape their attackers. In front of the cathedral there is a very ancient chair carved out of stone said to be the Throne of Attila. Allegedly, this is where he sat and got madder and madder that he had come all this way and could not destroy the sea people. As I sat on his chair, a strange, eerie chill came over me. But, that was possibly because it was about 38° outside, and that stone was *cold.*

We boated back to the island of Murano, the center of glass making for much of the world during the town's heyday. It became the glass center of the realm because the Venetian leaders kicked the lowly artisans out of the city lest they burn down the town with their furnaces. In a twist of economic irony, the glassmakers eventually became some of the most prominent families in Venice. Then, because Venice was so dependent on the mirror, goblet, and chandelier trade, the glassmakers were not allowed to leave the Republic. There are still glass foundries there, but now they are mostly dedicated to creating works of art made out of nothing but Italian sand from the nearby beaches.

Our hotel was in the Ghetto[7] where the Jewish merchants (of Venice)[8] were forced to live and were actually locked in every night. Today there are five synagogues around a charming piazza, a yeshiva school, and several kosher restaurants.

I had chosen our hotel on the suggestion of the conference director (based on his personal experience and recommendation) as well as its adjacency to the conference location. It was quaint and historic, as the Italian equivalent of Georgio Washingtoni had slept there. It also had been awarded a three-star rating by the Association of Three-Star Rating Professionals, which they displayed on a plaque behind the reception desk and in every hallway.

---

7 Where the word comes from.

8 Where the play comes from.

Once we were settled in, the sordid points of the hotel soon became apparent. It was one of those hotels where the charms of the fellow guests we had met earlier in the evening diminished as the night continued, as their most intimate noises provided the sound track for our room. The walls had no insulation, and the plumbing of both the building and the travelers in the rooms next door was more apparent than is conducive for favorable impressions.

We heard those sounds so clearly that I was able to diagnose the internal problems of the building, and especially the concern of the gentleman next door in room 118. I suspect it had to do with his prostate. However, I would have gotten a second opinion for the troubles of the guest above us, who seemed to be suffering more from lower gastro-intestinal issues. The design of the rooms, with their elegant 14-foot ceilings, merely added to the duration of the sound of the water flow from the floor above. (The builders of the hotel also installed the drainpipe next to the headboard of the bed, so it was much more convenient for us amateur diagnosticians.) After spending three nights in the hotel, I had my own suspicions as to why Venice so often floods.

The marble-floored hallway amplified every footfall, boot trod, and haughty (or heavy) high heel. The noises of post-partying couples as they ambled or staggered down the hall, (sometimes with laughter, sometimes with singing) would echo cavernously.

In our bathroom, the towels and hand cloths all had holes in them making easier to grip and hold on to. The hotel was very involved in the environmental sustainability movement. Some days we had our soap and shampoo replenished, some days we did not.

I think that our neighbor next door must have been somewhat inebriated most of the time. He tried using his key in our door one night about 2 a.m. before discovering his mistake. He eventually found his room but could not get the door to close (as he was in it) requiring an elevated voice of what we took to be comments concerning the door's questionable lineage. He then must have slipped the door's deadbolt accidently. Slamming the door in a loud and repeated manner did not attain the closure he was trying to achieve. It was still ajar when I left for the conference the next morning.

As a courtesy to some of the guests, the hotel management allowed smoking on the non-smoking floor. This did help to fumigate the rooms and served to irritate (but not kill) the black flies that came up through the drainpipes to complain about the noise. How could they be expected to attract a mate if they couldn't be heard? To make their point, they demonstrated (continually, I might add; it was most impressive) by flying around the room and buzzing in various pitches. It certainly was effective from an attraction standpoint as many of their colleagues eventually joined them. Although I don't know how successful it was in attracting females since all the flies that gathered in our room gave off the same buzzing noise and we did not see any actually *in flagrante delicto.* (Not that we were looking, mind you.) I suspect other male flies, hearing the larger noise, came up to see if there were any better opportunities topside. We all shared in their disappointment.

We did not know when the European Union was going to convert to the new high-definition television standard, but the unit in our room had not even passed the transition from black and white to color. Had we been in the U.S., the NBC peacock would have looked like a dead pigeon. It was unknown how many channels the TV was supposed to receive, but they had thoughtfully placed the sound of snow and low-level static on all 33 of them. I believe this was to have some "grey noise" which might assist in getting to sleep. The other guests on the floor did not have this amenity as their TV's bombarded them with comedies, sports events, and, what we took to be election results. The latter provided no end of elation to the group in, what we think, was room 216 above us. Evidently, it was the local custom to celebrate electoral success for a period of no less than 24 hours. I do not know what their party affiliation was; but, when the festivities began, it would appear they supported privatization. However, as it continued into the night, spilling out into the hallways and other rooms, they became quite communal and socialistic. (I was going to say left leaning, but, when they walked, they actually leaned to both sides.)

As the room already had a television set, I am sure the management felt that the presence of a radio would merely be looked upon on as outdated technology and give the impression of an establishment that was not up with the times. To protect guests from harmful electromagnetic waves wrought by Wi-Fi transmissions, hotel management thought it best to just direct the guests to the computer café half a mile down the street where it was far enough away not to pose any danger to their guests. (It turned out that the café was closed for the season.)

The front desk attendants had cleverly fixed their phone so if any guest called from one of the rooms, it did not ring, and therefore did not disturb the receptionist as she served people who were checking in or fretting over the clue for fourteen-across. The continental breakfast the hotel served consisted of hard rolls, butter, burned croissants, and cereal with milk. The milk was being served long past the expiration date intended by the cow who had donated it. There was also tepid coffee and orange flavored water the management playfully called "juice." [9]

When we checked out at 8:15 a.m., I thought it best not to disturb the sleeping receptionist and just leave the key on the front desk. I did not fill out a comment card. After all, they were so proud of their three-star rating.

•

The academic conference was one of the most unusual I have ever attended. It was jointly sponsored by the French and Italian governments, and alternated each year between Paris and Venice. There were attendees and fellow academics from 23 different countries. The conference was held at the *Università Ca' Foscari Venezia*, founded in 1868 as Italy's first university dedicated to economics and commerce. (It was named after the first building, the Foscari Palace.) This university has about 20,000 students in a variety of majors. In the building where the conference was held, there were signs for classes in Economic Philosophy, Economic Psychology (Consumer Behavior? Freakonomics?), and the Economics of Entrepreneurship. The entire university is scattered across Venice in ten different buildings. It is the only university in the world where students have to take boats to get their next class. Our building was at the end of one of the canals facing the mainland. I got to spend time with new friends and colleagues from Poland, India, England, Spain, Lithuania, Slovenia, Ukraine, and, of course, Italy and France.

The vast majority of the presented papers were theoretical. This is the opposite of American conferences where almost all the papers are empirical studies with very complex statistical models and analysis. The Europeans called any research "empirical" studies if they contained proposed hypothesis. Very few of the papers had even the most basic descriptive statistics. Many were dedicated to a philosophical or political analysis of a marketing phenomenon. When I asked why this was the case, they responded they did not have the money to spend on surveys.

"We ask the government, but they are only interested in paying for research that contributes to economic development. So, we write theoretical papers because they don't require any funding," said one delegate.

---

9 We never needed to set an alarm to get up because every morning the kitchen staff would consistently burn the breakfast croissants at 6:30 a.m. This would set off the fire alarm, which, fortunately, was installed in the hallway outside our door.

The conference presentations could be in French, Italian, or English but the presentation slides had to be in English. This was very hard to follow, because most of the presentations were not in English. At U.S. conferences, you are expected to give a summary presentation of your research with time for questions. Here, everyone else (except me) actually read his or her entire paper. The translation of these into English kept you very alert. It might have been some time into the presentation before I "broke the code" and the entire meaning of what I originally thought the research was about would completely change. Some of the notes I took included:

"Low price and low cost are used interchangeably. Hard to know if they are spending or making."

"'Competencies' really means 'competitors.' Review these slides when there is time."

"Opposition = comparison."

"Rehabilitation means 'return' to or 'revisit'."

"Significativity = significance. (But they are not using it in the statistical sense.) What is this?"

"Emergency is really emergence. Now I get it."

I eventually realized in one paper (which was presented in English) the words "exhibition", "expedition", and "exposition" were used interchangeably and I never did understand what they were trying to say. I'm not sure anyone else did either. After the presentation, there were no questions.

A Day of Wien and Roses

Flying back to Podgorica, we had a one-day layover in Vienna *(Wien)* and took time to see the city of Mozart, Brahms, Liszt, and little bitty sausages in a can.[10] We flew Austrian Airways where they served *kuchen* for an on-board snack, had newspapers in three different languages, and the cabin music always played a Strauss waltz.[11] The hotel we had chosen was named *Rathaus*. I was worried about choosing a hotel named Rat House until I discovered it really means City Hall. When we arrived, there was only about two hours of daylight left, so we headed to the *Stephanplatz*. The cathedral there was lovely but was no warmer inside than it was outside (25°F).

---

10 Vienna sausages were probably invented by a resident of Frankfurt, Germany named Johann Georg Lahner. Not missing a chance for publicity, the Austrians renamed them *Wiener*, meaning "from Vienna".

11 It made you feel like Dr. Heywood Floyd riding the moon shuttle in *2001: A Space Odyssey*.

We toured the historic church very rapidly, so we could run down to the Hofburg Palace before it closed. There we saw the Spanish Riding School that trains the famous Lipizzaner stallions (which are bred in Slovenia). The Palace has been the seat of government in Austria since the late 1200s. It was the palace of the Holy Roman Empire, the German Nation, and the Habsburg dynasty. The opulence of the palace and its treasury had a very profound effect on me. The artwork, décor, and treasures were rarely Austrian. They were from regions all over the Austrian (and later the Austro-Hungarian) empire—gifts to the royalty, tribute, and spoils of war.

As we were new in town, we headed back toward the Rat House to eat some *weinerschnitzel, bratkarttoffeln, und wiener apfelstrudel.* After four days of pasta and pizza in Venice, it was *wunderbar*.[12]

---

[12] As we met local Viennese, and told them we traveling, they wished us "Gute Fahrt!" which sounded a little potty to us but it turns out to mean, "Have a good trip." This may explain, why, five stops out of Vienna on the U3 subway, there is a stop labeled Gasometer.

Road Trip!

Universities in Europe provide students (and faculty) with a much needed Spring Break. It is scheduled not really caring who needs a break from whom. This is a very civilized practice, something my previous institution did not believe in. Having looked out over students in classrooms most of my adult life, I can tell you, once spring begins to bud and a young man's thought turns to beaches and bikinis, they are pretty much lost to even the most inspired lectures. Their behavior continues until their primeval need is satiated, and they can return once again to the chalk-filled lecture halls of higher learning with sunburns, bleached hair, and open minds. Montenegro is a civilized place, and we were given a week off in March, efficiently placed in the exact middle of the semester.

Spring had definitely sprung and so had our wanderlust. We had saved just enough money for one more trip while we were there, but where to go? We had always wanted to see the Holy Lands but there was trouble there again. Istanbul, the intersection of eastern and western civilization was certainly alluring. Beth Lynn had always wanted to see dismal Moscow. But, after much debate, we finally decided on the birthplace of western civilization—Athens.

I expected making travel arrangements would be easy as there were two tourist agencies on our own street. The first one I entered had posters all over its walls promoting trips to London, Pariz, and Moskva with excursion packages to local favorites like Budva, Ostrog, and Lake Ohrid. In the office there were four desks, all empty.

I called out, "Dobar dan?"

No answer.

There was nobody in the backroom or the *toaleti* either. I took a brochure about Adria Airlines off a rack and let myself out.

I went to the other agency in the next block and asked if they spoke English.

The manager said, "Ne."

"Mogu kupiti karte u Atinu?" (Can I buy tickets to Athens?)

"Ne. Beograd."

"Thessaloniki?"

"Ne. Beograd."

Okay. "Hvala." (Thank you.)

I walked back past the first office on my way home. It was now locked with a "Zatvoreno" (Closed) sign on the door at 2:30 in the afternoon.

Through the good graces of a friend at the embassy, we found a travel agency where the manager spoke English and was most helpful. We told her what we wanted to do; and she asked, "Why don't you drive? You can save a lot of money."

"Drive? Is that safe?"

"Sure, I just got back from there. Just stay out of Kosovo, the mountains of Albania, and downtown Tirana if you can help it. Oh, and Athens traffic is terrible."

The more we considered driving, the more appealing and exciting it sounded. As middle-aged people of previously dubious adventuresomeness, we decided we would finally go backpacking across Europe. Our creaking middle-aged bodies and Beth Lynn's irrational need to sleep on a mattress and have porcelain fixtures nearby, tempered the backpacking plans. Thus, instead of actually backpacking, we rented the car and decided to drive.

After many nights of strategic planning which included pouring over maps of the Balkans spread out on the kitchen table and much moving of little men on horses around with sticks, we decided we could live out our fantasy and still stay within budget. We could plan a trip to see some countries most Americans would never see, edify ourselves intellectually, and still be back in time for me to administer a pop quiz the following Monday. We consulted Google maps, travel guides we had brought, and asked new friends who had made such a trip. From this intel, we calculated we could drive down through Albania, across the Greek Peloponnesian mountains, into Athens, then island hop to some exotic dot in the Aegean Sea, motor up to Meteora, muscle our way into Macedonia, bisect Albania once again, and pop home to Podgorica.

I located a friend of a friend who had a car he would rent us at a reasonable price. He worked full time for the government but owned two cars that he rented (to foreigners) to make extra cash. The car he provided was a small Opel. It had all the required papers, a safety vest, and requisite number of tires. It also had a standard transmission, something that (given the nature of the roads we were to encounter) would keep me shifting gears almost constantly for the next ten days. When we eventually returned to Podgorica, I looked like a fiddler crab.

Another friend had kindly offered us her GPS navigation device that turned out to be a godsend in the larger, confusing cities. The device had a female voice that had the strangest sounding Montenegrin accent—as though she was from somewhere up near Cambridge. Beth Lynn's parents had already named their GPS unit, "Garmina." We appropriately named ours "Garmica."

Before I left the States, I had studied very hard to obtain the distinguished and coveted International Drivers Permit.[1] In preparation to drive in Europe, I had practiced continuous honking and certain hand gestures. I also knew there were very different European Union traffic signs that had no explanatory words. We had not gotten far from Podgorica before we encountered road signs we had never seen before. We interpreted them as follows:

1 Which can be obtained for a smile and fifteen bucks at any AAA office.

We left Podgorica heading south skirting the east shore of Skadar Lake on a small country road and crossed the Albania border at Han i Hotit. There, the remnants of a police state were still apparent with barbwire, high fences, and empty gun turrets pointed our way. Our first trans-country segment was to cover the length of Albania on its National Highway. We discovered that national highways in Albania were much like dotted lines on a map. The same road would go from a modern four-lane highway and become a two-tread dirt road a few kilometers later. Often a perfectly good freeway would suddenly, and without warning, inexplicably end. The road would then become a pothole-pocked, crater-covered, dusty gravel lane until it decided, many miles later, to become cured concrete again. Yet none of this was marked on any of the maps or the GPS. Every road in Albania was under construction. Those that weren't, should have been. When the "highway" became gravelly and there were no lane designations, traffic became more like an organized demolition derby with cars approaching you on both sides careening through the dust.

Cars would follow so close behind us that the hood of their car would completely disappear in our rear-view mirror. Then, I would see a man with very thick glasses glaring at me, mentally estimating the distance between our car and the oncoming traffic to see which side he could pass on. The really fast drivers on Albanian roads had sports cars with Italian license plates. They zipped by us and the impotent police officers that were on foot.

Based on comparative satellite imagery, NASA believes there are more pothole craters in Albania than are on the moon. What I wouldn't give to have the shock absorber concession there. You would have to only stock Mercedes Benz parts since that seemed to be the ride of choice among the natives. We would see brand new Mercedes sedans tootling down the road spewing diesel exhaust, the open trunk filled with produce, and a goat sticking his neck out of the back window.

The Battle of Bunker Hill (That Never Was)

The first thing that strikes anyone visiting Albania for the first time is the presence of thousands of cement bunkers planted across the entire country. The communist dictator, Enver Hoxha, constructed them during the Cold War in anticipation of various imaginary invasions that never came. Every dictator has to have a boogeyman from which to protect his people, and Hoxha was no exception. Every other country was eventually Albanian's supposed enemy. Most of the bunkers were small, built for one soldier and a machine gun. They were domed, cast-cement structures about six feet in height with four of that sunk into the ground. The bunkers had a small, approximately 12 by 18 inch, horizontal slit in the top, just large enough to sight out of. It was said they were designed to withstand a tank attack. Some were slightly larger and could hold several soldiers.

As we drove south, we noticed that the bunkers dotted the entire Albanian landscape scattered across fields and meadows. They appeared in the middle of farmland, hugged mountain cliffs, and littered the beaches. Some appeared singularly and others were in clusters. In the Gjirokastër District, along the Drinos river valley, there were hundreds of bunkers lined in parallel rows aimed at Greece, just in case there was an invasion of Greek soldiers decked out in their ceremonial skirts and pom-pom shoes. Hoxha told the world he had built 700,000 bunkers, but the official count is more like 60,000. This means he probably billed Russia and, then, China for 640,000 that were never constructed. We stopped several times to explore a few that were just off the road. Some of the farmers now used them to store hay or rocks cleared from the fields. Others were obviously outhouses. We particularly liked one bunker we saw sticking out in a wheat field. It was bald and had protruding concrete "ears." We named him Archie.

Going to Shkollë in Shkodër

Our first Albanian stop was the University of Shkodër in the town of the same name. Shkodër is considered the "soul" of Albania because it is the home of Mother Teresa's parents. At the university, I had the opportunity to speak to a graduate Marketing class where my lecture was interrupted by the call-to-prayers coming from the loudspeakers of the mosque next door. The students were a small but very dedicated group. They had to have been because the class met from four to eight every Friday evening.

Shkodër is the Albanian gateway to the large lake of the same name that is shared with Montenegro. It is situated in a fertile valley with overlooking hills, perfect for protecting the area. The basis for the city's name is lost, but there are ancient Illyrian and Greek references to Shkodër. Some believe the name comes from the phrase, "*Shko në Kodër*" which means, "go to the hill" and refers to the Castle of Rozafës.

The next morning, we took a quick tour of the castle fort that sat 300 feet high above the city and lake. Shkodër was the Illyrian capital until Queen Teuta fled to Risan on the Bay of Kotor in Montenegro. As with the rest of the Balkans, the Romans added to the fort, but it fell to the Slavs who were then conquered by the Byzantine Empire who were run out by the Venetians. They ended up evacuating in 1478 to overpowering Ottomans' forces. The Turks held it until 1913 when expansionist Montenegro defeated them and devastated the city. (Montenegro was then forced to give it up by the Great Powers the next year.) Every invading nation wanted Shkodër because of the strategic importance of the castle fort.

As with everything in the Balkans, Rozafës is not without its legend. During the Ottoman times, the walls of the fort kept falling down. An Islamic mystic told the builders they must sacrifice someone by encasing them within the walls if they wanted the castle to stand. A woman was chosen who took the news stoically but had one request—that a hole be built in the wall, so she could continue to nurse her baby son. Since that time, at the entrance of the fort, the walls seep a white, milky liquid. In January and February, when the flow is the strongest, nursing mothers come and rub the water on their breasts. Rozafës was the name of the woman.

We dined in the castle overlooking the Drin River valley where it merges with the Bunë River before flowing into the Adriatic. On the bridge over the river were signs which read, "Forbidden to horse drawn carts," "Forbidden to hunt and fish on the bridge," and "Gathering medicinal plants is not allowed." We wondered what medicinal plants would be growing on a bridge. Below the Rozafës castle sat the Lead Mosque (*Xhamia e Plumbit*), built in 1773 by the Bushatllinj dynasty, the family of the ruling Vizier (who lived in the Castle up above). It was so named because the Vizier wanted a lead roof to protect the building from the elements. The roof proved too tempting to almost every subsequent generation, and the Austrians removed the last of the lead for their bullets in 1916. In 1967 its minaret was struck by lightening and destroyed. This was the same year Hoxha's Communist regime closed all the churches and mosques in order to declare Albania an atheist state. During that time, most of the religious buildings were destroyed. For some reason, the Lead Mosque survived. Because of the weight of the building required to hold up a lead roof, the mosque had sunk into the ground and was surrounded by water. When religious freedom was allowed again in Albania in 1990, the first spiritual rally was held at the Lead Mosque.

When we departed Saturday, it was market day. Shops were open to the street; tents and umbrellas were set up in all available spaces. Friends and family were clustered together exchanging news. Stoop-shouldered women in scarves lead donkeys laden with hay, kindling, or PVC pipe down the dusty streets. The men at the market wore old sport coats over threadbare sweaters with dress slacks and Wellington boots.

We had to veer around the sheep, goats, donkeys, and dogs that were sunning themselves on the highway. Driving through Lushnjë, we barely missed hitting a legless man who was sitting on the pavement. He was begging—getting attention by banging on the sides of the cars that were swerving at the last minute to avoid hitting him. Old women in black blouses, black stockings, and white scarves were selling live chickens in crates and homemade olive oil in used plastic Coke bottles. A man stood between lanes of high-speed traffic offering a dead rabbit for sale that he had just shot. As we got closer to the port of Durrës, fish vendors lined the sides of the road. Fresh fish were being sold out of the trunks of Mercedes-Benz cars. They were not on ice.

Closer to Durrës, we drove over mainline train tracks covered with weeds. Hoxha built trains in his country, but they always stopped well short of any border and never connected to the rail system of any other adjoining country. You could take trains within Albania but not to Albania. His regime encouraged the people to take trains in an effort to curb the use and desire for private transportation. Up until Hoxha's death in 1985, there were very few licensed drivers in Albania as only top members of the Communist Party were allowed to own cars. As late as 1986, the U.N. estimated there were only 150 authorized drivers in a country of 2.8 million people. This was good considering there were very few paved roads anywhere. After the Communist regime fell, the demand for driver's licenses skyrocketed. Everywhere we drove, there were hundreds of cars with the sign "*Autoskollë*" mounted on top. In the cars there would be an instructor with as many as six students crammed inside. The students' ages ranged from teenagers to grandparents. We learned to be particularly cautious around them because when they would change student drivers, the car would immediately jackrabbit onto the road and take up two lanes as a safety buffer. Evidently, guts and intimidation were as much a part of the curriculum as was signaling and shifting.[2]

Acting Under Durrës

We continued south from Shkodër to Durrës where, after the fall of Communism in 1990, hundreds of thousands of Hoxha's cronies stormed its harbor, hijacked boats, and forced the owners to take them to Italy. It was so dramatic that the Italian government took over the foreign port to prevent further pirating of their ships. We then motored down along the southern coast through Vlorë heading to Sarandë[3] with a slight dusty detour to Berat, *"Qyteti*

---

2 Ironically, *autoskollë* also means being bullied.

3 In Albanian, road signs might read "Sarandë", "Saranda", or "Sarand". They don't

i njëmijë dritareve" (The Town of a Thousand Windows)[4], so named because of the retained Ottoman architecture.[5] In the Mangalemi neighborhood, the old houses are stacked one on top of another rising up a steep hill that overlooks the Osum River. Each house had as many as 12 front windows staring out into space. The river is the division for two mountains that were once giants, Tomorr and Shpirag. They fought and killed each other over a beautiful young woman who, then, drowned herself in her sorrow. The river is the accumulation of her flowing tears.

•

Google Maps is a wonderful tool but carries with it the optimism for which Americans are known. It told us we could drive the complete length of Albania in four hours. It took ten. Garmica, the GPS, was much more pessimistic; she said it couldn't be done at all. It was not that she didn't know about Albania, she just didn't realize there was any Albania south of Vlorë. The road went up the mountain and came down the other side with hairpin turns (and one paperclip turn) and nary a beep from Garmica. She showed us driving somewhere out in the ocean between the Greek isles of Mathraki and Othonoi. It was then we realized if you haven't driven in an isolated southern Balkan mountain range at midnight on a moonless night, down an unlit, winding, single-lane road, dodging old women dressed completely in black who were herding donkeys and sheep down the middle of the pavement, not knowing where you were because the GPS system showed your car in the middle of the Ionic Sea, and you did not know the local language, well, you really hadn't traveled.

And, up to that point, I guess we hadn't.

As we drove down from the mountain crest, we were presented with a romantic view of the moon over the ocean and the lights from the Greek island of Corfu. Unfortunately, the road did not lend itself to rubber necking. The scenery was breathtaking but so was the absence of a shoulder or any guardrail. We called it "The Road of A Thousand Foot Drop." It was dusk when we started our descent, and pitch black when we got to the bottom near the ocean. This was only to find the road climbing back over winding, rolling hills, some with sheer

---

spell any better than I do. It turns out that if the ë is the last letter on the word, it is silent. (*Then why do they use it?*)

4 Not to be confused with Gjirokastër, "The Town of a Thousand Steps" (because of the climb to its citadel).

5 It may mean one thousand (*nje mije*) or it may mean "one over another" *(nje mbi nje)*. It is hard to say as Albanians talk pretty fast.

cliffs into the sea. In some of the villages we passed through, the road was the only street in town with just footpaths to the houses above or below. We would pass through villages of old stone structures, and then come across acres and acres of the cement shells of houses that were begun but never finished after the financial collapse of 1997.

We made it to Sarandë about one in the morning and found our hotel just up from the water's edge. We had booked ahead. The owner had stayed up for us, and was waiting in the lobby, smiling. He only had one reservation for the night. We were the only ones there in a nine-story, ninety-room hotel.

Contrarians that they are, Albanians, have an interesting habit of nodding to mean no and shaking their head to mean yes.[6] In addition, in Albanian, "yo" means "no" as opposed to meaning "hello" as it does in Philadelphia.

Not knowing this little cultural tidbit, I read phonetically from the Albanian guidebook, "Do you take euros?"

The owner shook his head.

"You do not take euros?"

He nodded.

"So then, you don't not take euros?" I asked in English.

At this point, I pulled some euros out of my wallet to show him, and he gave me the official international thumbs-up sign. He did not speak any English but asked, "A flisni Italisht?" (Do you speak Italian?) Beth Lynn spoke up and he chatted with her for a few minutes before he gave us the room key, and we headed upstairs. During the Cold War, when there was only one official Albanian television channel[7], Albanians along the coast jerry-rigged their TV antennas to pick up Italian broadcasts. They can quote many Marcello Mastroianni movies by heart.

To decompress that night, I flipped through all the cable channels on the TV set. I couldn't imagine there was a lot of money to produce Albanian TV shows, so I was impressed to see *Big Brother Albania.* It turned out that was not what it really was. It was the Big Brother *Albanian Fan Club.* This show was aired after the Big Brother broadcast from the U.K. was finished, and featured a local panel dissecting the important events from that night's episode.

At breakfast the next morning, we pleasantly discovered Sarandë sat on a lovely bay overlooking Corfu. Before leaving Albania, we made a stop at *Syri I Kalter* or Blue-eyed Spring. This was a deep iris-blue spring that fed into the Bistrica River and produced water the color of blue we had seen only in the

6 After observing this several times, the no is more of a slight diagonal motion.

7 The Communist Channel, coming to you in living color—red.

Caribbean. Driving around a dam on the Bistrica, we got stuck behind a repair crew that was grading and paving the road. They would tamp down the steaming asphalt that had just been shoveled out of the bed of a blackened Toyota pickup truck. Every hundred yards or so, the crew would stop work, go back and pick up ten beehives which they hand carried along the road, and set them beside the next section they were working on.

Greece

Leaving Sarandë, we headed east into the hills and, then mountains of southern Albania, which is the Greek minority section of the country known as Northern Epirus. In an hour we went from palm trees on the beach to snow dusted mountains. Along the road were memorials to individuals killed in car accidents. They looked like mail boxes in the shape of little churches, and were filled with flowers, lit oil lamps, bottles of water, and a picture of the deceased.

After crossing over the Greek border, the road signs now looked like really long fraternity names. To our left (up the hill) were olive trees, and to our right (to the shoreline) were orange groves and miles of strawberry fields (which almost lasted forever). The weather was mild, the breeze refreshing, and the scent from the fruit fields was intoxicating.

While we took a lunch break in the town of Ioninna, our waiter asked how far we were planning on driving.

"We are trying to make Pátra before dark."

"You have full tank of gas?"

"No, we are going to fill up before we leave here."

"Strike."

"*What?*"

"Strike. Petrol stations all on strike. All closed."

"Closed?"

"*Nai* (Yes). All closed as protest."

"What are they protesting?"

"Who knows? Taxis, airports, ships, they get to strike. But not restaurants. It's not fair." (He digressed.) "How much you got?"

"About an eighth of a tank."

"What is eighth?"

"One over eight," I said, drawing it in the air.

"You get mebbe Arta. No get Pátra. Pátra two hours. You need place to sleep. I got cousin in Arta."

"Thanks anyway, but we're going to press on and see how far we get."

Sure enough, every gas station we passed had "*ΚΛΕΙΣΤΑ*" (Closed) signs or had the pumps taped off. Their convenience stores, bars, restaurants, and repair bays were all open. Everybody was still working; they were just not pumping any petrol. We passed several BP stations. I thought *surely* the Brits would be open. We had prepaid the hotel in Pátra. If we didn't make it, we were out €100 and several hours on tomorrow's schedule, which meant canceling some of the things we most wanted to see. We pressed on toward Arta and Amfilochia watching the gas gauge fall closer and closer to the "E." I didn't want this to be one of those cars that hovers forever at 90 percent empty and then immediately comes to a stop at the same time a 400-ton Hellenic Freight truck barreled up behind us.

The sun was setting in the Ionian Sea, and we were losing light—getting to the point of having to make a decision. I directed the navigator to scan for the nearest hotel on the GPS, and I would look as best I could for a hotel sign or even a room to let. We were just about to pull over, evaluate the "situation," and place blame, when I noticed a very small gas station where a woman was filling up a scooter. I whipped in and pulled up behind it.

"Dezil?" the woman whispered.

"Unleaded," I whispered back.

"Fill?" I nodded.

While she was pumping the petrol, she crouched behind the car occasionally peeking over the roof at the on-coming traffic. I crouched down with her, not knowing who it was we were avoiding. The pump came to €45.01.[8] She took my fifty-euro bill, ran into the office, shut the door, drew the blinds, and didn't come back.

We got back on the road and headed toward the new Rio-Antirio suspension bridge that links Peloponnese with mainland Greece. The longest cable-stayed bridge in the world was completed in 2004, and they are still proud of it—very proud. It was a $30 toll to cross it into Pátra. But they don't charge you a thing to leave, which says a lot about the town.

That evening, at the hotel, we dined on skewered *griskin* and ladyfingers (okra). We met a fellow American who had discovered the joy of *tiganita*, the deep-fried vegetables they serve there.

He gushed in Tony the Tiger fashion, "They're great! But, you know, you usually don't associate fried foods with Greece."

I don't think he even realized what he said.

Standing in Oly Places

[8] Gas there was €1.42 per liter or $7.40 a gallon

The statue that dominates the entrance to the Olympia Museum depicts the goddess of victory, Nike. Evidently, she has been the official sponsor of the Olympic games since they were first held in 776 B.C. The ancient Olympic site is tucked in a little valley southeast of the Peloponnesian Mountains. The village was originally an Assyrian outpost. Its architecture, even through Roman times, depicted the Assyrian eagle. The Olympics began as a tribute to Zeus and continued uninterrupted for 1,170 years. Theodosius I, the last Emperor of both eastern and western parts of the Roman Empire, abolished the games in 394 A.D. For some strange reason he believed that grown, naked men running, wrestling, and throwing things in the air was "too pagan." Go figure.

Olympia was a training facility, wrestling stadium, bathing house, gymnasium, an outdoor track, and had its own Temple to the big guy himself, Zeus. The only thing they didn't have was Astroturf. Even Philip II of Macedonia sent money and people to build a monument to the games.[9]

Seeing this site had special meaning for Beth Lynn. She got to stand in the exact spot where, every two years, the Olympic torch is lit and begins its journey to the site of the next games. The original stadium is still there with its embanked, grassy viewing stands (it hosted the shot put events in the 2004 Games). In the space of a month, Beth Lynn, the ultimate Olympic fan, got to watch the 2010 Vancouver Olympics, see where the 2004 Athens Games were played, and visit the site of Olympia. This was a big deal for someone who has, among other things, memorized the hometowns of all Olympian speed skaters.

Leaving Olympia, we drove across the mountains, finding the weather was now so nice that cafes and restaurants had set tables up outside. Driving through the art colony of Kourtesi, our car passed so close to the patrons we would brush against their tablecloths. One man, who was reading a newspaper, would lean his chair to the right as cars would pass and not even bother to look up.

Europeans have to drive small cars in order to negotiate their small centuries-old urban streets. After seeing all the compact, sub-compact, and sub-atomic compact cars that were on the roads, I am sold on them. Some Americans argue small cars just are not safe. "Why, if you got hit by one of those big tractor-trailers, you'd be dead!" News flash: there are just as many tractor-trailer rigs in Europe as there are in the U.S., so I don't buy that argument anymore.[10]

---

9 It was called the *Phillipeon* and had to be finished by his son, Alexander the Great. It is the only structure in Olympia dedicated to an actual human. Another example of what the gods would have done if they had only had the money.

10 We did see a vehicle we couldn't figure out-a Smart Car ambulance. How do you get a stretcher in one of those things?

Paul's Letter to the Corinthians

I Corinthians 3:19:2010

Dear Corinthians,

How ya'll doing?

Had a great time. Saw the canal and was impressed. Those French do good work. The ruins were great. The Roman artifacts were lovely and I was impressed to know that Corinth was larger than Athens way back then. The view from the Acrocorinth was incredible! Thought you might be interested to know that somebody has knocked over several of the columns on the Temple of Apollo and has left loose marble rocks on the road from Lechaion to the Agora. I tripped over several of those stones myself. You might want to replace those because somebody could hurt himself or herself.

- Paul

Up the Greek Without a Paddle

Unbeknownst to us, we had entered Athens two weeks into the public frustration generated by the Greek financial crisis. We suddenly discovered that strikes, protests, and riots were a daily occurrence. We crossed the Corinthian Canal and approached Athens via the toll road. The Communist Labor Union, *ΠΑΜΕ*, had broken all the tollgates and taken over the booths allowing vehicles through for free. I pulled up and the toll attendant would not even make eye contact with me when I tried to pay. The protestor who had commandeered her booth was yelling political slogans at the drivers who passed through. When I did not respond, he rushed outside, thrust a pamphlet in my face, and then proceeded to stand in front of the car waving a red flag. Over the traffic noise, I yelled "English?" At this, we saw his shoulders slump; and he dropped his flag. Crestfallen, he moved to one side and waved us on.

•

Like the German autobahn, the posted speed limit on Greek highways is 130 kph (81 mph).[11] Cars will constantly pass you exceeding that speed by 30 mph or more. Some even approach testing the theory of relativity. (I think they could get Greece completely out of debt if the police would just invest in more radar guns.)

We were making great time with our schedule until we arrived in Athens during the evening rush hour. Our travel agent was right about Athens. It was best to arrive before dawn and leave in the dark of night, so you did not have to

[11] Their racing team is Grecian Formula 1.

deal with most of the traffic. Chaos theory is alive and well in Athenian traffic. We would come to streets where the intersections were clogged with cars coming from all directions. The signal lights were working, but they were completely irrelevant to controlling the traffic. Motorcycles would weave between the stopped cars and were the only vehicles making any headway. Ignoring the cross walks, which were covered by cars, pedestrians walked between and around them on their path to the subway. Like some smog-belching ooze, the traffic would eventually, but slowly, begin to flow downhill where it would meet up with another collection of stagnant traffic at the next intersection. Police were posted at all intersections, but it was mostly for their own amusement. Traffic circles became the Greek Swirling Dance of Death Defiance.

"Death, I spit in your eye."

"Death, try and catch me!"

"Death, you must wait just a leetle longer, I made it home tonight!"

Greeks (and Athenians) are actually very good drivers, in a NASCAR sort of way. Every culture has its own set of driving rules and we observed that Athenians drove in the following manner:

1. If there were designated lanes on the street, they were merely there to keep the road painters employed. Three lanes meant at least three lanes of cars, two motorcycles in between them, and additional room to pass on the two feet of shoulder especially if there were only a few people with bicycles on it.
2. When the light changes to green, all cars must jackrabbit off and race to the next intersection where they have to stop and idle only a block away.
3. Motorcycles must dart around and between all traffic, moving or not.
4. Motorcycles must work their way through stopped traffic, edge to the front of the line, and then run the stoplight.
5. Little old ladies have the right of way no matter what else is going on even if they are slowly crossing a 130-kph freeway leading a reluctant donkey with sacks of oranges on its sides.
6. The sidewalk is not a DMZ (De-Motorized Zone). There are cars parked there permanently. A driver may pull up on the sidewalk, leave their car idling, and then walk to get a pack of cigarettes at the nearby kiosk. (It is safe to leave the car running because no one could steal the car with the traffic backed up the way it was.)

In Athens, we observed a reoccurring psychological phenomenon that we dubbed the *Law of Physical Reductionism.* That was when the driver believed the vehicle they were driving was actually smaller than it really was.[12] We came to the conclusion that this is the way Athenian drivers think:

"This bus is really just a car and can go down this tiny alley or fit between those two parked cars whose owners are talking through the windows."

"My car is not a car, but is really a motorcycle. It happens to have four wheels, but I can park it on the sidewalk and no one will notice how big it is."

"My motorcycle is just a bicycle with a little motor, so traffic rules don't apply to me, and a cop car can't catch me in this traffic anyway."

Athens is the only place I have ever driven where other cars got so close that I wanted boat bumpers hanging off my car. Other drivers got so near our car that they could tune *my* radio. Beth Lynn died a thousand anticipatory deaths in the Athens traffic. After the first three near collisions, she slid down on the floorboard, assumed a fetal position, and began sucking her thumb. I had to unfold her when we got to the hotel. We parked the car there, and did not move it until we left Athens a few days later—in the dim light of early dawn.

•

Athena must have been a complex woman, being the goddess of both weaving and war strategy. Her namesake city of 4.5 million people (40% of the country's population) sprawls across most of the Attic plain stopped only by the Saronic Gulf.[13] The historic heart of Athens is, of course, the Acropolis. That beautiful 500-foot butte conveniently placed in the center of town on top of which, beginning in 447 B.C., ancient Greeks built the Parthenon as a tribute to their patron goddess, the function for which it served for almost 1,000 years. (There was an older Parthenon before that, but the Persians destroyed it in 480 B.C.) The Parthenon has served as a Greek temple, a Christian church, and a Turkish mosque (with minaret), before being destroyed by Venetian artillery in 1687. (To be fair, the Ottomans *were* using it to store gunpowder at the time.)

In 1801, Lord Elgin, the British Ambassador to Constantinople, got permission from the Sultan to survey the Parthenon. He proceeded to remove most of the remaining statuary and ship them home to jolly old England. Not

---

12 This must be from looking through the side-view mirrors so often that they make close objects appear smaller than they really are.

13 As opposed to the *Sardonic* Gulf, which was the distance between me and the facial expressions of the other drivers.

being a philanthropic man, he then *sold* them to the British Museum. Since Greek independence in 1832, their government has been trying to recover the "Elgin Marbles" with negotiations continuing to the present day. The British argument against returning them was that the Greeks did not have a suitable place to display and protect them. To that end, the Greeks built the Acropolis Museum to the tune of $165 million. It is now one of the finest designed museums in the world. The Brits still have the statues.

Construction on the museum was started in 1989. After three false starts, it was finally opened twenty years later. During construction, the museum was found to be situated on top of the ancient ruins of the town of Makrygianni. The architects then redesigned the museum's building plans, so visitors could look through glass floors and watch archeologists working below them. If you examine a Greek one-euro coin, the owl on the reverse side is a copy of a *tetradracmae* coin that was excavated at the bottom of the Acropolis. Thus, Greek currency has not changed all that much in 2,500 years.

From atop the Acropolis you can see all of Athens. Looking down you can find the wandering streets of the Plaka and the expanse of the Agora. (That is, if you are not afraid of heights.[14]) From here you can see why the Athenians thought they were above all other civilizations, second only to the gods on Mount Olympus.

•

We spent two days wandering around downtown Athens, including the base of the Acropolis, the Plaka, Athens Central Market, and the neighborhood around the hotel that was on the waterfront in Alimou. We would take the tram from our hotel to downtown, while trying not to forget what return stop was ours.[15] On the tram, old people genuflected every time they passed a church. They did not even look up; they knew where each one was on the route. One day, the tram was particularly crowded because it was Greek Independence Day, and people were headed downtown to see the children's parade. Flags were out, and all the kids were in colorful costumes.

The next day, at the end of the tram run at Syntagma Square, across from Parliament, we jumped off only to find the police in black balaclavas holding riot shields. We quickly jumped back on again. Riots began to be a daily occurrence. We began to watch for police vans parked a few blocks out from the square

---

14 Known as *Acropophobia*.

15 Our slogan was "Remember the Alimou."

where officers would be suiting up. Then we would get off at the next stop and grab the next tram traveling in the opposite direction.

In these times of economic and civil uncertainty, it paid to call the front desk every morning and have, what I began to call, the Daily Baseball Conversation.

I would ask, "Kali méra (good morning). Are there any strikes today?"

"Trains and busses no run."

That would mean Delphi was out, but the Acropolis was safe.

•

Perhaps we got wishful after seeing the movie, *Mama Mia*; because we, too, wanted to have a couple of dreamy days on a Greek island in the Aegean Sea. We did not have the time or budget to island hop; we could only visit one. After exhaustive research, we chose Santorini, the island that might hold the secret to the lost city of Atlantis.

A short thirty-minute flight from Athens landed us on the eastern slope of the island, the southernmost of the Cyclades nearest Crete. We had booked a hotel over the Internet that looked small, quaint, and out of the way. From the airport, we hailed a taxi and told the driver where we needed to go. After a very bouncy ride on an old road, he pulled up at a building that was the same color as the beige soil that surrounded it.

The cabbie asked, "You got reservations?"

I assured him we did as we were getting out of the cab. He shook his head and drove away. The hotel was the Santa Mare. I should have suspected something with the hotel being named after an old nag. The front door was locked tight, and there were no cars in the parking lot. We walked around the building calling out "hello" as we went. Peeking through the windows into the rooms, we saw that none of the beds had sheets on them, and the swimming pool in the back was completely drained. It was apparent the hotel was closed for the season, and we were several miles from the nearest village. I went to the front door and dialed an emergency number. A man answered, said, "Yes, yes" and hung up before I got a chance to speak. I didn't know what else to do except pick up our luggage and start walking into town. Immediately, two short fellows appeared out of nowhere. The slightly taller of the two introduced himself.

"Hi. I am Dede from Bali." (So was Dede's friend who didn't talk.)

"You talk to boss."

He unlocked the front door, let us into the reception area, and motioned for us to wait. He dialed the phone and repeated, "Yes, boss. I know, boss," several times.

Dede asked me, "You got voucher?"

I shook my head.

"They no have voucher."

"Yes, boss. I know, boss," three more times.

"He want to talk to you," he said handing me the phone.

"Hello?"

"Read me voucher," a voice growled.

"I don't have a voucher. I made a reservation over the net."

"What company?"

"I don't know what company. I have a booking number."

"You not know what company? How I get paid?"

"I don't know. My booking number is MRTM452010."

"Okay, okay. I talk to Dede."

I handed the phone to Dede, and he said "Yes, boss" about seven more times before he hung up, got a room key, and grabbed our luggage. It turned out that the owner of the hotel ran the entire operation from Athens over his mobile phone. Yet again, we were the only two people in the entire hotel. Every morning there was a complete breakfast buffet with eggs, pastries, and juices set out for our two place settings at a single table.

If you want privacy, we recommend the Hotel Santa Mare.

•

We wanted to see all the sights and join in the festivities on the island, but they were at one end of the island and we were at the other. It was hard for me to justify renting a second car on top of the one from Montenegro that I was already paying for. That car was still in Athens probably lounging around the hotel pool and running up a tab. After extensive financial analysis, we decided renting a $15 scooter from Marco across the street would not break the bank. His wife, Daniela, who was from Romania, drew us a map of the island showing where all her favorite spots were. Because of the volcanic activity on the island, there were romantic deep red beaches as well as black ones that had patches of white from pumice.

We first rode to the southernmost point of the island where the naval lighthouse was, and we sat at, what seemed like, the very end of the world. From there we viewed a panorama of the sea and the ancient caldera that is Santorini.

It is a crescent-shaped island surrounding the cone of a now dormant volcano in its lagoon. The water near the center is always teal green due to the sulfur flowing up from the bowels of the earth. After estimating the slope of the island from the edge of its remaining cliffs, the original atoll must have been almost 4,500 feet high when the volcano erupted 3,600 years ago. The explosion was estimated to be ten times that of the Krakatoa eruption. It probably was the disaster that wiped out the entire Minoan civilization on the isle of Crete.

Travelling back on the road, we saw three huge construction cranes down in a gulley behind a locked gate. This was the archeological excavation of *Akrotiri*. Certain archeologists think this settlement was the basis behind Plato's tale of Atlantis. There was enough circumstantial evidence to that effect to convince Jacques Cousteau to mount an underwater expedition in 1976. The structures in the town are very well preserved like those in Pompeii and for the same reason. The difference is whoever lived on Santorini left in a very orderly and organized manner before the volcano erupted. There were no unburied bodies, and there were very few gold items left indicating the residents were not surprised by the eruption but left the island before it occurred. The Greek government built a covered roof over these ruins that later collapsed killing a visitor. Thus, the site has been closed for the last eight years.

The two major towns on Santorini, Fira and Oia, sit on the edge of the cliffs overlooking the caldera and bask in sensuous sunsets. Cruise ships dock a thousand feet below Fira and disembarking tourists have the choice of taking a cab, a cable car, or a donkey up into town. The Dorians (the column folks) claim they founded the island in the 9th century B.C. and named it after their reluctant leader, Theras. The Greeks call the island Thira. Tourists refer to it by the derivative of the Venetian name of the Church of Santa Irene in the village of Perissa on the south part of the island or Santorini.

Therans, being an island people, had no choice but to be sailors. The poorest crewmembers lived in cliff caves as troglodytes. The mates, having more money, built homes that extended out from the caves. Captains constructed houses and windmills on the tops of the cliffs. Most of these homes were plastered white with blue doors and roofs that glowed in the sun.

Being a Sunday during the off-season, very few businesses and restaurants were open. Hungry, we puttered around in the dark until we heard a loud and boisterous noise coming from the Aquarius Café in Perissa. It seemed the entire town was there, enjoying the Greek National Soccer Championship. The patrons' allegiances were clearly divided. Chairs and tables had been moved to create two camps, one for each team, and a buffer zone aisle in the middle. One group would yell and cheer, and the other would moan, and vice versa. We made sure we sat in the neutral section back near the restrooms. The only other man back there was Anthony, who owned the place. He had his laptop out so he could get caught up on his bookkeeping while keeping an eye on customers. He was actually an artist and had bought the café so he could have a place to offer his pictures for sale. It did not work out very well; so he opened a gallery in Fira where the crowds were, and now he was stuck with this café on the remote part of the island. Andreous, another gallery owner we met, lived on the island seven months a year and in Athens the rest of the time. He was hoping the lower prices from the financial crises would bring more tourists than last year. He said he gets visitors from all over the world, but only Americans buy art. He also said the economy was so bad most Athenians were only eating one meal a day.

•

Greeks are very passionate about life. Their personal animation is enthralling and endearing. A typical conversation between two men will go something like this.

"Ti κανίς!" (Greeting.)

"Πώς είσαι παλιός φίλος μου? Δεν έχω δει εσείς για χίλιες μέρες!" (Commence hugging and kissing.)

"Χίλιες μέρες! Περισσότερο σαν ένα εκατομμύριο! Πώς είστε μόνοι σας κρατώντας? Πώς είναι η οικογένεια; Πώς είναι ο Αλέξανδρος, ότι η μη καλή ξάδελφος σου?" (Faces nose to nose with elevated voices.)

"Αλέξανδρος! Το ένα που είναι πολύ τεμπέλης για να κύμα μακριά μύγες?" (Foreheads touching while holding each other's shoulders.)

"Αυτό είναι το ένα! Τι διάβολο τεμπέλης. Θα ήθελα να τον ταΐζεις για τα σκυλιά!"

"Ίσως χρειαστεί να αν γίνει νέα γιος-το-δίκαιο σας!!!!" (Much wild gesticulation.)

This was just to ask a friend what time it was.

•

Somewhere in Santorini, Beth Lynn acquired that unfriendly fungus of female plumbing, *candida albicans*. Upon returning to Athens our first order of business was to find something to alleviate her discomfort. All touring was put on hold while we searched out the nearest pharmacy. The concierge directed us to one just a few blocks away, and we arrived at 2:05 p.m. Pharmacies in Athens close every weekday from two to four o'clock for lunch and a siesta. This was not good. The best I could do was to distract her for the next two hours while we waited for the drug store to reopen.

We window-shopped up the high street until the commercial district petered out and became tall apartment buildings. We crossed the street to a small bakery. This late in the day, they only had one pastry choice left—a floradina, an almond paste croissant covered in powdered sugar. We bought two, walked out to the sunlight, took one bite each, and immediately went back in the shop and bought the remaining four.

Having sold all her inventory, the shopkeeper locked the doors behind us. We walked down the hill to the next bakery and bought all the floradina they had, too. We were now the proud owners of twelve floradina and had powdered sugar all over our mouths to prove it. In Athens, there is a bakery on every street corner; and we decided that might not be enough of them. We sat down on a park bench across the street from the pharmacy and proceeded to fatten up on floradina while we waited for the store to open up. Caught up in the enthusiasm of our new discovery, we had somehow forgotten to get napkins; and we were both covered in white powder. Eventually, the pharmacist and clerk arrived to unlock the door.

Because I had less powdered sugar on me than Beth Lynn did, I went in to buy the medicine. I asked the clerk if she spoke English, and she shook her head. Our limited English-Greek ("With Popular Phases Sounded Out") Language Guide covered such medical issues as heart attacks, broken bones, and STD's; but yeast infections didn't even make the top ten. I pointed outside to Beth Lynn. The clerk looked out the window; and Beth Lynn waved back with a floradina. I then pointed between my legs. The clerk smiled and handed me a box of condoms. I shook my head, pointed back to Beth Lynn, and began vigorously scratching my crotch. The clerk called the pharmacist out from the back room. I repeated the gestures, and both women looked at me and tilted their heads in unison. I will not go into details, but I will tell you the mime class I took as an undergraduate 36 years ago finally paid off. When it dawned on them what we needed, they smiled at each other and handed me two small boxes. It was then that I noticed I had been thoroughly entertaining six women who had quietly entered the store behind me. I thanked the pharmacist profusely for her understanding.

"Sas ef□charistó□! Sas ef□charistó□!" (Thank you! Thank you!)

"Here. You two want a couple of floradina?"

•

Charming Andreana, a woman in her twenties with deep brown eyes, coal black hair, and a contrasting pearl complexion, staffed the reception desk at our hotel in Athens. She exemplified the effervescent essence of the local hospitality industry by being friendly and optimistic every day. One morning I called down to get the weather report, so we could dress appropriately.

"What is the weather today?" I asked Andreana.

"Nice, very nice," she replied.

"And the forecast?"

"Even nicer."

Not the specific answer I was looking for, but she was always right.

Andreana's helpful instructions always took on entertainment value all their own. Not wanting to drive in Athens any more than was absolutely necessary; we needed directions to get to the airport on public transportation. She took out a blank piece of paper and began to draw.

"These is the hotel. These is the street, out there (motioned to the front door with her pen). These is the other street. These is the ocean (drew wavy pattern). These is the bus station. These is you two (drew two stick figures). And, these is your luggage—the pullllll around bags and the leettle bag. You and your luggage are gunna to go through these door (motioned to front door with pen again), down the street here, across these light here, and across these street here. Donna cross without light, you donna make it. Take the X96 bus. Don't take the X95 bus. You no like him, he no like you. Only the X96 bus. Buy the tickets on the bus. Then the bus gunna go down these street, turn on these street, and get on this beg, beg street. Then the bus gunna stop here and you not gunna know why. Then the bus gunna get on the highway (for this she had to get a new piece of paper) and go allllllll the way down to the airport here. And here is you and here is your luggage, happy at the airport!"

We were already happy.

A Funny Thing Happened on the Way to the Agora

The Romans called them Forums; to the Greeks they were *Agora*—the center of almost all activity in town as it was the marketplace. What marketing professor would not want to see the Agora? The Athenian Agora sat at the base of the Acropolis intersected by the Panthenaic Way, the ancient main road in and out of town. This was the center of ancient Greek commerce and communication. There were at least 28 buildings in the area. It was in these buildings, their courtyards, and gardens that political gatherings, debates, athletic competitions, theatrical performances, and election campaigning took place.[16] Elections were held on the street corners. It was a true democracy with everybody (at least all the male citizens) voting on every issue. It took 6,000 people to have a quorum. Voting either was done with a show of hands, or, if it was close, by putting white or black pebbles in a vase. The wheels of legislation must have turned slowly indeed. The only building that has been completely reconstructed is the long white *Stoa of Attalos* that also serves to house the archeological museum. (The Rockefeller family paid for the restoration in the 1950s).

In the 6th century B.C., the *Agora* was redesigned to include most of the legal courts as well. In this area, archeologists have found bronze election ballots, a marble *kleroterion* (an allotment machine), which was used to randomly select jurors and clay *symbola,* which were the jurors' pay tokens. It was here that the early Greeks posted *tabulae* proclaiming new laws, contracts agreed upon, civil litigation settlements, arbitration agreements, as well as the interesting practice of ostracism. If someone was a real pain, an election could be called. People would pick up broken bits of pottery (it being free and plentiful, the Athenian equivalent of litter) on which they would scratch the name of the person they hated most. Again, if there were 6,000 votes against the person, they voted him off the island; and he was forced to leave Athens for ten years. This had nothing to do with the legal system, but it did help get rid of unwanted political rivals.

After the Romans conquered the Athenians, they donkey-dozed the *Agora* and built their own forum a few blocks to the east that ended up including Hadrian's Library. This is the palace he built when he was not busy constructing his wall to reduce Scottish immigration into the Roman Empire. The building was more than just a repository of parchments; it was a cultural center that contained a garden, works of art, and several lecture halls. Just a bit of Dear Old Rome to enlighten the heathens who had to live in the outposts of the Empire and had no culture whatsoever.

While examining these ruins, I chatted with one of the archeologists at the site. He explained that they were working on uncovering newly discovered sarcophagi and trying to restore some of the columns by carving matching pieces of marble. From the progress they were making, I did not think their grant money ran out anytime soon. The invading Herulians destroyed Hadrian's

---

16 The last two sometimes being indistinguishable.

Library about 267 A.D.[17] Viewing these ruins brought back the painful experience in my youth of having to wade through both the *Iliad* and the *Odyssey*. The only thing I remember thinking at the time was the entire war was fought over a girl. Geez. A *girl!*[18]

In the dense Plaka neighborhood below the Acropolis, I couldn't figure out how the restaurants got their supplies. The walkways were too narrow for a delivery truck to pass through. The honking of a scooter behind me interrupted my pondering about this. It was piled high with four crates of vegetables and bags of fruit hanging off the handlebars. The driver rested his feet on four cartons of eggs. He would pull up halfway into the front door of the restaurant, hand someone a box or bag, get a signature, and back out to make further deliveries.

The Plaka had brand name stores, and it abutted to the Athens Flea Market with its blanket-draped kiosks that hocked souvenirs. It seemed very touristy to us, so we hoofed it over to the Athens Central Market below Omonoia Square. Here we found displays of olives (24 varieties at one of the vendors), sacks of spices, and bags of dried sponges.19 There were varieties of raw fish, chickens hanging from hooks, and skinned, decapitated sheep heads for sale. We also stumbled on a store where you could start your own Olympics. They sold custom-made laurels made out of precious medals. In ancient times, the winner of the games would receive a humble olive laurel (not one of gold, silver, or bronze). The judges would present the champions with a laurel and hardy handshake.20

Meteora Shower

Leaving Athens in the drizzling rain early on our last morning, we drove north past Kozani, where they grow saffron and electricity. Kozani is the coal and electrical center of Greece. DEI, the country's power company, has 15 power plants in the one valley.

Before we left the States, I had asked my one and only big, fat Greek friend what we should see in Greece, and he said not to miss Meteora. Everyone

---

17 "Hi! We're the Barbarians and we do light sacking and heavy pillaging. We specialize in enslavement and plundering. Looks like you've got a lot work for us here, so we'll just get started. You weren't keeping that old large marble building for any reason, were you?"

18 Geek (not Greek) measurement: What is a millihelen? It is the face required to launch *one* ship.

19 Reminiscent of that famous movie, *Absorba the Greek.*

20 (Thank you, Mr. Brooks.)

else we spoke to who had traveled to Greece echoed this sentiment, whether they had visited the place or not. Meteora is the collection of Greek Orthodox monasteries that are perched high atop stone pinnacles, which overlook the town of Kalambaka at the base of the Pindus Mountains. Every Greek restaurant in America is required to have at least one picture of these unusual structures on their wall in order to maintain their certification.

In the 6th century, hermit Orthodox monks crawled up these rocks into the caves and never came down. By the 14th century it was an ideal place to hide from the Turks, and at least 20 monasteries were built in the next 100 years (six of which survive today). Access was only by very loooong ladders (several stories tall), which the monks took in every night or by a rope pulley system. It was not until the 1920s that walkways were cut in the rock to allow for visitors. Now, tourism is the monasteries primary source of income. (We noted the roads at the monasteries were better paved than streets in the town below.)

Ladies were requested to wear skirts in the monasteries, and they can provide them for you. The Great Meteron[21] was open the day we were there and it housed the monastery, rooms that provided an insight into the monastic way of life, and a museum of Greek military history. There was an ossuary holding the remains of previous monks who faithfully had served a spiritual life. Of the six monasteries still open, five are active; and one is a nunnery. Each one has only about ten active inhabitants. At the end of the tour, I stood at the edge of the precipice looking 1,200 feet down and wondered what monastic life would have been like isolated from the rest of the world, spending it in solitude and meditative prayer.

Wandering around Kalambaka, the small town below the spiritual aeries, we discovered the dessert, *χαλβά* (halva), a gelatinous concoction much like the main body of a pecan pie. There were two types, one made from honey and one from olive oil, both equally as sweet. The dessert is so ubiquitous in the Balkans that in Bosnia and Herzegovina the phrase "prodaje se kao halva" ("sells like halva") is a colloquial expression similar to the American saying, "sells like hotcakes."

Macedonia or (FYROM—The Former Yugoslavian Republic Known as Prince Macedonia)

The country of Macedonia has an image problem. It does not know how to brand itself. Since splitting from the former Yugoslavia, it proclaims it is the Republic of Macedonia. However, in its effort to achieve membership in the United Nations, Greece disputed the use of the name as they already had three administrative regions known as West Macedonia, Central Macedonia,

---

21 Sounds like a Vaudevillian magician.

and East Macedonia and Thrace.[22] The Greeks argued that the Republic of Macedonia couldn't lay claim to the name as most of ancient Macedonia lies within the current borders of Greece and that Macedonia *is* Greek. In 1992, the International Monetary Fund, the World Bank, and other international organizations proposed the new country be called the Former Yugoslav Republic of Macedonia (FYROM). However, the Macedonian government did not want to be associated with the former Yugoslavia, but accepted the "reference" (not an official name, mind you) so they could achieve U.N. Membership in 1993.

The dispute didn't stop there. Greece then protested that the Macedonian delegation could not be seated alphabetically with the other "M" countries. Macedonia did not want to be seated with the "F" countries, as that would legitimize the word, "Former." They compromised and sat the delegation next to Thailand—"T" as in "*The* Former . . ." Additionally, Greece had a problem with the new Macedonian flag, which bore the Vergina Sun, the 16 pointed emblem that was allegedly worn by Philip II of Macedon, father of Alexander the Great. Macedonia changed its flag in 1995 due to Greece asserting intellectual property rights on the symbol. Macedonia renamed its capital airport in Skopje, "Alexander the Great." Trade agreements refer to the countries in such circuitous fashion as "The Party of the First Part having its capital in Skopje" thereby avoiding having to use the word "Macedonia" at all. Now, the two countries are at a political stalemate, perhaps converging on the name, "Northern Macedonia."

Crossing over the Macedonian-Greek border, we entered the town of Bitola, RoM (or FYROM) in the southern part of the Pelagonia valley below the Baba Mountains. The Chamber of Commerce claims the city to be the important junction that connects the Adriatic Sea to the south with the Aegean Sea and Central Europe. Certainly true during the days of the caravans, but modern freight logistics have diminished its importance.

From Bitola, we drove over the mountains and began descending from the Gomo Krushje Mountain pass. Cresting the top, we heard a loud clunk under the car and I realized I no longer had use of the manual transmission. We coasted 12 miles down the windy mountain road until there was finally a place to pull over. I flagged down a passing ambulance that was serving as a taxi for about 15 people. The driver and I communicated through sign language. He punched in the phone number for emergencies, handed it to me, so I could then dial it on my phone.

The police dispatcher on the other end didn't speak much English but told me he would call me back. Twenty minutes later, a woman called and

[22] Since 2011, the three have been combined into one district called Macedonia-Thrace.

she explained that the police had sent someone down to the high school to get an English teacher in order to translate. She helped arrange a tow truck into town. Within an hour, a young man with long hair in a ponytail (very rare in the Balkans) showed up driving an old and very large flatbed truck. He hoisted our car onto the truck, and we climbed inside the cab. Beth Lynn had to sit on my lap, because a toolbox full of rusty chains on the front seat was too heavy to move. The driver spoke English, and he told us he was a law student who worked as a driver on weekends. All of his family members were tow truck drivers. He was proud of the fact that even his sister had her tow truck driver's license. We introduced ourselves and found out we had been rescued by Philip—of Macedonia.

He drove us down the hill and into the number one tourist destination for Montenegrins, Lake Ohrid. The simple reason for this is it is the cheapest place to vacation in the Balkans. You can stretch your euros while you sit on the esplanade overlooking the deep waters of the blue lake.

Philip took the car and us to the local Opel dealership where the staff was very helpful. They had already arranged a hotel for a taxi to take us to a hotel. The hotel happened to be in the charming Ohrid Old Town that sat on a bluff overlooking the water. After three passes through the few narrow streets of the old, walled city, our cabbie finally had to get out and ask a pizza delivery guy how to get to our hotel. He just pointed straight up. Sure enough, we couldn't drive to the hotel. It was up an alleyway even a scooter couldn't ascend.

We spent the next day exploring Ohrid including its amphitheater that was built before the Romans came conquering in the 2nd century. It is still in use today for plays and concerts. Samuil, the king of the First Bulgarian Empire, moved his capital here and built a castle on top of one Philip of Macedonia had built 1,200 years earlier. Ohrid also claimed to be the spot where Saints Cyril and Methodius converted the Slavic people to Christianity and invented the Glagolitic alphabet that one of their protégées named *Cyrillic.*[23]

Our car was fixed late the next day. As we were leaving town, we were repeatedly stopped on the road by gaggles of teenage girls in folk costumes. After finding one who spoke English, we found out it was the Macedonian National Give Money to Girls in Folk Costumes and the Gods Will Smile on You Day. At least that was what she said it was.

The Republic of Vevčani

---

23 If the protégée had liked the other saint better, I guess they would all be spelling in Methodist.

Although the sun was already setting on a long day, and we had even a longer way to go that night (over the Albanian mountain pass, through Tirana traffic in the dark, across the Montenegrin border, and return to Podgorica), I wanted to see the verdant village of Vevčani.

Sixteen kilometers north of Lake Ohrid lies Vevčani, whose blue springs bubble up in the mountains above it, and streams rush through canals in the center of town during the spring. The water is incredibly sweet and delicious. According to the last census, Vevčani is populated by 2,419 Macedonians, three Serbs, and one Aromanian.[24] Although it is located in a beautiful part of Macedonia, the people are the attraction.

The Vevčani are an interesting and independent people. In 1987, when the Yugoslavian government wanted to route the water from their springs into a pipe to provide water to the Ohrid and Struga metropolitan areas below, the townsfolk protested. One of their arguments was that the water was too good for the brutish palates of city folk who could not appreciate the finer things in life. This resulted in what became known as the "Vevčani Emergency" in which government soldiers were dispatched to the area. The tiny village, knowing they were soon to be overpowered, fought back in the only way they could against an overwhelming number of Yugoslavian troops. They sat all the village grandmothers on the dirt road to block the threatening bulldozers from coming into town. In the Balkans, nobody messes with grandmothers. The Beograd government backed down. This success spawned a strong sense of independence in the villagers.

Four years later, when Macedonia declared its independence from the former Yugoslavia—Vevčani decided to declare its independence *from Macedonia*. They formed the "Republic of Vevčani" and immediately issued their own passports and currency. The smallest bill had a picture of the mayor on it. The largest denomination had a nude woman sprawled in a Rubenesque pose. One of the main evening conversations in town was to speculate which local maiden posed for the thousand-dinar bill.

This time, when the new Macedonian government troops showed up to put down the rebellion, the Vevčani people said, you don't understand, this is just promotion for our annual carnival. The "standoff" made worldwide news. They gave tickets to all the soldiers and invited them to come back in January. These people know how to party; their annual carnival has been going on for 1,400 years.

24 The one Aromanian must get rather lonely. Aromanians are one of the last legacies of the Roman civilization.

We drove up the winding dirt road where the grandmothers had sat, crisscrossing the whitewater canal several times before reaching the little town square. As usual, I didn't have a plan except to obtain one of the passports and some Vevčani currency, as I wanted to be the only kid in homeroom with one of these for Show and Tell. We stopped in front of a small market and a large man with an even larger moustache came out carrying a bag of groceries.

"Dobar dan," I said.

He paused and scowled because I was speaking Serbian and not Macedonian.

"Engliski?" he asked.

"Ne. Americanski," I replied.

"Ah," he said smiling and nodding as if that explained everything.

"Srpski okay?" I asked.

"Srpski okay," he said putting down his groceries.

At this point, I realized I didn't know the Serbian word for "currency", "bill", or even "money." I raised my finger and said "Samo minutu" (just a minute) in order to return to the car and fetch my Serbian-English phrase book. I walked back across the street to the car and he followed carrying his groceries. The dictionary wasn't in the handy cubbyhole (where I normally kept it when touring), the glove box, or my camera case. This required opening the trunk, removing the luggage, and digging through the laundry in order to realize I didn't pack that dictionary for this trip. Why would you pack a Serbian-English dictionary when you are driving to Greece?

My new friend was leaning on the car. Evidently, he was a very patient man with nothing else to do except to help strangers. I shrugged my shoulders and said, "Žao me je." (I am sorry.) He shrugged his shoulders, but he raised his eyebrows in an offer of help. I shrugged again, shook his hand, and said goodbye. I was getting back in the car very discouraged when I remembered I did know the word for passport.

"Pasoš! Vevčani pasoš!" I yelled.

"Ah!" said moustache, smiling again. He took out his cell phone, phoned a friend, said "da" and hung up.

He then pointed up a small street and beat his chest twice then motioned to the right. He then beat his chest three more times and made the international gesture for moustache. I didn't get it the first time. I pointed, beat my chest three times and was about to continue when he grabbed my wrist.

"Ne," he said emphatically.

He then took my wrist and pointed my hand up the street, beat my chest with my hand twice, pointed to the right, and beat my chest three more times. And he wasn't particularly gentle.

"Razumjeti?" (Understand?), he asked, still gesticulating with *my* hand.

"Da . . . . da . . . . da," I said. I got it—up that street two buildings, turn right, and continue for three buildings, and then something about a moustache.

"Hvala!" I said, thanking him, retrieving my wrist, and patting him on both shoulders.

He beamed, bowed, grabbed his groceries, and sauntered down the hill.

I got back in the car. Beth Lynn had not been pleased with the needless excursion I had foisted upon today's trip.

She asked, "What was that all about? Do you know how to get back to the main road? Do you even know what time it is? Do you know how late we are? Do you even know where you are going?"

"As a matter of fact, I do know where I'm going. Give me your wrist and I'll show you."

I drove up the small road past a church and a civic building, turned into an alleyway and went past three small structures. There, in the middle of the alley was another large man with another large moustache. He motioned me to follow him. Blocking the alley by parking the car, I followed him into a quaint little hotel. In the middle of the foyer was a banquet set for a large and exquisite dinner. I really wished we could have stayed. He went behind the bar and pulled out a new Vevčani passport and some currency. He did not have any more bills with the maiden on them, so I had to settle for a smaller denomination with a water jug on it.

A few minutes later, when we left Macedonia, I gave the border guard my best smile and my new Vevčani passport. He gave me a look that made "deadpan" seem alive. It *had* to have been the first time a tourist had ever done that. However, I am a now a dual citizen of the United States *and* the Republic of Vevčani.

For ten euros you can be, too.

Prištinë, Kosovo

At the age of 77, Beth Lynn's parents finally decided to make their first trip to Europe. They flew to Rome where she was waiting for them in order to spend three days visiting the Vatican, skipping down the Spanish Steps, and throwing coins in the Trevi fountain. From there they flew on to Montenegro where we whisked them away to the Adriatic coast to show them a wet Budva, a damp Kotor, but a very sunny Dubrovnik.

On their last night, we were having dinner on Kotor Bay in an old mill that had been converted to a very romantic restaurant. We were loosening our belts when a friend from the embassy called and asked, "Since your parents can't get home, we wondered if all of you wanted to come for lunch tomorrow?"

I excused myself from the table so as not to unduly alarm anyone.

"What?!? They can't get home? Whaddya mean they can't get home?" I whispered.

"All the flights in Europe have been cancelled because of the ash from the volcano in Iceland," he explained.

Now we were faced with some major decisions to make beyond just that of dessert. We were now a few of the millions of people affected by the output from an Icelandic volcano no one outside of Reykjavik could pronounce.[25] (Although I was certain that had not kept many of the stranded travelers from coming up with their own names for it.)

We returned to the hotel and found the receptionist knee deep in rescheduling problems, but she did confirm the worst—nobody was going anywhere. The in-laws were supposed to fly from Podgorica back to Rome the next morning, have a one-day layover, and then head back to the States. I immediately tried to call the airlines that was supposed to take them to Rome. If you are a small, regional airline and you do not know what to do when such a meteorological crisis occurs, you can do what this small, regional airline did—just disconnect the phone and shut down your web site. That way you are not troubled by any annoying customer inquiries.

The hotel receptionist told us that Podgorica Airport was making the go or no-go decision for all flights the next morning at 9 a.m. The in-laws flight was at 10:30 a.m., and we were two hours away by car. We left early enough the next morning in order for them to try to make their scheduled departure. What we did not know was that on Sunday mornings, the highway department performed maintenance in the two and a half mile long Sozina tunnel. This caused a 60-minute delay while the large repair trucks stopped both lanes of traffic. Anxiety was now running high in the car.

Arriving at the airport, we found the flight had indeed been cancelled but was rescheduled for two days later. We were able to book her parents into one of the last hotel rooms in town. Arriving home, we turned on the BBC to watch the latest updates from the Volcanic Ash Advisory Center and catch the results of the KLM Airline test flight into the voggy atmosphere.[26] After many frantic

---

25 It is Eyjafjallajokull and it will be on the final exam.

26 KLM was so confident about the flight results that their CEO, Peter Hartman, went

trans-Atlantic phone calls, it was determined the soonest the in-laws could return to the U.S. was the following Sunday.

Our planning was further complicated by the fact I was to speak at the American University in Kosovo (AUK) in Prištinë in two days, and we had already purchased our tickets. It was obvious we could not leave the Parental Units alone in Montenegro by themselves for a week. So, what do you do when your in-laws are stranded in the Balkans? You take them to a war-torn United Nations-occupied country and show them a good time. With a bit of trepidation (but with them getting the benefit of bragging rights among their friends for the rest of the year), we booked them to fly with us.

I had originally wanted to drive there to see the Alp-like mountains on the border, but we were discouraged from doing so because of snow, road conditions, questioning U.N. KFOR (Kosovo Force) troops, and bandits. Everyone said there were bandits operating in the mountains, but they were always over the next ridge. When we spoke to people who had actually made the Kosovo trip recently, they asked, "Bandits? What bandits? There were bandits?" The most trouble they reported was great weather and being stopped by KFOR soldiers wanting to know why anyone would want to drive from Podgorica to Prištinë when any sane person would fly because it's only an hour and, "You don't have any American cigarettes on you, do you?"

•

The Kosovar capital is a town in progressive turmoil. Unfinished freeways have been erected above tiny, dusty streets filled with cabs, old Mercedes, and KFOR jeeps. Newly constructed high-rise buildings tower over war-torn ruins from a decade ago. Kosovars speak Albanian, are primarily Moslem, and the lilting calls to prayers can be heard throughout town. We stayed north of town near AUK in an area at the base of Germia National Park. We were told to stay on the park pathways, as there was still unexploded ordnance in the woods especially near the old Serbian army headquarters.

The President of AUK was kind enough to send a driver to pick us up at the airport. The driver played American music for us from station K-F-O-R "Cares for Kosovo" radio. As we passed through downtown, Beth Lynn asked if I noticed anything unusual about the people on the streets. She remarked how young they were as the average age of Kosovars was 28. I suppose that because I've spent life on a college campus, they just looked normal to me. Many of the

---

aboard the flight as an observer making him the first Dutch Ashtronaut.

older generation were killed in the war or died from the rigors of refugee life fleeing to Macedonia or Albania. After the war, almost a third of the adult male population left Kosovo to find employment.

Because of U.S. involvement in the NATO bombing of the Serb army that attacked Kosovo in 1999, Kosovars *love* Americans. We were driven up the main avenue in order to get to our hotel. We couldn't miss seeing the three story Bill Clinton poster hanging over the Bill Clinton statue that stands on Bil Klinton Boulevard. Every cabbie wants you, as an American, to see it. (Clinton is only slightly less revered than the other adopted daughter of the region—Mother Theresa.) We saw KFOR soldiers from Sweden, Denmark, Italy, Ireland, Turkey, France, and, of course, the U.S. The ones we saw were off duty, sipping cappuccinos on the main promenade; but they were fully armed. We saw the Kosovo Security compound and drove past the KFOR headquarters north of Prištinë. Troops and police were ever-present but not intrusive. They were not on every intersection as in Albania, but patrolled the streets in jeeps with mounted automatic weapons. The town was packed with European Union and United Nations officials from all over the world. We thought Kosovo could certainly boast more bodyguards *per capita* than any other country we had visited.

The architecture was a mix of cement, early—and late-Communist era construction and very few new buildings. The structure that gets the most attention from visitors is the National Library building. It is a multi-level structure with mushroom domes sprouting out of the various level roofs completely surrounded with, what looks like, oversized chicken wire. The story goes that when the official from Beograd came down to dedicate it, he told them to go ahead and take off the scaffolding and covers. There weren't any.

AUK has two modern buildings, and its faculty teaches all the classes in English. It is presided over by Chris Hall, an Oxford scholar and former politician from Maine. He is the consummate diplomat, and many people think he ought to be running the local government. He has proclaimed the school's motto as "Friends of Everyone, Allies of None." The AUK buildings happen to be on the site of the former Serbian Army torture center. After the war, the Kosovo government tried to sell the building, but no one local wanted to buy it. The Rochester Institute of Technology purchased it and thought it best to change the reputation of the place by making it a center for education. They acquired the site, rejuvenated the buildings with modern classrooms and offices, and began to welcome students.[27]

---

[27] When they prepared the back area for a basketball court, the school was told not to dig too deeply.

Wanting to try genuine Kosovar food, we took a suggestion and a cab down a dark street and an even darker alley to an unmarked restaurant named *Tiffany's.*[28] It was a traditional Albanian restaurant, but there was no menu. The waiter came over and looked at all of us thoughtfully for a moment without saying a word, raised his finger in the air, and disappeared. It was the first restaurant where they serve you *what they think you should have.* The waiter returned with bread and an herb pâté of carrot, dill, and hot peppers. This was followed by a stream of small individual ceramic pots containing börek (baked pastry) filled with sour cream, pork with yogurt, beef with local vegetables, and cabbage leaves stuffed with saffron rice and lamb. We noticed every table was served something different.

On the afternoon of our second day in Kosovo, the university thoughtfully provided an armed security guard and driver in order to tour some of the sights just out from town. We toured the Gadime caverns that were discovered in 1969 by a man trying to expand his house that was built up against a hill. He broke through the cave wall and then tried to claim the entire cave as part of his homestead domicile. The cave contains examples of strange aragonite speleothems,[29] stalactites that grow down in various directions, but not *straight* down. It is as though the cave is spinning and gravity does not exist in it at all.

From there we visited the Gračanica Monastery located in the village of the same name, a small Serbian suburb of Prištinë. (The neighborhood businesses take euros or Serbian dinar.) Built in 1321, this structure is the definitive example of Byzantine brick architecture. As this is a Serbian Orthodox church completely surrounded by Kosovar Moslems, the compound is guarded by the Swedish troops (as the locals consider the Swedish neutral) and ringed in barbed wire. I asked the guard there how tough the duty was, and he said he did not think the place really needed a guard; but a man with a lot of stars on his uniform came by and told him to do it. Serbian King Milutin built the church with a promise he would construct a new church during every year of his reign (which he did, all 42 of them). Not oblivious to the power of history on his people, he had his entire family genealogy painted in the monastery frescoes next to saints and the Madonna.[30]

The historical highlight of the trip was our visit to Gazimestan, the site of the Battle of Kosovo Polje. Armed Serbian police guard the Gazimestan

---

28 And, yes, they do serve breakfast.

29 This will definitely be on the final exam.

30 Which should thoroughly confuse any newly minted hagiographologist (one who studies saints.)

monument, and we were required to show our passports as though we were entering Serbian territory.[31]

This was the site of the deciding victory of the Turks over the Serbs in 1389. It was the beginning of the Ottoman domination of the Balkans as well as the beginning of the end for the Serbian empire. Most of the conflict in Yugoslavia goes back to this single battle. Serbian Prince Lazar had 20,000 troops and Ottoman Sultan Murad I commanded 30,000. The Ottomans were victorious although both the Prince and the Sultan were killed in the battle. On the towering monument are the words Lazar proclaimed in an effort to rally all Serbs to stand against the Turks.

"Whoever is a Serb and of Serb birth,
And of Serb blood and heritage,
And comes not to the Battle of Kosovo,
May he never have the progeny his heart desires,
Neither son nor daughter!
May nothing grow that his hand sows,
Neither dark wine nor white wheat!
And let him be cursed from all ages to all ages!"

It was at this location on the 600th anniversary of the Serb defeat where an ambitious Yugoslavian politician named Slobodan Milošević said Kosovo was for the Serbs, not the Albanians. It was the rallying cry for the growing Serbian nationalistic fervor that caused the break-up of the Yugoslavian republics and the beginning of the tragic war. Kosovo is the emotional heart of Serbia as it was the ancient capital of their Balkan Empire, and where the Serbian Orthodox Church was founded. It is very difficult for Serbians to see Kosovo as anything but their ancestral home and their rightful territorial claim. Slobodan Milošević[32] was a low-level Communist Party bureaucrat until he riled up the Serbian Yugoslav majority in Kosovo. This propelled him from the President of Serbia to the President of the entire Yugoslav Federation.

Milošević sent 40,000 Yugoslavian troops into Kosovo to replace the existing police force. Serbs were dispatched to take over administration of the Kosovo Republic. Albanian (Muslim) newspapers, television, and radio were

---

31 Coincidentally, if you land by air in Prištinë and then try to cross the northern Kosovo border, the Serbians won't let you because you have entered Serbian territory *illegally*.

32 In an irony of ironies, *Slobodan* means freedom.

banned. The University of Prištinë was virtually shut down with all of the non-Serbian faculty fired and 97 percent of the students expelled.[33] At the time, Kosovar unemployment ran as high as 80 percent. Kosovars formed insurgent groups to attack army strongholds and Serbian neighborhoods. As with all of the fighting in the recent wars, neither side was blameless in perpetuating the prevailing prejudice or the ruthless slaughter of innocent individuals. (Watching this drama unfold, Montenegro's government under Milo Đukonović distanced itself from Milošević's policies. Montenegro felt enormous economic pressure as the cost of the war and the embargo took its toll. Hyperinflation was rampant, and the suffering of the people was apparent to the entire world.)

After sending troops into Kosovo, Milošević then dispatched his army into Bosnia-Herzegovina, which began the Yugoslavian Wars of 1992-1999. Almost a million Albanian Kosovars were displaced into neighboring countries including Montenegro. Still, during this tragic time the Montenegrin sense of humor persevered. The Montenegrin joke goes that Milošević dies, and he arrives at the gates of Heaven.

St. Peter stops him and says, "I can't let you in. You are a big sinner. You have to go to Hell."

Milosevic turns around and heads down to Hell. A moment later, a row of sinners led by Lucifer himself comes up to the gates of Heaven.

St. Peter is astonished and asks, "What do you want?"

Lucifer replies, "We're refugees."

Milosevic was deposed in 2000. He was subsequently arrested for crimes against humanity but died in his cell awaiting trial in The Hague.

•

Across the highway from the Gazimestan monument, the conquering Moslems created a tomb (türbe) to the fallen Sultan Murad I, honored for defeating the Serbs and expanding the Ottoman Empire northward. Whereas the Serbian monument was protected by six armed Serbian troops, the türbe was simply looked after by *Mrs.* Sanija Türbedari (whose last name means "caretaker of the shrine"). The care for the shrine had passed down from father to son and,

---

33 In order to allow their students to complete their degrees, Albanian faculty members took the university underground. They held classes in homes, warehouses, and abandoned buildings. They hid the entire university from the new authorities for over two years and were never paid.

currently, it was her husband's responsibility. Times being tough, he had another job, and she had to do it.

The tomb contained only the Sultan's internal organs (his body having been shipped back to Bursa, Turkey to be buried among the other royal türbi). When we arrived, it was being visited by a Turkish NATO public relations regiment who were passing out gimmie caps with the Turkish flag to the neighborhood children.

Legend has it after the fighting was over and thc battlefield was strewn with the tens of thousands of bodies of the fallen warriors, large flocks of ravens came to pick at the bones of the dead soldiers.

Kosovo means, "Black bird."

Croatia

Croatia is a beautiful boomerang-shaped country that wraps itself around Bosnia-Herzegovina (abbreviated locally as BiH) to the north and seals it off from the sea. This is due to the history of the sea-faring Venetians who conquered Croatia versus the Ottomans and their land-based armies who invaded BiH. When the Slavs arrived in the 6th century A.D. they split up with some going south to the mountains and the Montenegrin Littoral (Serbs) and some going north to the sea (Croats). (The Croats will tell you it was the smart ones that went north.) Both groups plundered and razed most of the previous Roman settlements, basically starting a civilization from scratch. The refugees from the Dalmatian coast in Croatia who fled the Slavs escaped southward and were the founders of the town of Dubrovnik.[34]

Dubrovnik

Dubrovnik is a yellow walled-town with orange tiled roofs that instills a deep sense of history (some of it recent). It provides entertaining eye candy and lofts a leisurely spirit that puts the vacant into vacation. The town (and previous city-state) owes its entire existence to wheat. The town was the main granary for most of the eastern Mediterranean. It was such a significant port of call that warring nations would declare the Republic of Ragusa, as it was then known, off-limits to fighting. It was also known as a fair trading harbor. Above the

---

34 Allegedly, it was on the border of Dalmatia and Sardinia that the first municipal firehouse was built. That is why a Dalmatian dog is the *de facto* mascot of every firehouse. As they say in the movie, *State and Main*, "Just a few more miles and the mascot would have been a sardine."

customs house is the ancient inscription, "We are forbidden to cheat and use false measures, and when I weigh goods, God weighs me."

The *Placa* is the main street that goes from the large Pile Gate south to the clock tower near the docks. It is crowded with strolling people; and loud with chatter from outdoor cafes. Dubrovnik, like the rest of Croatia, is Catholic—vested in its Venetian heritage on the edge of the Orthodox frontier. Near the Pile gate is the Franciscan Monastery. In its cloisters is a pharmacy that has been in continuous operation since 1391.[35]

Under the clock tower sits the St. Blaise Church built in 1715 to replace the one that was destroyed in 1667 when an earthquake leveled the town but not the city walls. St. Blaise is the patron saint of Dubrovnik and adorns the city flag. Above every gate and building was a sculpture of him cradling the city in his arms. The city's 75 foot tall walls were built between the 13th and 16th century and encircle the city. They are about a mile and a quarter long not including the constant stairs that take you from level to level. They provide both a view of the Adriatic and the town inside. Stopping for numerous, spectacular photo-ops of both sea and scenery (and a refreshing glass of fresh-squeezed orange juice at the halfway point) we walked the walls in just under two hours. Behind St. Blaise Church, a morning market filled our senses with splashes of color from bouquets of spring flowers, dried figs and fruit, and the fragrance of locally grown lavender.

In 1991, Dubrovnik was the target of Serb (and Montenegrin) artillery shelling because Croatia was now a breakaway republic of Yugoslavia. Maps at Dubrovnik's gates show you exactly where the damage occurred and what buildings were destroyed. (This same map was in every classroom at the university where I spoke. Croatia does not want their citizens to forget anytime soon.)[36]

The Rector's Palace in town served as jail, court, assembly house, and home for the most powerful man in Ragusa. City fathers had an interesting approach to prevent anyone from getting too power-hungry. The Rector and the Captain of the Guards were elected from the nobility to serve *for only one month at a time.* This Rector was constantly reminded about his civic duty as, emblazoned over his office, was the motto *Obilti Privatorum, Publica Curate* ("forget private matters, look after public ones.") In Dubrovnik, there is a ghetto just like the

---

35 He just would *not* retire.

36 We were told not to drive a car with Podgorica license plates into Dubrovnik because it would get keyed. It was suggested to rent one in Herceg Novi, the Montenegrin town closest to the Croatian border, as those citizens refused to join the attack on Dubrovnik.

original one in Venice where its Jewish merchants and moneylenders were allowed to live but not leave.

While we were there, the city was hosting the European Extreme Fighting Championships. Staying at our hotel, in several rooms across the hall, were the eight members of the Russian Extreme Fighting (and, it turned out, Inebriation) Team. After losing the former and trying desperately to win the latter, they would return to the hotel sometime after 4 a.m. In their slightly impaired condition, they were still cognitive enough to know which floor they were staying on, but not which rooms were theirs. They tried their keys in all 24 doors on the floor, arguing and cursing until finally achieving success.

One of the academic colleagues we met while in Dubrovnik told us about serving on the Croatian privatization council. He was in charge of selling former Communist government businesses and assets to foreign investors. He was in the middle of such a deal in Dubrovnik when the Yugoslavian government declared war and the artillery shelling began to rain down. He immediately called his supervisor and told him he was heading to his home in Pula to be with his family. He was told in no uncertain terms to stay put and consummate the transaction as his country desperately needed foreign currency in order to buy arms to defend itself.

"Do you know how hard it is to sell a hotel to a bunch of Germans when you have to yell over the bombing noise outside?" he asked us rhetorically.

Split Decision

Up the coast from Dubrovnik sits Split, the ancient Roman resort. Unbeknown to us, the high season had just started, and nary a room was to be had at any of the major hotels. However, a helpful receptionist located a "cousin" who could rent us a room; and, presently, Mrs. Rosas appeared in her car and escorted us to her apartments. Just so we would not get lost, she then drove us to dinner at a cozy little restaurant. The restaurant owner then drove us back to the apartment. You just don't get that kind of service at the local Holiday Inn and Denny's.

Split was the summer home of the Roman Emperor Diocletian, who, when he wasn't slaughtering Christians, worked on planning his retirement on the Croatian coast. The palace he built was a massive structure along the lines of a Roman fortress covering ten acres and was home to 10,000 people. He retired in 305 A.D. (the only Roman Emperor ever to do so) after ruling Rome for 21 years. When the Tetrarchic government he established imploded a few years later, a delegation was sent to encourage him to return as Emperor. He was reputed to have asked them, "[you] wouldn't dare suggest I replace the peace and happiness of this place with the storms of a never-satisfied greed?" He died a few years later but was vilified in Serbian Orthodox mythology as the evil *Dukljanin*, an adversary of God. He was so named because it was thought he built the town of Duklja, near Podgorica.[37]

One of the heroes of Split was the Bishop of Nin, a Croatian who disagreed with Rome on many issues. He is one of the first dissenters to hold religious services in a local language (as early as 926) instead of the required Latin—which no one could understand. It is because of this that the Catholic religion has been such a long and strong influence in Croatian culture. The Bishop's statue stands 22 feet high, and he is depicted with his finger in the air, holding a Bible, preaching fire and brimstone. The statue was originally in Diocletian's Palace; but the Italians, during their occupation at the beginning of World War II, moved the huge statue outside the wall because of the Bishop's ancient argument with Rome.

Hvar

There are over 700 islands on the Dalmatian coast, but only about 50 are inhabited.[38] The islands hug the coast and range from Krk, the largest and most northern (which sits on the 45 parallel, exactly halfway between the equator and the North Pole) down to Mrkan[39] across from Cavtat near the Dubrovnik airport. The islands rise out of the Adriatic and span the horizon, capping the blue sea with bands of ecru shorelines below a green ridge-crests of trees. The average temperature on these wooded rocks range from the 80s in the summer to 50s in the winter.

A lazy ferry sailing through red water from the setting sun took us south from Split to the island of Hvar. The island claims to have 2,800 sunny hours a year meaning you can catch rays 62 percent of the time.[40] Between the town of Stari Grad where the ferry docks and Hvar City on the south side, the island rises up to the Stari Grad Plain. The Plain has two features that are astonishing. The first is an agricultural patchwork of stone walls (*chora*) and shelters that are adjacent to ingeniously designed rainwater recovery systems. Greek colonists first built these features sometime about 350 B.C. They have been in constant use

---

37 The legend states he stole the Sun from the sky and Saint John the Baptist fooled him into putting it back. *Dukljanin* then chased John and tore a piece of flesh from his foot. This is why humans have arches.

38 The children's story was originally entitled "One Hundred and One Dalmatian *Islands.*"

39 Pronounced like Texans do when stating their patriotism, "Hi, I'mma Mrkan."

40 That makes it sunnier than Nice, France. So Hvar is especially Nice.

for the last 2,400 years. Each succeeding farmer since ancient times has utilized this walled system to enhance crop production. Modern plowing methods have not improved on its efficiency. Within the cadastral walls are an occasional shelter hut called a trim ("treem") that is made entirely of flat corbelled, stacked stones held in place without any mortar or support beams. The trims would be for sheltering humans, and, later, livestock. These buildings might be from the Bronze Age but are certainly from the early Greek period.

Local farmers still grow the same crops as in ancient times—grapes, olives, with cultivated and wild lavender. The Stari Grad Plain is *covered* in lavender and hills of purple waves blow in the mistral winds. The entire island carries this sensuous fragrance. (Even the men smell that way.)

We decided Hvar City was the most romantic place we had ever found. A tourist town of 4,000 souls, the tiered, red-tiled buildings surround a bay of boats that bob lazily in the water. All are watched over by the *Tvrđava Španjola* (Spanish Fort) on a cliff above the town. Especially enchanting in the evening are the fort's brightly lit stonewalls which makes the fort appear to float in the darkness above the city. The town faces out to the Adriatic and the small chain of (almost connecting) *Pakleni Otoci* islands serve as rocky respites for those who want to do absolutely nothing. A promenade hugs the harbor and ends at a church square full of artists, restaurants, and, sometimes, film crews, as it is so picturesque. The square is a serene site to sit and slowly sip (or shop).

The emphasis on tourism as an economic engine began here in 1880. The locals decided to diversify their income base so they developed a marketing entity to bring cash customers to the island city from various populated parts of the Austro-Hungarian Empire. To promote the health giving properties of sun and sea, the locals named their town, *Higijeničko društvo u Hvaru* or the "Hygienic Society of Hvar."

Full Disclothesure

It is no news that Europeans are much more casual about their bodies and nudity than are Americans. Even I knew that. Where the surprise comes is the first time you actually see hundreds of vacationing bodies on the beach *au natural* especially when you are not expecting to come across said not-so-huddled masses as you cross over the dunes from the parking lot. There is actually very little nudism in Montenegro. However, Croatia, their neighbor to the northwest, *owns* nudity.

The story goes that King Edward VIII (during that brief year of 1936 when he actually was the King of England) cruised the Adriatic on the steam yacht,

Nahlin, with his then-married lover, Mrs. Wallis Simpson (for whom he would abdicate the throne later in the year). They liked to go skinny-dipping and asked the captain to lay anchor off the Croatian island of Rab. Due to his royal prerogative and influence, the local functionaries immediately declared the beach "clothes optional." The area was already appropriately named *Rajska Plaža* or Paradise Beach. Because of the cavorting king, it became known as "English Beach."

In an effort to attract foreign currency during the 1950s, Tito encouraged his regional bureaucrats to designate more beaches as nudist resorts in order to entice continental tourists to the area. At last count, Croatia had at least 30 nude beaches or facilities on its coast. That is one almost every ten miles of its shoreline. Europe's first full-service nude resort was opened in the Istria region near the town of Vrsar in 1961. It is still thriving and can accommodate 18,000 guests in its facilities and on its three miles of beach. Interestingly enough, the nude bodies at these places are not Croatian. They are probably German, Austrians, Italians, or Spanish. It is estimated that 15 percent of tourists that come to Croatia, come to get naked.

Nudists are not nudists anymore. They are *naturists*. Or, in the German, *Freikörperkultur*, which means "Free Body Culture" or FKK for short. This is something one needs to know when touring Europe as a sign with FKK is the standard designation (no matter what the local language is) for "Naturist *Autokamp* Ahead—2 km." or "Slow—Nudist Crossing."[41] Pure naturists derogatorily refer to those people who keep their clothes on as "textiles."

Some beaches are set aside as purely "naturist," meaning no clothes allowed. Others are "clothes optional" which means you can choose the extent of your tan. However, you may need to ask the locals how a certain beach is designated on any given day as they may alternate between naturist and textile. Due to not understanding the local schedule, you may get a shock, delightful or not, depending on your point of view.

There are no cameras allowed on naturist beaches. Window-shopping or acting as if you are just admiring the landscape does not go over very well either. On every beach there is at least one self-designated "textile police" who, if you don't drop trou quickly enough, will approach and lecture you (in whatever their native language is) on the local dress standards with much gesticulating and shouting. This individual will usually be a man in his sixties wearing a white beard and ponytail, shell beads, flip-flops, and the brownest, most leathery skin

41 Which is probably unnecessary; as you would think people would slow down anyway.

you have ever seen. It will pass through your mind he was born on this beach, has never left, and he would be a lot better looking wearing a codpiece.

•

With a touch of the "When in Rome" attitude, we had decided to give overall tanning a try. Neither one of us could actually bring ourselves to completely birthday suit it in front of strangers[42], but the idea of an Eden-like frolic did have its appeal. We rented a small boat and motored out past the island of Jerolim with its large nude beach (which consisted of large boulders and rocky beaches) and headed out to the island chain in front of Hvar to find our own private piece of this paradise.

As it was the beginning of the summer season in early June, the islands were mostly empty with few boats in the coves and fewer people on the shore. However, the islands were solid rock and the trick was landing ashore on one of the islands without putting a hole in the hull. Presently we found a small break in the boulders just large enough for us to land. It was on the north side of Veli Vodnjak, the last island in the chain, whose sole occupant was a distant lighthouse. We pulled up very carefully and tied off.

There was not a soul in sight. The nearest island was a mile away. We had the entire world to ourselves. We took off our clothes and stood there *sans vêtements* feeling quite free. One of Beth Lynn's accomplishments is that she holds a brown belt in tanning. She loves to swelter under a searing sun but is very safe about it. She has her formulated sunscreen and applies it liberally. She also has her specific music playlist, which, evidently, helps even out the bronzing.

It was a perfect place on a perfect day—or what the Italians call, *piccolo paradiso*. We lay down under the sun on the warm rocks and felt the slight breeze caress our skin. Beth Lynn put in her ear buds, and I drifted off into that nap nether land where I was not quite asleep but drifting peacefully at the edge of unconsciousness, lost in my thoughts but sensuously feeling the elements. I do not know how long I was in that serene stupor but was eventually disturbed by a loud splash in the water. I looked up to notice a very large catamaran now sitting about 15 yards away. The crewmember who had just thrown the anchor in the water casually waved at me. I casually waved back. He turned his back on us and began to help the other 20 or so people on the boat who had come to scuba dive. I looked over at Beth Lynn, who still had her eyes closed. The divers on the boat

[42] Or friends, for that matter.

paid absolutely no attention to the nude couple on shore. They were preparing their gear, checking their tanks, and rolling off the back end of the boat into the water.

When there was nobody visible onboard the catamaran, I nudged Beth Lynn and pointed.

She grabbing her towel and gasped "Where did that boat come from?!?"

"From the flag, I'd say Slovenia."

She glared at me and hissed, "That's not what I meant. How long has it been there?"

"Long enough," I replied.

We reluctantly put our bathing suits back on and lay back down. Paradise is a very short-lived phenomenon.

Bosnia i Herzegovina

From a map, it appears Bosnia and Herzegovina (BiH) is a land-locked country, cut off from the Adriatic by a gerrymandering Croatia. However, on closer inspection you find the town of Neum, whose coast is surrounded on the north and south by the same, but non-contiguous, country—Croatia. The reason for this bit of creative cartography stems from 1699 when the Ottomans suffered their first major military setback in the area, and the Austrian Empire rose to power. The short, three-mile access to the sea at Neum was granted to the Ottomans in the Treaty of Karlowitz merely as a deterrent to the aggressive Venetians who had designs of the remainder of the eastern side of the Adriatic.

Theoretically, this little toehold could give BiH its own port to the sea; but the coast is made of formidable rock and a deep-port access is economically out of the question. Even today, this tiny bit of territory provides a bit of trouble. BiH and Croatia both staff two crossing checkpoints, one at Klek and the other at Zalton Doli. On many current maps the Adriatic Highway (E65) wanders down the Croatian coast from near Ploče, but disappears when it hits the BiH border, and magically reappears in Croatia as it approaches Dubrovnik. During the high tourist season, these crossings can create miles-long traffic jams with people traveling to and from Dubrovnik. This is such a problem the Croatia government is contemplating building the Pelješac Bridge over to a peninsula it owns to circumvent this issue and completely cutting off Neum from the main stream of traffic.

Post-war BiH government is a strange political patchwork only a negotiation committee could love. It is a country of three political entities (territories): The Federation of Bosnia-Herzegovina, Republika Srpska, and Brčko.

Bosnia-Herzegovina is the interior of the country including the capital of Sarajevo. It covers 51 percent of the total landmass of the country. It is mostly Muslim but contains territories that are also majority Croat (and, therefore, Catholic). Republika Srpska contains the 49 percent of the land, that part which is dominated by Serbs (Orthodox) and occupied by them after the close of the 1992-95 Bosnian war. This is made up of territories on the north, east, and south parts of the country. Its capital is Banja Luka to the north. The overlapping of these two entities occurs in the Brčko District in the northeast part of the country bordering Serbia. It is about half Bosniak and half Serbian, and is currently occupied by a United Nations peacekeeping force. As we drove through BiH, we saw villages with homes flying the flag of the Serbian Orthodox Church. The next little town, just eight miles down the road, houses were hoisting the Turkish flag, denoting their Ottoman heritage and Muslim allegiance.

The new BiH government has a Parliamentary Assembly that is bi-cameral. Its House of Peoples consists of an equal measure of five Bosniaks, five Croats, and five Serbs. The House of Representatives is two-thirds Bosniak and Croat and one-third Serb. The country is presided over by the Chair of the Presidency of Bosnia-Herzegovina. The Presidency consists of one elected Bosniak, Croat, and Serb. They each hold the Chair's position for eight months at a time during their four-year term of office.

Leaving Hvar City, we drove the length of the lavender island east to Sućuraj to catch another ferry that landed at the mainland at Drvenik. From there we entered BiH again. This time, instead of a newly constructed border guard and customs office with a wide strip of no-man's land between two countries, the guard station was a detached garage. I had to go into the hut to get the passports stamped because the game was on and the immigration agents were too engrossed to bother coming out. Entering the country, we passed armored cars marked with the Canadian flag carrying mine-sniffing dogs. This was 15 years after the war was over, and the work was still not completed.

Mostar

The city of Mostar is divided by the Neretva River, which flows north to south through the town. Looking north at the famous reconstructed *Stari Most* (Old Bridge), you see the minarets poking up over the buildings on the east bank and white crosses adorning the green hills to the west. The Bosniak Muslims live on the east side, and the Croat Catholics live on the west. Mostar is a perfect example of complex post-war BiH.

For the most part, the residents of Mostar historically got along. When BiH declared its independence from Yugoslavia in 1992, the Yugoslavian People's Army (JNA) began an 18 month long artillery siege of Mostar. They had canon batteries located on the hills above the city. The city was united in an effort to push back the JNA, and they were successful with the Bosniaks Muslim BiH army on the front and the Croat army on the rear flank. As soon as it was apparent the JNA was routed, the Croat army began firing on their allies, the Bosniaks.

The Ottoman ruler, Suleiman the Magnificent, originally constructed the old bridge in 1558. It was the symbol of the city and the two cultures that lived side by side. The bridge has stood through countless battles from Ottoman times through the Austrian takeover and two World Wars until 1993 when it was destroyed by the inter-fighting after the JNA was repelled from Mostar. The Croats destroyed the bridge, but it was the first thing to be rebuilt after the Dayton peace accords were signed. It was reopened in 2004 in hopes it would serve as a future physical and figurative connection between two different peoples warily sharing the same city.

One of the few historical buildings that was not destroyed in the recent conflict was the Muslibegovic House, a National Monument owned by Taj ("no Mahal") Muslibegovic. It is an original Ottoman house consisting of a large home, an out building, and two Turkish courtyards. It serves as an example of Ottoman residential architecture, a National Museum, as well as his family's home. The structure is made of white plastered stone with dark brown, hand-carved wooden windows and doors from the 18th century. There are also a few rooms open to the public as a hotel. Taj is the ninth generation of his family to live in this historic home.

Walking through Mostar, we could still see bullet holes in the walls, the burned out shells of buildings, and the artwork made of war materiel. On the Muslim side, there was a large statue of a proud woman. She is entitled the "Maid of Mostar." The sculpture was molded out of the brass artillery shell-casings that were collected after the war. Someone takes time to polish her every day.

Speaking engagements in other countries had taken us to exotic and delightful places. Now, we were going to have to wait for semester classes to end until we would have time to begin discovering Montenegro.

Magnificence in Miniature

Lord Byron wrote:
"At the moment of the creation of our planet, the most beautiful merging of land and sea occurred at the Montenegrin seaside . . . When pearls of nature were sworn, an abundance of them were strewn all over this area . . ."

The small, but stunning, country of Montenegro sits on the east side of the Adriatic Sea. Its brief coastline has 117 separate beautiful beaches[1] that rise straight up to a coastal mountain plateau that gives way to the Zeta plains from which you can detect a hint of the spectacular, Alps-like Durmitor mountain range to the east. The landscape rises from sea level to 8,300 feet in less than 40 miles. Sixty percent of the country is made up of mountains that are 10,000 feet or higher. Montenegrins like to boast that if you ironed the country flat, it would be as big as all of Russia.[2]

Because of its superlative beauty, Beth Lynn and I wanted to start by driving the scenic coast of Montenegro—all 87 squiggly miles of it. It was to be a week of old, broken down, citified, middle-aged travelers traveling to see old broken down cities from the Middle Ages as every coastal town has a *stari grad* (old town).[3]

We started by driving along the northern shore of Lake Skadar which took us past the twin peaks (the locals refer to them as Sophia Loren) above Vranjina, into the sleepy fishing village of Virpazar and on into Skadar National Park. Skadar is a large, fresh-water lake situated just over the mountain ridge from the coast. It

1 Twenty-five percent of its coastline is beach.
2 That is, of course a great exaggeration—India perhaps, but not Russia.
3 It was a feudal effort.

is 27 miles long, 9 miles wide, and is split by the Montenegrin-Albanian border. For centuries, it served as a smuggling route but now is popular with birders as it is home for one of the last species of pelicans in Europe. Along with the inflow of the Morača River, 50 active springs including the largest, Raduš, keep it filled, and, sometimes overflowing. Near Vranjina, there was a monastery that King Nikola built for his daughter, Jelena, where she could live out her life as a nun. The King knowing that besides being very tall, Jelena was not the prettiest of maidens. In a tale worthy of fairies, she did marry and became the Queen of Italy.

The first time we visited Lake Skadar was on a spring Sunday when the day actually lived up to its name. Friends who had a Volkswagen van invited us to ride with them across the top of Lake Skadar to the fishing village of Virpazar. There we met the owner of the Pelikan Inn who showed us his drying fish and herbs. Every time we would visit his inn, he would give us a plant (mint, lavender, or basil) as a gift. His business was down but only because the lake was up. Much of the town was under water due to all the rain previously mentioned.

We then proceeded up and over the hills to the backwaters of the lake in search of an old bridge that was located in a quiet and relaxing spot called Rijeka Crnojevića. We traveled on a narrow, one-lane road that hugged the side of the mountain. Ruins of stone houses dotted the landscape, and there was a church on every ridge. It was said one of the rulers of Montenegro wanted their people to see an Orthodox church wherever they looked, so he instructed them to be built just this way. There were flocks of sheep feeding below isolated terracotta-tiled stone houses. We spotted one village that sat on the edge of the lake whose only access to civilization was a donkey trail down from the road.

Arriving at Rijeka Crnojevića, we realized that the flooding situation at Virpazar was merely a foreshadowing. This town, too, was under water. The hotel was serving lunch on the upper floor since the restaurant on the ground was completed flooded, To provide patrons access to the hotel, the proprietor had thoughtfully placed empty, plastic milk jug containers upside-down in the water, so you could step from the dry parking lot to the hotel's front door. We enjoyed grilled trout while we sat in front of a fireplace looking over the river channel that was now a large lake. Afterwards, we walked along the sea wall and argued with geese that thought they had the right of way. One house that now stuck out over the high water was in the midst of spring-cleaning. The resident would stick a mop out the window, dip it in the lake, and swab his floor with it.

•

Our next stop on the trip was Godinje, a tiny, almost abandoned, hamlet resting on a hill above Lake Skadar. It was built by the Montenegrins but improved upon by the Venetians. This was very apparent by the Crmnica architecture in which the houses were built with adjoining walls and connecting tunnels so residents could escape during periodic Ottoman raids. Some of these medieval houses had porches built to enjoy the view of the lake—about a century before it became commonplace in European house designs. Out some 500 yards into the lake sat *Grmožur*, a fortress-island built in 1834 that was the Alcatraz of Montenegro. The motivation for the jailers to be vigilant was simple; if any prisoner escaped, the guard had to finish out the prisoner's sentence.

In 1907, a European beauty contest was held in London, and every country was invited to send a representative. King Nikola I, eager to show off Montenegro loveliness to the rest of the world, sent messengers to all the towns searching for the perfect Montenegrin female specimen. She was found in Godinje. The King ordered her to go and represent their small country on the world stage. She won. Because of the exposure, she was paraded around Europe and had several proposals of marriage from millionaires and near royalty. However, she returned home and wed a local boy. When asked by the King why she did not accept the proposals, she is said to have told him, "You sent me to show the beauty of Montenegro, not to get married." In a small house in Godinje, there was a room with a shrine to this woman. It was covered in newspaper and magazine clippings from 1907 and 1958 when she turned 70. Her name was Milena Delibasić, and she was quite a looker.

The tiny road above the lake took us through fishing villages, herds of sheep, dark enchanted forests of chestnut groves, and high above isolated island monasteries including Ostros. This is home to the monastery *Precista Krajinska* ("Pure Land") erected by Vladimir, prince of Duklja—perhaps the first monastery to be built in Montenegro. After Vladimir was killed, his beloved Kosara, a daughter of the Macedonian King Samuil, brought his remains to the monastery where she lived as a nun until her death. The devoted couple is buried there together.

At the south end of the large lake, we began to parallel the Ada Bojana River that serves as the border with Albania. The river's delta forms an expanse of black sandy beach created by the mysterious 1858 shipwreck of the schooner *Merito*. Halfway between Lake Skadar and Ada Bojana are the ruins of the Bishops' town of Svač that was laid waste by the Mongols when they could not capture the city of Ulcinj, a few kilometers to the north. Svač was so pious a town that it had a church for every day of the year. The foundations of eight of them can still be discerned.

We spent our first night on the road in Ulcinj—the pirates' lair. The population was over 80 percent Albanian Muslim, minarets could be seen atop the cityscape, and calls to prayers were heard. Every town in Montenegro has a central fountain. This one had a Turkish crescent moon over it denoting its Ottoman heritage. Ulcinj sat at the base of a long draw that ended at a naturally protected curved harbor and beach. The town was probably also an Illyrian city that was taken over by the Greeks in the 5th century B.C. and then by the Romans in the 2nd century B.C. It was part of the Byzantine Empire until the Venetians conquered it in 1405. They named it *Dulcigno* (Ulcinj being the Albania translation of Dulcigno). The Venetians then lost it to the Turks in 1571 in a crap game. The Ottomans were able to retain control over the city for 300 years. Control might not be completely true as this was the pirates' homeport for the eastern Mediterranean because the town is located on the Strait of Otranto—the gateway from the Adriatic to the Ionian Sea. At one time, there were over 400 ships harbored at Ulcinj, and plundering was its main industry. As such, it also had a slave market and almost a hundred slave houses. The Slave Square (*Trg Robova*) still stands as a silent monument to this period. Because of this aspect of its history, when many North African slaves were freed, they took Albanian names and stayed. Ulcinj is the only town in the Balkans to have a significant African-heritage population.

After being captured by the pirates in 1575, a young Spanish soldier named Miguel Cervantes was thrown into prison in Dulcigno, as the town was then called, until he was shipped off to Algiers to be ransomed several years later. It might just be coincidence that he gave his most famous fictitious female in the novel *Don Quixote* the name, "Dulcinea."

Just south of Ulcinj was the Milena canal where fishermen used large nets which they merely dipped in the water to take fish "in passing" (*kalamera).* To the south is the longest sand beach in Montenegro, *Velika Plaža*, (Big Beach) at over seven and half miles long. During the months of July and August, there may be as many as 150,000 bathers lounging about. There is also Ladies Beach (*Zenska Plaza* in Montenegrin, known locally in Albanian as *Zonja Plazhi*), which is only for the fairer sex. Because of the sulfur arising from a spring and the radium in its sand, the beach is said to increase fertility. For some reason, Beth Lynn said she did not need to stop.

In Ulcinj, the old, walled city rises out of a natural rock jetty and overlooks the beach; and the new town overlooks the old town. For us, it was the first of many *starim gradovima* (old towns) that lined the coast of Montenegro as well as the entire Adriatic. Some were still thriving communities, and others were historical ruins decimated by invading hordes or brought down to earth by seismic seizures.

In 1979, Montenegro experienced a devastating earthquake that measured 7.2 with its epicenter located on its coast. All its seaside towns from the Croatian border south to Ulcinj were heavily damaged. Over 400 villages were completely razed. One hundred and twenty-one people were killed and about 1,000 injured. One hundred thousand people were left homeless, about one-fifth of the entire Montenegrin population. The impact of that quake can still be seen in buildings all along the coast. To pay for the reconstruction, every employee in Yugoslavia was required to donate one percent of his or her wages to the relief effort for the next ten years.

Dining that first evening in Ulcinj, we met Ishmet, the hotel manager, who felt obligated to supervise his one waiter and his only two dining guests. During dessert, he joined us at our table for conversation. He lamented about the years of Communist rule.

"Here everything was okay, but in Albania it was so sad. So many people wanted to join their families here where it was good. But, even the birds could not fly from Albania to here."

He bragged about the local landscape.

"Ada Bojana River iz strong like Muslim man."

But, times were tough and there were too few guests for the hotel.

"There is no money in Ulcinj. Not like Podgorica with the mafia and all those rich people. Why don't they come down here? The water is good and it is much cheaper."

Then he sighed and said, "I'm in debt like Greece."

Passing the Bar

Up the coast from Ulcinj was the town of Bar. After the fall of Yugoslavia, it was Serbia's only port on the sea. Montenegro got custody of it after the two countries' divorce in 2006. Thus, it was the terminus of the only railway in Montenegro: Bar to Beograd, Serbia via Podgorica. Goods arrived in Bar from Italy and elsewhere, were placed on containerized train cars, shipped to Beograd, sorted, then reloaded onto trucks and *shipped back* to Montenegro.

Stari Bar sat on a hill above the modern town. It had a strategic view of the port as well as being located in a choice defensive position that could also fend off potential attacks from the mountains. It was a city surrounded by ancient cyclopean walls, all fitted stones without the use of any mortar. All the *stari grads* in Montenegro are located overlooking the sea with the exception of *Stari Bar* that is three miles inland and halfway up a hill at the foot of the Rumija Mountain. Originally built by Byzantine Emperor Justinian in the 6th century, it was referred to in the 10th century as *Antibaris* (or "across from Bari") in Italy. It was taken by Venice in 1443, retaken by the Turks in 1571, and given to Montenegro in 1878 after the Ottomans virtually destroyed all the buildings. The lion of St. Mark, the patron saint of Venice, has a prominent place on the entrance to *Stari Bar,* and the Turkish aqueduct still descends from the top of Mount Rumija but no longer provides running water to the 600 buildings that were once inside the now crumbled walls.

Montenegrins claim they have a tree that is the oldest one in Europe. It is the *stara maslina* or old olive tree that sits in Mirovica, a suburb of Bar. The tree is approximately 20 feet in diameter and still bears fruit. Not bad for a tree that was planted about the time Christ was born. To make one wax philosophical, an olive tree always lives longer than the civilization that it supports. Because of the immense shade the tree provided, feuds and civil matters would be settled under its shrouded canopy.[4]

Coasting Along

Heading north from Bar along the coast, we lazily passed by beautiful beaches and playful inlets that allowed the waves to perform their magic to entice these mesmerized travelers. It was a drive worthy of any coast in the world. The first town we passed was Sutomore which hosts The Church of St. Tekla, built in the 14th century. The church has a special feature that holds an ecumenical lesson even for today. It has two altars—one Orthodox and one Catholic.

The next town was Petrovac, the family-oriented seaside destination. It had a quaint boardwalk with restaurants and shops that curved around a large beach. Many people remember Montenegro as the location of the latest incarnation of the James Bond movie, *Casino Royale,* with Daniel Craig. The plot all takes place in Petrovac. If you rent the movie, you will fall in love with the breath-taking scenery and architecture.[5]

North of Petrovac was Reževići, with its historic monastery swathed in the scents of green olive, laurel, and oleander. Around the next curve was the

---

4 Recent lab analysis from the University of Venice has confirmed there is an entire olive grove on Rumija Mountain that is at least 2,000 years old.

5 Unfortunately for the Montenegrin Tourist Ministry, all of those scenes were shot in Prague.

Venice-like walled town of Sveti Stefan that sat out from the shore. Just a bit beyond and hidden below was Przno beach. It is said to be so beautiful there that, according to Roman and Greek mythology, it is where the ancient gods came to make love.

One of the first times we visited the coast, we wanted someone else to do the driving so we could see the sights on the trip. We took a 5:30 a.m. bus out of Podgorica and the journey was uneventful until after we passed through Cetinje when the road dropped down off the mountain, and we could see the shoreline below stretching to the horizon in the distance. The swaying motion from the descending serpentine roads combined with the constant side-to-side G-forces acting on our bodies prevented us from being able to read or nod off. We were conscious but too numb to even converse with one other.

The return bus was a private affair owned by a husband and wife. She took the tickets, made change, counted passengers, loaded the luggage, and checked the oil. His job was to drive the bus and smoke cigarettes. They would argue about such things as the bus's air-conditioning. He (and the passengers) wanted it on as the windows did not open, and the air was stifling. After repeated requests to the driver, he was glad to turn it on. She promptly turned it off again to save fuel. He turned it back on. She flipped it off again. He said the passengers were hot. She thought it was a waste of money. There was an honest and earnest exchange of views that increased in decibels until the driver made an overly dramatic gesture with his arm and turned it on one final time. Some women have no sense of mutiny.

Big, Happy Budva

Budva was the "happ'nen spot" of the country. It had a very active nightlife with discos, clubs, and entertainment—both within and outside its own *stari grad* walls. A few kilometers up from Budva was Jaz Beach, the location for outdoor rock concerts. Budva's resident population is 15,000 people. During the summer season, the town may host as many as 330,000 visitors. Sometimes the summer guests literally overpower the infrastructure, as, for hours during peak season, there might not be tap water or electricity.

Budva was built on Greek ruins on top of Illyrian and Roman on top of those. According to legend, Budva was founded by Cadmus, the son of Phoenician King Agenor, who was expelled from Thebes. He arrived in an ox-drawn cart and stopped because of the spectacular sea and landscape. Even Sophocles wrote about *Butua,* the beautiful town of the Illyrians.

When the Great Catholic-Orthodox Schism occurred in 1054, the Roman-Byzantine boundary was drawn through the center of Budva. The town was acquired by Venice in 1443 and stayed as the last major port and outpost of Catholicism against the edge of the Ottoman Empire, which sat at the south end of Montenegro's coastal mountains. From up on the mountains, the Turks stared longingly at this town for 400 years. Subsequent years found Budva under Austrian, French, Russian, and then Austrian rule again.

Boka Kotorska (The Bay of Kotor)

> "I wonder how the sun can even set, when nowhere can such beauty be met."
>
> —Ljuba Nenadović

> "When you go up north (in the mountains), you feel as if you have come to the very end of the world. Here in Kotor Bay, you find yourself at the very entrance to the world."
>
> —Dušan Kostić

The city of Kotor is the crown jewel of Montenegro's historical and foreign tourist destinations. It lies at the farthest inland point on the Bay of Kotor, what some report as Europe's southernmost fjord. Although not technically true (as Kotor Bay is a riverbed, not carved by glacial erosion), the dramatic drop of the mountains straight into the water create breathtaking views as well as pacification for the soul. The bay is a doubly protected inlet with numerous ways to defend against invading ships and armies. The easiest way was to string a huge chain across the 900-foot gap at the bay's narrowest part in the inner bay and close up shop for the night.

Kotor is nestled under a mountain that gives nurture to almonds, agaves, palms, mimosas, oleanders, kiwis, pomegranates, eucalyptus, and cypress trees. Sailors transported magnolias and camellias from Japan around 1771 that still grow wild in the area. The camellias were brought back to their loved ones, so the flower is now given as a sign of love and loyalty.

The walled city and fortress was an independent republic between 1391 and 1420. Its obelisk-shaped pillory, just inside the main gate served as the town meeting point and dates from 1602. As it states above the city's Sea Gate entrance, the exterior walls were constructed in 1550.[6] Inside the walls we

6 When Tito, in World War II, recaptured the city, he placed his own inscription over the entrance that reads, "That which is others', we do not want. That which is ours

experienced a delightful discovery of its varied architecture—from 12th century Franciscan churches standing beside French provincial buildings constructed when Napoleon took the city in 1805. Besides the strategic significance of Kotor's protected port, much of the desire to possess it (even dating back to Roman times) came from wanting to control *Uvala Solila*—the salt works to the south.

Like many of the well-preserved ancient walled-cities in the Adriatic, this one is an active town of residences, shops, and sights. The twin towers of St. Tryphon's Cathedral were completed in 1166 (some 300 years after Tryphon was named the patron saint of the city). The church was damaged in the earthquake of 1667. As there were never sufficient funds to rebuild the damaged tower as it was originally built, they did the best they could. St. Tryphon's is the only church in Europe that has twin bell towers that do not match.[7] The protective fortress of Kotor climbs from sea level to 3,600 feet up the mountain behind. Its walls extend for almost three miles up past the Church of Good Health (which you need in order to make it up that far) to the Church of Sveti Ivan, a total of 1,350 steps to the top.[8] This gigantic wall was to protect the town from attacks by the savage Montenegrins who lived over the mountain. At night, the entire city and fortress wall was lit providing an awe-inspiring sight from across the bay.

Not So Risan(t)-ly

Further around the east side of the bay is the small town of Risan, one of the oldest settlements in the Balkans. It was the royal residence of Queen Teuta of the Illyrians and it dates back to 300 B.C. If there was anybody here before the Illyrians, they did not leave any evidence of themselves for posterity. Either that or they were very tidy. The Illyrians (or *Illyri*[9]) were a loose confederation of tribes who lived throughout the western Balkans from about 1,300 B.C. to 600 A.D. They epitomized the Bronze Age as they left many bronze weapons, bronze and amber jewelry, and third-place medals lying around. The Illyrians were threatened by the Greeks in the 5th century B.C., then run off by the Romans in the 3rd century B.C., to be eventually killed by the Slavs in the 7th century A.D. A hardy bunch, it is believed the remnants of the civilization may now be vested in Albania.[10]

---

we will never surrender.")

7 The church had to be restored after the 1979 earthquake as well.

8 On a hot day, you can get very sveti.

9 No relation to Kuryakin.

10 Although if they are there, they aren't telling.

The odd thing about Illyria is that it is believed to be the only civilization named for an *imaginary character*. In Greek mythology, Illyrius[11] was the son of Cadmus and Harmonia. It is also believed, due to the threat of potential starvation, the Illyrians migrated south from Hungary about 1300 B.C.[12] In pre-Roman times there might have been as many as 42 distinct tribes occupying the Balkan Peninsula. The Celts to the northeast and the Gauls to the northwest surrounded them. Their principal industry was also piracy—the one aspect of the legacy they left to their progeny that lasted for another 1,800 years. The Romans finally got tired of the Illyrian's thieving incursions and waged war against them for six decades until finally subduing them (except for a brief revolt under Caesar Augustus when he formally split off Dalmatia as a separate protectorate).[13]

In about 228 B.C., the Illyrians either enslaved or ran the neighboring Thracians off to the east until they hit the shore of the Black Sea (carefully avoiding waking up the Macedonians who were to the south).[14] This caused the Greeks to actually ask the Romans for protection from the Illyrians. The first two diplomats the Romans sent to Queen Teuta's court, she murdered. The Romans responded by sending two armadas in order to discuss the matter. She countered by climbing Mount Orijen above Risan and peter-panning into the bay, committing suicide in front of the invading Romans and all of her subjects. Before she died, she placed a curse on her people—they should never be sailors again. The conquering Romans left Risan the heritage of a large house called *Villa Urbana* that was unearthed in 1930. In the master bedroom is a rare depiction of *Hypnos*, the god of sleep. What makes this mosaic of Hypnos so unusual is that he is *awake*. Risan also has the oldest street still in use in the Balkans, Gabela Street.

By 100 B.C., all the Balkans, from the Danube to Athens, was under Roman rule. They mapped out the area as Illyrium. When the Roman Empire could not save itself from marauding bands, such as the Ostrogoths, Emperor Diocletian split the Empire into two uneven halves with the eastern portion having its capital in Constantinople. This would eventually become the Byzantine Empire, which lasted 1,000 years longer than its western counterpart in Rome. Montenegro

11 His grandsons were Triballus (from whence we get the word, *tribe*) and Scordiscus (the god of Frisbees).

12 Ironic, huh?

13 The area is now known as Split, Croatia.

14 We know this because there is not a thrace of them left there anymore. (Surely, you saw that coming.)

would be at the dividing line of these two empires, and destined to almost continuous conflict from then on.

Perast as Prologue

"It is as though a chunk of Venice has floated down the Adriatic and anchored itself onto the bay."

—Peter Dragičević

Exactly half way across the interior bay of Kotor sits the quiet and peaceful village of Perast. It possesses 18 churches (16 Catholic and 2 Orthodox) or one for every 19 of its 350 residents. This fact alone signifies Perast's previous importance in the Venetian Empire.

It was there in the mid-1700s that Marko Martinović inaugurated the first nautical and cartography school in the Mediterranean. At the water's edge were four shipbuilding docks; and the town had over a thousand ships that called Perast their homeport. The school was so famous for its naval officer training that the Russian czar had all of his captains attend school there.

Perast is also across from the only two islands in the bay, one housing an Orthodox monastery, Sveti Đorđe, and the other is the *Gospa od Škrpjela* (Our Lady of the Rock) Catholic church built in 1630. It is the only man-made island in the Adriatic. As scrapped ships were to be sunk, they were towed out from Perast to this spot, which built the base for the island church. For a small fee, we rode a boat out to see the Lady.

Among the church's treasury was an embroidered religious needlepoint of the Madonna and Child sewn by Jacinta Kunić that took her over 30 years to complete. In some places, she used her own hair as the locks of the cherubs. Looking closely at the stitching, we could see her donated locks change through the years from blonde to silver.

On one of our previous trips to the bay, we had discovered the Hotel Conte. The hotel building was 300 years old, and it has a restaurant that served good local seafood and wine.[15] The advantage to the hotel was that you could sit at a table on the promenade and have an expansive view of the bay to blissfully watch the sun go down. The drawback was you had to climb up three stories of outdoor

15 As there is only one main street in Perast, everybody has to cross in front of the Conte restaurant if they want to get anywhere in town. Many people, if they are looking for someone and can't raise them on their mobile phone, will come to the restaurant, have a drink by the window, and wait for them to eventually walk by.

stone stairs to arrive at the hidden courtyard where the rooms were. The hotel is attached to the Church of Saint Nikola.

In an astounding feat of civic pride, the citizens of Perast gathered together 441 *pounds* of gold in order to pay for the construction of the tallest campanile (181 feet) on the eastern Adriatic seaboard. The bell tower was constructed in 1691, but the church itself remains unfinished to this day. This ancient bell tower is next to the hotel. On our first stay, we had such a lovely time at the hotel, we booked ahead when parents and friends were to visit. During our next stay, we were surprised as at 6 a.m., all hell broke loose not ten feet outside our window. At first, we thought there was a fire. It was coming from the large bells that were ringing in the day. The bells had not rung at all during our first stay there. There were deep apologies to our visiting guests, but I still believe they thought is was a poor practical joke to play on someone who had flown so far to come see us.

Hitting the Cock

On May 15 every year, the village of Perast celebrates their victory over the Turks (which is something considering they were completely surrounded). The event is called "Hitting the Cock." When we were there, it had been raining all day, and the storm had knocked all the electricity out in town. Nobody on the celebration's organizing committee knew if they were going to have the festival or not which was supposed to begin at 5 p.m.

"Well," I said to the Parade Marshall, "We will keep our fingers crossed. Do you do that here in Montenegro?"

"We used to," replied the wet and discouraged official, "but it didn't work. So, we don't do that anymore."

However, at 4:55 p.m., they lined everybody up, cleared the street, and struck up the band. The festivities began with a short parade (as it's a very small town) which included women dressed in folk costumes, representatives from the Bay of Kotor Navy (ceremonial), and the City of Kotor Band (which brags it was first formed in 1842). The Navy sported costumes from the 18th century and muskets from the 15th century.

We were surprised that the band's first number was "The Battle Hymn of the Republic." This was followed by "She'll Be Coming 'Round the Mountain," and "Stars and Stripes Forever." When the band took a break, I went to ask the band director why they were playing American music. He said it was not American music and showed me the names on the sheet music were "Happy Band 1," "Happy Band 2," and "Step Lively." The band marched from the boat dock to the Church of St. Nikola, a distance of about three blocks, where a special mass was held. The Madonna from Our Lady of the Rock was honored by hoisting her onto the shoulders of the Navy guard who marched in a circle. Colorful flowers were given to all the women. The band then played national songs, and everybody danced and swayed to the music.

The highlight of the festival was the marksmanship contest in which a rooster was tied to a floating plank about a hundred yards out in the bay, and all the men took a chance at hitting the cock with an ancient musket. It was like a southern turkey-shoot with the world's biggest water hazard. First, the members of the Navy took honorary shots, and then members of the crowd got a chance for the donation of five euros. The cock was finally put out of his misery by number nineteen, a local strapping (but humble) lad who earned the honor of strutting down the street at the head of the parade holding his trophy rooster and in possession of all the bragging rights for the next year. Tradition required he also had to buy a *barrel* of wine for all the spectators. Not a lot of incentive to win as far as I was concerned.

Cetinje, The Real Montenegro

The road between Kotor and the small town of Cetinje connected a remote outpost of the Austrian empire to the small, but free, principality of Montenegro. Because the road has to go straight up three thousand feet from the sea, there are 25 switchbacks, each one providing a more breathtaking view of the bay and surrounding mountains. Constructed between 1879 and 1884, every meter of the road is said to have cost a golden ducat ($2.5 million in today's dollars). The road is known as the "Ladder of Kotor."

From the late 15th century until the mid-20th century, Cetinje was the capital of Montenegro. That was, until 1946, when the Communists wanted to re-orient the country away from its royalist past and toward a socialist future. So, they moved the administrative center to Podgorica.[16] Until that time, Cetinje was both the political (palaces and Parliament) and the religious (Cetinje Monastery) heart of the country. In 1880, the city had 15 foreign embassies lining its promenade. When you approached Cetinje from the coastal mountains up the Ladder, vibrant colors of the blue sea and dark green forest quickly change to become a desaturated and depressing setting with the landscape becoming covered in light grey boulders combined with denuded black trees and silver juniper. Our first time there, we understood why this city was successfully defended so many times—it was virtually impossible for any army to march

[16] The capital and Parliament were moved to Podgorica but the President's official residence is still in Cetinje, 25 miles away.

over the surrounding rocky terrain. It was the terrain that made the Ottomans in the south and the Venetians from the north think twice about attacking the Montenegrins.

Cetinje sits at the base of Mt. Lovćen, surrounded by so many loose boulders that visiting George Bernard Shaw once exclaimed, "People, am I in paradise or on the Moon?!" Montenegrin folk tales state that when God was making the world, He carried all the mountains in a large sack, placing them where He thought best. When He got to Montenegro, He was so stunned by its beauty He paused in awe. Unfortunately, at that moment the sack burst blessing Montenegro with a bewildering mass of rubble.[17]

Montenegrins say they only take seriously God and war. The two were intrinsically linked to the Montenegrin destiny for over 600 years. The Serbian Nemanjići dynasty began to crumble in 1389 when the Ottomans defeated the Serbs at the Battle of Kosovo Polje. During this time, the Crnojević dynasty ruled Montenegro inside the surrounding Ottoman Empire by moving its palace upland from lush river bottoms to rocky mountain nooks. The last holdout of which was one small part of the impassable black mountains of Montenegro, the ancient (and subsequently modern) capital of Cetinje.[18] There was a single path to the town, and the rocky area was described as a "petrified ocean." The Montenegrins, being the obstinate and hardheaded people they are, fought back from this position against the Turks in a long succession of successful guerilla attacks. Montenegrin king Stefan Crnojević signed an alliance with Venice, which bought a little power and some time. The last of the Crnojević line, Đurađ, married a Venetian noble's daughter and eventually fled Montenegro when his anti-Ottoman activities became known to the Sultan. Đurađ's brother, Stefan II, was more pragmatic. He changed teams, and ruled the area for the Ottomans. His progeny all became Moslem governors.

Interestingly, the first book of Psalms was printed in Montenegro only 40 years after Gutenberg printed his first Bible. The ruling prince had a printing press shipped all the way from Germany only to discover they had to hand-carve their own Cyrillic movable type. The year was 1492.

---

17 In 1739, when the Ottomans were demanding tribute from the Montenegrins, their ruler, Vasilije, sent the Turks a message that read, "The only currency my people have are rocks and you must come and take them yourselves."

18 Interestingly enough, in the same area were a clan of Vlachs, a separate isolated tribe of sheepherders who may have been the last remnants of the conquering Romans. Even as late as the 17th century they were still speaking Latin as their native tongue.

Before leaving for Venice in 1516, Đurađ made one last royal pronouncement. He named the first Prince-Bishop (*Vladika*) of Montenegro as his successor. Although the Turks attacked the capital repeatedly and even sacked it a few times, they were never able to completely conquer the Montenegrins. Their holdouts were somewhat effective in that the local Ottoman leaders collected less tax and allowed more self-rule in Montenegro than anywhere else in their Empire. Because Montenegrins were always at war with the Turks even after greater Serbia had long capitulated to the Ottoman occupiers, Montenegrins always thought of themselves as the "best of the Serbs." In the last decade of the 19th century, Montenegro repeatedly pushed back the Ottomans gaining lands to the east and south significantly contributing to the downfall of the Ottoman Empire. Montenegrins may have been dominated, but there were never tamed.

•

The late 1600s saw the rise of a long line of Vladikas, who ruled Montenegro until 1851. Before 1700, the clans of Montenegro had developed from mere extended families to become the political power base of the country. Squabbles among them were constant and rampant. Blood feuds were the *de facto* law. However, no one had more political power than the Petrovići, the clan that supplied the men who served as the Vladikas. These were Metropolitans of the Orthodox Church who also ruled the country and led the army. It is said they would forge into battle, blessing the enemy with one hand and chopping off their heads with the other. As the Bishops had to be celibate (since they were monks), the succession was passed from uncle to nephew. The Vladikas ruled for an average period of 12 years each. It took almost 150 years of Vladika rule to unite the clans into a semi-cohesive state.

When the Ottomans sliced through the Balkans, it decapitated the Byzantine Empire, but not the church on which it was based. However, the Ottomans controlled the Orthodox Church by naming a loyal Greek as Patriarch, but this man was not trusted or recognized by the autocephalous churches outside of Greece. The Ottomans went on to abolish the Serbian Orthodox Church in 1766. Because of this, the Montenegrins looked toward Russia as the last remaining Orthodox super-power, the two countries united together in their Christian beliefs—like a mouse and an elephant. It was said that Montenegro thought of Russia as her Mother although Russia did not know Montenegro was her son.

In 1715, Danilo I was the earliest Vladika to curry favor from the Russian court to support Montenegro as the most active Christian holdout against the Muslim Turks. Russia gave Montenegro lots of moral support, a few cherished religious icons, but not a lot of money. Russia had its eye on a port on the Adriatic and Montenegro could serve that strategic purpose. (This was part of Russia's centuries-long design on Constantinople so it could control trade through the Bosporus and into the Black Sea. It was in preparation for such a move, that the Russian navy trained many of its officers at Perast.)

In one of the oddest periods of Montenegrin history, a man emerged from the mountains claiming to be the long, lost Russian Tsar, Peter III (who, in fact, had been murdered several years before). His sobriquet was *Šćepan Mali* or "Šćepan the Small." Through what must have been one of the greatest con artist acts in antiquity, this very short, but suave man, got himself elected to the Montenegrin ruling body. He then proceeded to calm inter-clan disputes, build roads, create a national census, and regulate trading markets. He was so popular and successful that the ruling Vladika finally had to have him murdered.

In 1797, Napoleon Bonaparte defeated the Venetian Republic,[19] and the Austrian Habsburgs[20] were forced to give Belgium to France and take Croatia and Dubrovnik. This agreement did not last long because Napoleon defeated the Austrians eight years later and took all of Croatia, making it part of his Kingdom of Italy. In 1813, Montenegro attacked Kotor and ran off the French, but the Congress of Vienna made Montenegro cede it back to Austria who got the entire coast of Dalmatia and an outfielder to be named later.

During the remainder of the 1800s, it seemed all of Europe conspired to keep Montenegro from having access to the Adriatic. European governments were convinced this move would give Russia its desired naval base, something Austria especially did not want to occur. In 1838, Montenegro's most beloved Vladika (and poet), Petar II Petrović-Njegoš, bought property from the Paštrovići clan along the coast in hopes of building an Adriatic port.[21] The Austrians immediately forced him to sell it to them for about $100,000. This gave them

---

19 It is said that Napoleon only finished off the Venetians. What really destroyed them was Columbus and steam power.

20 Due to intermarriages, the Habsburgs were known for genetically passing along the famous Habsburg jaw, a bone that stuck out so far, that no portrait painter dared depict it in its full majesty. It is said Charles II of Spain could not even chew. For that, he had a Royal Masticator.

21 Petar II became Vladika at 17. He spoke and read five languages. His personal (and state) library was very similar to Thomas Jefferson's at Monticello. He also stood close to seven feet tall. To accommodate his presence at the Palace, the staff had to raise all the furniture by six and half inches.

even more power over the tiny and continued land-locked principality of Montenegro.

Petar II was very progressive. He opened the first school, created the first Senate (made up of the tribal chiefs), formed a set of circuit judges, and established a police force that upheld national laws, superseding that of traditional local clan justice.[22] He also found time to pen what might be the most important epic poem in Montenegrin (and Serbian) history, *The Mountain Wreath*, an elegy about the struggle against oppression. During this time, Peter II designed a new ensign for his country. The Orthodox Church wanted him to have the Montenegrin eagle with its wings down like the flag of Serbia. Petar II wanted it with the wings up because the Montenegrins had never completely fallen to the Turks like Serbia had. He won.

While Petar II ruled, Montenegro was a poverty-stricken country. He, being a monk who had taken a vow of poverty, kept the entire state treasury in a cigar box under his bed. An austere man, he had but one vice—billiards. Petar had the first table in the country installed in his palace, which is known today as the *Biljarda.*

When he died from tuberculosis in 1851, he was only 38 years old. He was buried at the peak of Mt. Lovćen (5,500 feet) that overlooks both Cetinje and the Bay of Kotor. At least it does when the weather is clear. When we paid our respects, the mountain mausoleum was wrapped in dense mountain clouds, so the tomb was a surrounded by a soupy, mysterious gray fog creating the sensation of experiencing the passing from this life to the next. Mt. Lovćen is the smallest National Park in the country and is the Mount Olympus of Montenegro. Petar II's mausoleum was designed by Ivan Meštrovic, a Croatian (which caused more than a little stir in Montenegro). But, they brag that he asked for only a piece of famous Njeguski cheese and some local pršut as his fee.

Petar II's only nephew, Danilo II, was already engaged to be wed, and, thus, could not become Vladika. Instead, he was crowned Prince. Danilo II fought many successful battles against the Turks but was assassinated in Kotor in 1860, probably by the Austrians. He was succeeded by 19-year-old Nikola Petrović.

Nikola Petrović, now Prince Nikola I, had been tutored in Venice and Paris and favored the French culture, its language, and etiquette. His wife, Milena, was an entirely home grown Montenegrin gal; and the two provided an air of

---

22 German scientists from the 19th century stated that Montenegrins were like the new religious group in America, the Mormons. The commonalities included: the family was most important; they were faithful, honest, fought for their freedom, and loved genealogy.

sophistication mixed with humble simplicity. When they married, he was 19 and she was 13 and illiterate. Nikola I ruled Montenegro for over 50 years and led the country through five wars. It is said Nikola knew the names of each of his subjects. He created the first post office, the first school for girls, established the first constitution and freedom of the press, crisscrossed the country with telegraph lines and railroads, and, through a series of battles, doubled the size of the country. After uprisings against the Turks in Bosnia, both Serbia and Montenegro joined in and effectively broke the Ottoman hold over the Balkans. Under Nikola's rule, Montenegro was finally recognized as an independent state in 1878.

During this time, foreign correspondents stationed in Montenegro were sending dispatches back home about the little country's brave struggle against the Ottoman armies. These romanticized reports were published regularly in American, French, and English newspapers. They were especially relished by British readers who galvanized entire parishes to pray for the triumph of Christianity over the heathen Turks. Even Alfred Lord Tennyson wrote the poem, "Montenegro," in 1877, which further ignited interest in the affairs of the tiny Balkan country.

> They rose to where their sovereign eagle sails,
> They kept their faith, their freedom, on the height,
> Chaste, frugal, savage, arm'd by day and night
> Against the Turk; whose inroad nowhere scales
> Their headlong passes, but his footstep fails,
> And red with blood the Crescent reels from fight
> Before their dauntless hundreds, in prone flight
> By thousands down the crags and thro' the vales.
> O smallest among peoples! rough rock-throne
> Of Freedom! warriors beating back the swarm
> Of Turkish Islam for five hundred years,
> Great Tsernogora! never since thine own
> Black ridges drew the cloud and brake the storm
> Has breathed a race of mightier mountaineers.[23]

He wrote the poem *in absentia* as he never set foot in the country.

On the anniversary of Nikola's jubilee in 1910, he proclaimed himself King. He and Milena had nine daughters (two died, two did not marry) and three sons.

---

[23] Alfred Lord Tennyson, from *Ballads and Other Poems*, 1880.

With the cost of the wars and Nikola's own extravagant living, Montenegro was bankrupt.[24] The King had taxed everything he could. His solution for continued cash flow was to marry his offspring to titled European families who, in turn, would keep their newly acquired royal in-laws in the manner to which they had become accustomed. His children married no less than Romanovs, Battenbergs, and Mecklenburg-Strelitzs. Princess Jelena became the last Queen of Italy and Princess Zorka married Petar Karadjordjević I, the prince of the royal family of Serbia. Because of this premeditated propagation campaign, Nikola is known as "the Father-in-law of Europe." His son-in-law, Petar I would go on to become King of the Serbs, Croats, and Slovenes, which became the first Yugoslavia (the Kingdom of). He would eventually annex Montenegro out from underneath his own ex-father-in-law as his wife Zorka died in childbirth at the age of 25 and he had no sentimentality for the country.

"I was born by cruel fate in a little Balkan state," is one of the signature lyrics written by Basil Hood and Adrian Ross for the 1907 London version of the opera, *The Merry Widow*, by Franz Lehar. The opera takes place in the French Embassy of the bankrupt country "Pontevedreo," a mythical country whose delegation includes a Baron Zeta, Count Danilo Danilovitch, and Njegus, all conspiring to keep the country's cash flowing by arranging a suitable marriage. When the opera debuted in Vienna in 1905, the audience had no doubt whom the show was parodying. During intermission on opening night, The Montenegrin legation to the Austrian Empire left in a huff.

World War I was precipitated when Gavrilo Princip assassinated the future King of the Austro-Hungarian Empire, Archduke Ferdinand, in Sarajevo in 1914. Princip was a member of the Black Hand, a shadow organization within the Serbian government. The Empire then declared war on Serbia, and Montenegro immediately joined on the side of its religious ally. King Nikola used the war as an excuse to attack Albania, which failed as he was forced to give it up soon after. With Austria-Hungary soon invading his country, Nikola escaped to the protection of his son-in-law, the King of Italy. He had reigned for 58 years and had always gone to battle in the National Costume. Serbian King Petar I entered Montenegro with his troops. He placed the country under his protection refusing to allow his former father-in-law to return. Because of this, Montenegro became the only Allied country to lose its freedom because of the First World War.

Wiped off newly printed maps, Montenegro was governed by Serbia, which turned itself into the Kingdom of Yugoslavia in 1929. This lasted until 1941

24 It didn't help any that the royal family budget had to maintain seven palaces. Some were even across the street from other palaces. Again, it's a small country.

when King Petar II signed an alliance with Germany and Italy hoping, as did Britain, to achieve a lasting European peace. This move proved unpopular, and a military coup sent the King fleeing to London. Germany invaded Serbia just weeks later. Montenegro and its coastal region were handed over to the Italians who were welcomed by the populace until they had to begin implementing the bloodthirsty acts mandated by the Nazis.

•

In Cetinje, next to the Bilardja Palace, is a huge 1:10,000 relief map of Montenegro made out of cement. It measures 30 by 30 feet and has a large walkway around it. Constructed in 1916 by the occupying Austrian army, it was built so they could explain to the Emperor what a monumental task it would be to invade any further into this mountainous country. It was the best place to get an idea of just how vertical the Montenegrin terrain really is.

Due to its historical significance, Cetinje is also the country's museum center. It hosts the Monastery Museum, the State Museum, Njegos' Museum, the Museum of Ethnography, the Historical Museum, and the Art Museum.[25] The latter boasts art by Picasso, Renoir, Chagall, and Dali.

Nearby is the Cetinje Monastery, completed in 1701, with its valuable treasury. This large, gray-stoned, multi-storied building runs along the base of a hill. Owing to the intercession of a new friend, we were able to tour the Monastery and saw its most precious treasures: a wooden sliver from the cross on which Jesus was crucified, the mummified right hand of John the Baptist, and a hair from Christ's head (which was a gift from the Russian Metropolitan).

Needless to say, there are some very curious items on display in Cetinje. One particular item has a history of getting curiouser and curiouser. In the National Art Museum is a bejeweled icon of the Madonna, with a gold gilded façade exposing a painted face on canvas. It is known as the *Icon of Philermose* and, according to legend; the icon was created by St. Luke.

Following the Turkish occupation of the island of Rhodes, the Order of the Knights of Malta smuggled the icon, as well as the right hand of John the Baptist, to Malta where the knights could protect them in their own castle. The objects remained there until Napoleon conquered it in 1798. Pablo Gomez, a Knight of the Order, took the relics and fled to Russia. He then handed them over to Czar Paul I, the titular remaining head of the Orthodox Church. They remained there for two hundred years until the Metropolitan of Kiev, Antony Hrapovitsky,

[25] Don't forget the Montenegrin Museum of the Electric Power Industry.

brought them from St. Petersburg to Beograd, Serbia (with the fragment of the holy cross) and gave them as a gift to the new Yugoslav King, Aleksandar Karadjordjević, in the 1920s. When the Yugoslavian royalty had to escape the invading Nazis in 1941, the King left these relics in the Ostrog Monastery where they stayed in secret until 1952. Some believe this icon's history was the basis for the famous statue in Dashiell Hammett's *The Maltese Falcon.*

The icon has immense economic value as well as religious significance. It is studded with sapphires and rubies and its border is made up of 270 large diamonds. After World War II, the Communists kept it in the National Bank (and borrowed against it) until 1974. The Art Museum in Cetinje presently has the icon displayed in the Blue Chapel of the Government House. This was the end of the "silent war" between the Montenegrin government and the Metropolitan of Montenegro over who had the right to the relic for safekeeping.

Currently, the Montenegrin government is in a "discussion" with the Orthodox Church that claims, since the icon is a religious relic; they should have possession of it. They believe a secular government cannot appreciate the religious magnitude of such an item. The head of the Monastery wants it immediately moved to the Cetinje Monastery, about 100 yards away.

Ostrog Monastery

The most dramatic icon of Montenegro is Ostrog, the monastery carved out of caves on the Ostroška Greda Mountain between Danilovgrad and Nikšić, 28 miles northwest of Podgorica. We were told, "all religions will be there for Easter" as Orthodox, Catholic, and even some Muslims come here to pray.[26] The monastery is dubbed St. Vasilije's (Basil's) Miracle, since no one seems to know how it was constructed 1,800 feet up the cliff (or 600 feet down from the top). St. Vasilije arrived here in 1665 after the Turks decimated the Tvrdos monastery in Herzegovina. He died in 1671, and his body is enshrined inside Ostrog. (Some Montenegrins will stand up and cross themselves at the mere mention of St. Vasilije's name.) Ostrog is an active monastery. To pay homage, religious pilgrims start at the lower portion of the road and walk the last two kilometers, some choosing to do it on their knees. What can be seen now is the restoration of the monastery from 1929 when a fire destroyed all but the two cave churches.

---

[26] Modern Montenegrins are, for the most part, of Serbian descent, even those whose heritage includes the Ottoman invasion and subsequent Moslem conversions. Presently, about three-quarters of Montenegrins consider themselves Serbian Orthodox and about one-fourth Moslem with a smattering of other religions including Catholic, Roma, and the more recent invasion of Protestants.

The trip from the highway to the monastery can be a challenge. There is a one-lane dirt road that handles two-way traffic. It has 30 switchbacks but still rises at a 10 percent incline. In addition, there are no guardrails on the outside lane to protect a car from the shear drop off from the semi-paved road. There is a legend that no one has ever been killed on the journey up to the Monastery because God protects all those who visit. Before we visited the monastery, we did not understand why everyone made sure they told us that. When we eventually made the journey and would meet an on-coming car, both vehicles had to slow down and inch by each other. With the inside car next to a solid rock wall, the only one that could move over was the one that had to drive on the outside.

After negotiating past another car and feeling our right side tires float in mid-air, Beth Lynn started whimpering, knowing we had to keep going up since there was no place to turn around. Around one hairpin turn, much to our surprise, we looked upward and saw five large tour buses coming down the hill toward us. Although we knew that two objects could not physically occupy the same space at the same time, it appeared there was no other choice. Frankly, I do not know how we did it. After getting past the third bus, my confidence increased a bit and I paused to document our little accomplishment by driving and taking pictures at the same time. This did not sit well with my fellow passenger. (Actually, she was not sitting well at all as she was shouting at me from under her seat.) Our friends were right; God protects all those who visit Ostrog.

One of the benefits of visiting the monastery was being able to dine afterwards at *Ognjište* (The Fireplace), a unique restaurant on the way back to Danilovgrad. It was located in a cave under the highway and served wonderful meat dishes in iron pots heated under the ashes in their huge (what else) fireplace.

Riding in the Prijepolje Position

When we drove along the Morača canyon road northeast of Podgorica, we saw eagles soaring high above the river. On second glance, we noticed there was a train going into a tunnel on the side of the mountain *above the eagles*. The Bar to Beograd train is one of the most spectacular train trips in the world. Construction of the rail line was begun in 1958 but was not completed until 1975.

I had wanted to ride the train on its more scenic section, the part from Podgorica to just inside Serbia. We booked tickets to the first stop across the border, Prijepolje. The train we took into Serbia was the new Montenegrin train that would make any Tokyo-to-Kyoto shinkansen proud. Because of continuing construction on the tracks, the train took off on time but was an hour late arriving in Prijepolje. The tracks rose higher and higher above the Morača river canyon until the river disappeared from view and only mountaintops were visible. The railway line is so serpentine through the mountains that the full moon appeared on both sides of our car. This was our view until an elevated plain of Tyrolean-like scenery with farmhouses and haystacks began to pass by our window. After the town of Bjelo Polje, we passed over Montenegro's continental divide where the rivers began to flow in opposite directions. On this part of the 106-mile journey there were 128 tunnels.

We made numerous stops along the way in every town of any significance. Two of the stations had no towns—they were just monasteries. For one of the monasteries, there was no other way to get to it except by rail. After one of these stops, a large, bearded Orthodox priest joined us in our compartment. His massive white hair and beard were a contrast to his black robes. He nodded and we nodded—the typical beginning of a Balkan relationship. He spoke broken English and we responded in our artificial Srpski. He had a family in Serbia, but every day he took the train to his job at a monastery just across the border in Montenegro. Now, he was heading home for the day. He wanted to know why two Americans would come all the way to Montenegro just to ride his commuter train. I explained what we were doing in Montenegro and that I had a Montenegrin grandfather. Hearing this, the monk grinned from ear to ear and declared me Serbian Orthodox. He asked where my family was from. After I told him, he reached into the folds of his robe and withdrew a large deck of laminated cards printed with icons of saints. He thoughtfully flipped through them until he found the picture that represented the patron saint of my clan. He told me to put it in my wallet and keep it with me at all times for protection while I traveled.

I was admiring the card when the train stopped at the Serbian border. The imposing guards with their automatic weapons came into our cabin checking passports. They all knew the priest, but he still showed them his church identity card. He pointed to us and told the guards we were Serbian. They waved at us and immediately continued on to the next cabin. The priest smiled at the little favor he had done for us, but I was now very concerned about trying to get back into Montenegro without a Serbian entry stamp on our passports. I made a stamping motion with my fist and the priest just dismissed it with a wave. That night I didn't sleep much as I worried about crossing the border the next day. But, the priest was right. We had no trouble at all getting back into Montenegro.

Prijepolje, Serbia is a sleepy, little town on the banks of two drowsy rivers and serves as the governing center for the Zlatibor District of Serbia.[27] It is a town of 15,000 people, two rivers (the Lim and Mileševa), one monastery (Mileševa), and one Communist-era hotel (the Mileševa). Prijepolje has two claims to fame. It once served as a water stop on the caravan route linking Dubrovnik to Constantinople; and it is the birthplace of the NBA star, Vlade Divac. The town museum dedicates about half of its floor space to the seven-foot, one-inch hometown hero who was drafted into the NBA in 1989 even though he didn't speak any English. He held his own, playing on the same team as Kareem Abdul-Jabbar and Magic Johnson.[28]

For the sake of time, on the trip back to Podgorica, we took an older Serbian train that was one and a half hours late arriving in Prijepolje from Beograd. However, it actually got to Podgorica ahead of schedule—the advantage of traveling downhill all the way. The segment from the highest point, Kolašin, Montenegro to Podgorica has a grade of 25 percent. Only four years ago, there was a tragic train crash on the line above the village of Bioče, about seven miles above Podgorica. Forty-five people were killed and 184 injured when the train derailed and fell 300 feet to the river below. Reconstruction of that portion of the line is still on going. The complete trip from Podgorica to Beograd used to take seven hours. Now, to be cautious, it takes over ten. Other parts of the line that were bombed by NATO in 1999 are also still being repaired.

The highlight of the trip is traveling over the Mala Rijeka viaduct that is 1,600 feet long and rises 660 feet over the Morača River. It is the tallest train bridge in Europe and seems even longer when the train is going as slow as it does.

In the Mountain Greenery

Near the end of our stay we rented a car in order to see the last parts of Montenegro we had not been able to experience up close—the mountains in the north. We, drove up the meandering Morača River canyon with its rushing water, cave tunnels, and the train tracks above us. The Morača River splits Montenegro into two halves. It starts at the headwaters located at the base of Rzača Mountain, flows down through the mountain peaks, and joins the Zeta River at Duklja just before entering Podgorica separating the city into its old and

---

27 This last piece of information is completely irrelevant except it allows me to get in that great name, *Zlatibor.*

28 Divac is one of just a few players in NBA history to record 13,000 points, 9,000 rebounds, and 3,000 assists and play in over 1,000 games.

new parts. From there it slowly wanders on to Lake Skadar where the water is stored for about 30 days before being flushed out the Ada Bojana River into the Adriatic Sea.

Leaving Podgorica, it did not take long for us to enter the lush forest that covers half of the country. An hour's drive up the canyon took us to the white-walled Morača Monastery. The complex was built on a cliff over the river. Beside it, the Svetigora waterfall tumbles 125 feet down to the canyon floor. With the setting sun reflecting off the falling water, it is as though the Monastery floats on a glowing ribbon of light. The first small church there was built in 1252 and still has its original frescoes. The larger church was rebuilt in the 17th century over one the Turks burnt down in 1505.

Farther up the road past the monastery is the town of Kolašin, the mountain ski resort that also served as one of the headquarters of Tito's partizan army during World War II. During the war, Yugoslavia was politically split and fighting two wars at the same time. First, there were the *Ustaša*, a Croatian fascist regime that was aligned with Hitler. The remains of the former loyalist Yugoslavian Army formed the *Chetniks*, who fought for the routed royal family. The Communist Partizans were led by Josip Broz (Tito). All the while the latter two were fighting the invading Axis army all three were fighting each other for a civil war and the future of Yugoslavia. To paint the passionate picture of the times, the Ustaša wanted to kill one-third of the Serbs, expel one-third, and convert the other third to Catholicism. Between the three groups and the Axis army, 1.7 million Yugoslavs were killed, reportedly the highest percentage of any country's population during the war.

It took the Allies a long time to figure out which faction to support. After much consideration and pressure from Stalin, they chose to back Tito's Partizans. Much of Tito's fighting was done in the mountains of Montenegro with men of the same clans who had fought against the Turks for 400 years. Out of loyalty to these courageous Montenegrins, there was always a disproportionate number of Montenegrins in the Yugoslavian army leadership and a larger amount of internal funds headed to support the devastated Montenegrin post-WWII economy.

During the war, one of Tito's code names was "Walter" after the pistol he preferred, the Walther PPK. Ian Fleming took this tidbit and made it James Bond's personal weapon of choice. When Tito liberated Beograd in 1944, he literally had the country in his hands. An overwhelming majority then voted for him as Prime Minister, turning the country Communist. The new country of Yugoslavia consisted of Serbia (and Kosovo), Slovenia, Croatia, Bosnia and Herzegovina, Montenegro, and Macedonia.

Tito ruled "from Macedonia to Slovenia" a phrase that, for centuries, meant the entire world. He was quoted as having said he was the leader of one country that had two alphabets, three languages, four religions, five nationalities, six republics, surrounded by seven neighbors, hosting eight ethnic minorities. Of his neighboring countries, he spoke of Yugoslavia being surrounded by *brigama* ("with worries") an acronym formed by the first letters of Bulgaria, Romania, Italy, Greece, Albania, Hungary (or *Mađarskain* in Serbo-Croatian), and Austria.

Tito was a natural-born leader and a gifted military and political strategist. He was elected as Prime Minister, Secretary-General, or President six times. Tito was uniquely positioned to lead post-war Yugoslavia, as his father was a Croat and his mother, a Slovene. Political purging was rampant during Tito's reign, and no family was exempt including my own. However, forcing all of the former countries and cultures under one flag and one government was a challenge even for Tito.

He initially had close relations with Russia and Stalin but expected to be treated with more respect than a mere Politburo satrapy. Tito's famous letter of two roads to socialism got him and his government cut off from the Soviet-led Communist bloc and the associated foreign aid. Stalin saw Tito as a rival in world Communist leadership and signed an assassination edict to have him killed. Tito wrote back and said he had uncovered two Russian murder plots against him. If he discovered any more, he would send a team to Moscow to kill Stalin, and he would not have to send another one. From then on, Stalin tempered his rhetoric directed at Tito and his new Yugoslavian state. Tito then used this to leverage Marshall Plan funds from the United States. Communism was a costly endeavor; and throughout Tito's reign, Yugoslavia always had to be financially supported by one government or another, just like Montenegro under King Nikola.

Tito's unique "other road" to socialism included profit sharing for factory workers, freedom for citizens to travel abroad (including for work and education), tourism was encouraged, as well as an increased freedom of speech and religious expression (to an extent, but certainly more than in other Communist countries). By the time he was named President-for-Life in 1974, he had reduced the size of the secret police, had formed a legislative body with representatives from the entire country, and had established a collective presidency, which would rotate among an elected delegate from each of the country's republics. Upon Tito's death in 1980, the *New York Times* stated that, under Tito, Yugoslavia had gradually become a bright spot amid the general grayness of Eastern Europe.

•

Unique to the area in the mountains surrounding the resort of Kolašin are *savardaki*, conical (and comical) wooden huts made of long tree trunks and thatching. Above the town is Biogradska Gora National Park, which Montenegrins are proud to point out, became a National Park only a few years after Yellowstone. (There are four National Parks in Montenegro. To put this in perspective: the landmass of the entire country is less than the size of Connecticut.) Biogradska Park encompasses 14,000 acres. About a third of the park is primeval forest, only one of three such areas left in Europe. Trees here are 500 years old and may grow 200 feet tall.

Passing through the town of Mojkovac, we followed the Tara river canyon, where there was white knuckle, white water rafting. We drove on to Žabljak, the highest town in the Balkans and the gateway to Durmitor Mountain National Park.[29] Žabljak provides a stunning panorama of the mountains and the *katuni* (summer cottages) that dot its landscape. Inside its park are 18 glacial lakes each with its own mirror reflection of the jagged peaks. From there we crossed the plain south of the park in a casual search for *stečci*, large tablets with strange writing and symbols from the 15th and 16th century whose art carvings seem to be from a much earlier time. These stečci are scattered throughout the Balkans and their meaning is still not clear.

On day two, we took a right at Kolašin and crossed over the mountains on a washboard road on the way to Andrijevica. The constant rain had caused an avalanche to cover the road, but we could get our car around the fallen rubble if we put two of our tires in the shallow river. This took us to Plav with its beautiful lake. A short jaunt beyond was Gusinje and a view of the vertically rugged *Prokletije* ("accursed" or "damned") mountain range close up on the Albanian border.[30] Returning to Plav, we ran into the President of the Andrijevica fly-fishing club and his acolytes. Due to extensive bragging in sign language about large fish I had previously caught, they made me an honorary member and gave me a patch for my fishing vest.

---

[29] The word, Durmitor, is probably Romantic in nature and means "sleeping" from the same root word as "dormitory".

[30] I would think that if you were trying to cross them thar hills, "damned" would be the least of your epithets.

Every town we visited had one or more very large manufacturing plants that were closed and abandoned, the result of the collapse of Communism where the outdated factories were supported by government subsidies in order to keep local employment high. Now, over a third of the people in this mountain area are unemployed. Investment in new ventures is virtually non-existent, especially in these small towns. The mountains of Montenegro possess incredible natural beauty, few tourists, and no jobs.

In typical American fashion, we rushed through the Montenegrin countryside trying to cram as much sightseeing as we could in the little time we had left. We realized this educational excursion into the backcountry was just like all of our "work hard, then play hard" holidays where we have to allow an extra day just to rest up from the vacation. When we returned from touring parts of the country, we would show our Montenegrin friends pictures of all the things we had seen. They would chastise us and ask us, "When will you take a holiday just to enjoy?"

It was articulated best in the official tourist publication, *Explore Montenegro*:

"Where are they rushing to these modern nomads of the European, Japanese, and American metropolises, these speed junkies, going on holidays armed with digital camera and camcorders, wishing to capture as much as they can in the shortest possible period of time? Isn't a modern tourist, accustomed to looking at the outside through the lens of a camera, ready to stop, slow down, relax and enjoy the last oasis of intact nature and wild beauty anymore? There is not a camera in the world that can preserve the smell of a pine forest, dewy grass, cut hay, or taste of mead, dry strong Montenegrin wine or freshly baked bread."

This was a lesson we had to painfully learn; that the hurried American way of travel (and living) is not necessarily the best way. Taking time to enjoy life rather than rushing through it was a message that we were reminded of many times during our experience—especially by our own, newly discovered family.

The Clan

Finding Family

Montenegrins are all sons of—viches.

That is—*vić* with the *ć* sounded as in "ch." Surnames in Montenegro end in an—*ić*. Most are—*vić's* but others end in—*nić*,—*sić*,—*cić*, or—*zić*. They are all patronyms like "Mc" in Scotland and "O'" in Ireland. In Montenegro, they not only mean "son of" but they might also designate a clan, people from a certain area, or even a craft like the English name, Smithson. The surname Francović denotes they are sons of a long, lost Franc somewhere along the line. In my family name, Radović, *Rado* means happy. So, I'm the son of a dwarf.

•

It was just a month before we left the States when my St. Louis Radovich family said, "Oh, by the way, you have a cousin in Montenegro."

Nine years before, my American cousin, Melo Radovich, had received a strange and unexpected letter from an unknown, but, as it turned out, not so distant, cousin named Eva Radović. She is my grandfather's niece and my second cousin. When Eva turned eighty-five, mortality began to rear its shadowy head; and she began searching for her relatives to whom she could leave her house. She was determined it should stay in the Radović family and was bound by tradition to pass it to her closest male heir. Considering the house sits on the Adriatic Highway, overlooking the sea, in a prime resort location, many people (mostly Russians) have wanted to buy it. The neighbors said there was somebody knocking and inquiring every day. Eva was so adamant that her wishes be respected; she mounted a granite plaque on the front of the house that read:

THE HOUSE OF RADOVIĆ

These words are written on this house.
In honor of grandfather, great-grandfather, and great-great-grandfather Radović.
This house is believed to be two hundred years old.
It was preserved by my father and mother, Kata Radović.
And Mata, Tomo, Eva, and Stefan Radović.
They, too, adopted it,
Safeguarding and left it in good condition.
Mata is now deceased, as is Tomo and Stefan.
But Eva is still alive.
She asks on behalf of her brothers that the relatives Radović
Who are in America preserve this house and
Not sell it after her death.
And remain in the Radović house.
This sign was written by Eva Radović.
Do not remove this sign.
(This house is not for sale. Do not ask.)

I am sure there were a few Radovići relatives in the area who were hoping they would be the designated heir and inherit the house.[1] However, Eva enlisted the help of a close friend and began tracking down all the Radoviches in America[2] until she found Melo. Deeply empathizing with Eva's plight, Melo's daughters made a hurried trip over to meet Eva, so they could get to know each other and Eva could feel good about her "new" family. Melo's oldest daughter, Mary, is the cousin who is most sensitive to keeping alive our Montenegrin heritage. She has been there several times, took Serbian lessons for two years, and knows where the local Balkan restaurants are in St. Louis (and what is good where). She even learned to cook some of the national dishes, and, now, stays in regular contact with Eva.

Eva was ninety-two, set in her ways, and had strong opinions. Mary thought it best to send her a letter of introduction telling Eva to expect a letter from us asking if we could come meet her. Mary heard back from Eva who expressed surprise we were coming. We could now send our own letter of introduction.

---

1 My American cousins tell of having to patiently explain the family tree to several people who challenged Melo's position as Eva's closed male heir.

2 More than you'd think.

Eva was cared for by the Bantulić family. This was the family whom she has adopted. They owned and managed *Kuca Radović* that was Eva's brother's house in Petrovac that they had converted to a hotel. The Bantulići were Serbs who moved from near Beograd to the Montenegrin coast because of their son, Nenad's respiratory problems. Nenad was now 24 and spoke English very well. He was the youngest of the Bantulići children and Eva was very fond of him.[3] He served as the go-between and interpreter for us.

Nenad and his father kindly picked us up in Podgorica and drove us the fifty miles to the village of Drobnići where Eva lived. As we approached the little hamlet on the coastal Adriatic Highway we rounded a bend revealing almost vertical mountains on one side and a somber ocean on the other. The sky was a mix of dark clouds with bursts of sunbeams streaming down to illuminate the sea. The light created a rainbow against the mountains with one of its ends located behind a tall, three-story stone house that towered above all the other houses in the village.

"That is your family house," said Nenad, pointing to the structure.

It was a beautiful, 250 year-old, three-story, pale yellow stone building surrounded by Clementine oranges, olives, and pomegranate groves. The Radović house truly was the largest stone building in Drobnići (an endless source of pride among the family). The walls of the house were almost three feet thick. It sat at the foothills of the mountains facing the Adriatic. Looking eastward, it looked much like where we live, mountains shooting straight up to the sky. To the west from the front porch, there was an endless sea below a rocky coastline—reminiscent of the Pacific Northwest. My grandfather, Filip, was born in the house as was his father, Tomo, and his grandfather, Andrija. We suspect that phenomenon went back at least three more generations.

Ms. Bantulić greeted us at the door and showed us into the living room. Eva rose from her day bed and gave us a big hug and smile. Eva had long, silver hair, piercing blue eyes, a chiseled face full of history; and we shared the same large nose. Introductions were provided, and I told her how sorry we were my mother could not come and meet her. On Mary's suggestion, we had made Eva a photo book with pictures of my grandfather and grandmother, my parents' family, my sister's family, and our family. Opening it, she began to cry. When she would come across a picture of some relative she did not know, she would kiss the photo in the book. She had never seen a picture of my grandfather, much less my mother. My grandfather had sent many gifts to her from America, but he had

---

3 It was not unusual for the youngest male child to be named, Nenad. It means "Surprise!"

never sent a picture of himself. When Eva kissed the book, it was heartbreaking because it succinctly demonstrated the terrible separation of a family and the chasm of time and distance that had come between us.

Eva had lived in seven different countries (the Austro-Hungarian Empire; the Kingdom of Serbs, Croats and Slovenes; the Kingdom of Yugoslavia; the Italian [and then, Nazi] Occupation during World War II; Yugoslavia; Serbia and Montenegro; and, now, Montenegro). She had lived under five types of governments (kingdom, dictatorship, communism, socialism, and democracy) and all without ever leaving the house where she was born.[4]

Eva was dressed in a black skirt and blouse, which was the only color she ever wore. She was in mourning and had been since 1941 when the occupying Italian army,[5] on orders from the Nazis took her brother, Stefan, and ten other young men out in the street and shot them.[6]

Ms. Bantulić had prepared a lunch for us that was a mix of Serbian and Montenegrin dishes. It was a light spread—there were only five courses and seven entrees. She had prepared chicken, lamb, pršut, two other types of ham, salami, and beef. There was an egg and ham salad and a relish made from tomatoes, carrots, and red pepper that topped off baked bell peppers. The meal was finished with five different pastries and traditional Montenegrin cookies/ donuts, *malisorske priganice*, (like tiny beignets). The meal was exciting, adventurous, and delicious. After lunch, we let Eva rest while we were given a tour of the Radović house.

•

Typically, along the Montenegrin coast, three generations would have shared the same house. And, that was just the livestock. Animals were kept on the bottom floor, the family slept on the second floor, and the kitchen was on the third floor.

My great-grandfather, Tomo, had a brother, Mata, who made some money in Constantinople and sent it to Tomo to buy the house they lived in and to refurbish it. Mata never made it back to see his investment. Eva had taken great

---

4 As one pundit pointed out, "This is the opposite of tourism. You stay home and the countries come to you!"

5 The Italians thought they deserved Montenegro, as it had once been part of the Venetian empire. It is also rumored that Hitler promised Mussolini he could have it for a summer home.

6 Eva hates the Italians because of what they did to her brother. We were told not to mention Beth Lynn's maiden name, Martino. If it came up, she was a *Martineau*.

pains to keep the house from ever getting dated. She kept the original stone on the exterior, but through the years had plastered over the rough walls on the inside, sometimes leaving exposed a particularly distinctive stone or window feature. The first floor was now the living room and kitchen with stairs leading to the five bedrooms on the second floor.

Although the entire house was charming, it was the dusty attic that held most of the historic and emotional appeal. It was there we discovered a metal trunk (one of several) my grandfather and his brother had sent from America to his mother, Kata, during the Great Depression and World War II. The trunk had been full of sugar, coffee, clothes, blankets, and shoes that their mother, Kata, would eventually share with the other families in the village. We also found a corrugated box that had been full of Austex Chili con Carne my grandfather had sent to help out during the tough times after the war. It was a hint he was somewhat adapting to his new home in Texas and the native food. In the attic was a large window that looked out over the ocean. This is where *Baba* (Grandmother) Kata would sit for hours on end and wait for her sons to return from somewhere on the other side of the sea.

After the emotional tour, I excused myself and walked outside to the edge of the front porch and slowly surveyed the horizon on the ocean, the coastline below, and felt the cool mistral breeze on my face. I imagined my grandfather as a little boy playing in the dirt in front of me. I looked over at the orchard groves and saw him climbing the trees, first for fun and then to help with the family harvest.[7] I saw him running down from the house to the beach to play in the surf and catch fish with his father and brothers. Did the brothers play tag together? As the youngest, was he teased and taunted by the older ones? I saw him walking down the hill to the school on the road while his mother yelled after him in love. Did he like school as I did? I pictured him herding the family's goats across the road so they could drink from the cliff-side spring. I turned and looked at the mountains behind me and imagined him hiking on the steep trails and shinnying up the white rocks. I wondered how many times had he sat with his family and watched the sun set over the sea. What had he dreamed about? What had he wished for? I looked down and saw him sitting on the edge of this porch dangling his legs over the side, eating a pomegranate, and watching horse-drawn carts pass by on their way to Budva or Petrovac. This road connected the

[7] On subsequent visits I would have the indescribable experience of eating grapes and bitter olives off the very trees that my grandfather had helped to harvest over 100 years before. One of our most treasured possessions is a liter of olive oil pressed from the fruit of those same trees.

little village to the other local communities, but it was the sea that connected them to the world. I then thought about him as a young teenager, leaving this house for the very last time waving goodbye as he disappeared down the road.

When we were in Vienna and had visited the Habsburg Palace, I could not help but think that it was their desire for wealth and power (and the resultant opulence) that forced my grandfather from his home and family. They must have been in an incredibly dire and desperate situation for him to have to leave this home nestled in such an idyllic site and the family that loved him. I wondered what he thought as he spent his adult years in dry Arizona and, then, dusty west Texas remembering the wonderful coastal paradise of his childhood.

•

The Radovići originally came from the mountains of Serbia about eight hundred years ago. They wandered through the mountains of Montenegro before they got to the coast and could not wander any more. Fifty-four families (all with different last names) came and settled on the coast and formed what was to become the clan of the Paštrovići. This was when the inland territory was known as "Zeta" and was governed by the Serbian Nemanjići dynasty. As does every Montenegrin clan, our family has a patron saint. Ours is the Madonna, known locally as "The Little Lady."[8]

When we returned to the table after Eva's nap, the subject of common physical family traits came up. (Because I brought it up). I asked if I looked Montenegrin. Eva grabbed my head tightly, tilted it, and examined it closely from the balding pate to my clef chin.

She made the gesture of a curled moustache and stated, "*Crnagorski, ne*!" ("Montenegrin, no!")

She then stroked my eyebrows and said, "Paštrovići, *da!*"

This was my first lesson in differentiating Montenegrins from the mountains and our coastal clan, the Paštrovići. Traditionally, Montenegrins had dark, bushy moustaches that curled up at the ends. I have dark, bushy eyebrows that curl up at the ends. The rest of the hair on my head has fallen off or turned gunmetal, but not my eyebrows. They are as dark as my baby hair ever was and have now developed cactus-like spines that, unless kept in check, can hide vermin and

---

8 Montenegrins know that descendants of the diaspora do not know of their clan heritage. To find out which clan you belong to, they ask you "Who is your family's patron saint?" You are supposed to know.

puncture loved ones. The Paštrovići all have eyebrows that even Groucho would envy.

We knew our Radovići were from Drobnići, and we now knew we were part of the Paštrovići clan. Fortunately, the Paštrovići left legacies in the forms of 36 churches and five monasteries that were primarily built with pirated Ottoman money. The monasteries sit guarding the native lands safe from the Turks due only to the mercilessness of the Paštrovići warriors. (The clan members were experts in psychological warfare. They staked out the boundaries of their lands with tall staves that contained the severed heads of their enemies. They would leave them up for decades.) On a lighter note, the Paštrovići love to tell everyone that their hills, which overlook the sea, are so beautiful, that it is where the gods changed Cadmus and Harmonia into serpents and where they were destined to stay forever.[9]

The source of Montenegrin clans is still a mystery. It is thought that the Slavs, who became Serbs, and settled in Montenegro, may have taken the Illyrian tradition of extended families as a form of protection against other invading tribes. These clans are still a part of Montenegrin culture providing both a sense of historical pride and political influence. The President of the country frequently consults with clan leaders over major policy issues.

The one rogue clan among all the forty-six Montenegrin clans was the Paštrovići. Although they were Orthodox, they had sided with the Catholic Venetians (albeit against the Ottomans, the common enemy).[10] This placed them at odds with the rest of the neighboring clans who also wanted to go to war against the Venetians. The Paštrovići used the Venetians and the Venetians used the Paštrovići. The clan was ocean oriented, and, thus, economically dependent on the powerful Doge and the patrician families who had locked up trade on both sides of the Adriatic. Probably the Venetians gave the clan their ironic name because of the clan's sheep and goat herding activities. However, the clan was anything but pastoral. This Latin label belied the fact they were fierce warriors and even more fiercely independent.[11] The Venetians contracted with the Paštrovići to provide a buffer zone between the port of Budva to the north and the Ottomans to the south. By doing so, the Paštrovići did not have to pay taxes

---

9 Harmonia was Cadmus' wife. Harmonia means, "well assembled." She must have been really built.

10 When the Ottomans attacked, the Paštrovići would yell, "Here come the turkey legs!"

11 There is also a theory that the name was acquired from the ambassador that Serbian King Dušan sent to Dubrovnik in 1355, Nikolica Paštrović. However, Venice had conquered the territory along the eastern Adriatic prior to 1200 and the name was in use long before 1355.

to the Venetians for over 300 years and did not have to send their sons to serve in the Venetian military.

The clan's indigenous land lay on a small strip of Montenegro's coast that stretched from just below Budva south to Haj-Nehaj,[12] the Ottoman border north of Bar. Their pastures were mostly vertical as the clan's territory included all the shoreline up to, and just over, the Crmnica mountain ridge. Most of the clan's settlements were on creeks that descended from the mountains providing fresh water for themselves, their animals, and their orchards. They formed about twenty villages and thirty hamlets in the hills and along the coast.

The Paštrovići had their own language—a separate dialect and vocabulary from Serbian. The words for the months are particularly depictive. January is *siječani* (cutting wood); May is *svibanj* (dawning); and September is *rujan* (red like wine). When they wrote home to their mother, my grandfather and his brother penned their letters in a script form of the Paštrovići dialect.

The clan's people were nothing if not organized. They had communal sheep and goat pens and threshing floors. The latter were large round stone surfaces approximately thirty feet in diameter with stone benches along the sides. Threshing floors served the dual purpose of separating seed from chaff as well as providing a meeting area for the local elders. The structures can still been seen throughout Paštrovići land. Another distinctive feature of Paštrovići life was their unique homes. They took Venetian stone construction design and adapted it to their vertical environment. They built row houses of three stories with slanted roofs integrated into the mountain ridge. The rear of the house backed up to the mountain and had an entrance on the top floor. The kitchen was there with a hole in the roof to emit the smoke from an open fire pit. In the winter, they ate salted meat; in the summer, fresh vegetables seared in olive oil. The wealthy had whole wheat and the poor, corn bread. Across from the kitchen door was the outhouse.

The Paštrovići were hospitable people although leery of strangers. Sometimes built above the kitchen door was an opening used for flinging boiling water at unwanted visitors. The middle story held the living quarters. There were wood, and sometimes steel, frame beds with corn shuck pallets or an imported mattress. The bottom floor was for storage and a wine or *rakija* (brandy) still. That floor might also serve as temporary shelter for the family's animals. On the open side to the sea were windows, and perhaps a wooden porch on the second floor. As the family might have sons who would subsequently marry, an extension was built onto the house for the new couple who were also granted the land directly in front of their new home to garden. (The bride became a member of the groom's

12 Twin hills named "Fear" and "Fear Not".

family.[13]) Thus, a Paštrovići house may have multiple extensions for as many as three generations.

Although Venice claimed the area as its own, the Paštrovići territory was very much an autonomous region. The clan was also a class-based society. It was governed by 12 representatives (one from each of the major families) and four chosen judges. This formed the common assembly, the *Bankadu*, who met in regular session on Drobnići beach (where there was flowing fresh water and plenty of fish for those long legislative sessions). There were separate courts: the Elected Tribunal, for civil matters, and the Tribunal of Good People (which included 24 serfs), for criminal issues. The law of the land was the Code of Dušan. Interestingly, inheritance rights applied to male and female heirs and Paštrovići women had more rights than those of neighboring clans including the Venetians. Annually, they elected two ambassadors to Venice (probably to keep an eye on one another). As the Venetians wanted the Paštrovići to be their captive trading partner (so they could collect all the customs duty), they were prevented from trading with the city of Kotor (when it was an independent country). To keep some semblance of peace, Paštrovići were allowed to trade in Budva only two days a week and could enter only on the seaside gate to avoid any visiting mountain Montenegrins who viewed them as traitors.[14]

The Paštrovići raised goats and sheep, grew figs, olives, pomegranates, and oranges. They were also a seafaring group although they never built any ships. Why go to that much trouble when you can just steal them? The clan provided many legitimate sailors and captains, most sailing out of Constantinople. However, piracy may have been the clan's economic mainstay off and on for many centuries. For the most part, they liked pillaging Ottoman ships, particularly those that encroached on their waters and were a threat to their livelihood.

The grandest of the piracy stories is one that took place in the early 16th century. Word reached the clan leaders that several Ottoman war ships loaded with soldiers were sailing north to anchor at Jaz Beach in order to attack the city of Kotor by land. The Paštrovići rallied the men of the clan, and split their contingency in two. The larger group *ran* across the mountains to help defend Kotor (after sending an even faster messenger there to negotiate a protection

13 The clan had a saying, "In marriage, the woman should be smaller than a poppy seed."

14 Kotor similarly banned the Montenegrins. They were only allowed to trade in Kotor one day a week but had to leave before nightfall. They had a reputation for being uncivilized, continuing old feuds and starting new fights, and, afterwards, being the only ones left standing.

deal). The smaller group went to investigate the enemy ships harbored at the beach. The first group let the Ottomans mount an attack on the walls of Kotor, and then assaulted them from behind, slaughtering the attackers.

The second group found the ships virtually empty, boarded them, and sailed them back to their home harbor at Drobnići beach. Upon further inspection, to their surprise, the ships were filled with thousands of gold ducats—probably taken in an act of piracy on a Venetian ship while the Turks were on their way to Kotor. The clan had never had a windfall like this, and it took much thought and deliberation as to what to do. It was finally decided the Paštrovići would build its own city on the water, just like Venice. They hired Venetian architects and builders to construct a small walled compound just 200 yards off shore. It consisted of the requisite church and one large building for each of the twelve major tribes. Upon its completion, they christened it Sveti Stefan.[15] The Venetians built the small city and were, in turn, paid *with their own money.* Sveti Stefan is now the highlight of the Montenegrin coast and is an Aman luxury hotel.

My relatives all believe empires, governments, and armies may come and go, but there will always be Paštrovići.

•

My great-grandfather, Tomo Radović, and great-grandmother, Katarina (Kata) Gregović, were two very different people. Tomo was a physically powerful man, but gentle and easy-going. The village legend is that he saved two small children when he wrestled a bull to the ground—by its horns. His wife, Kata, on the other hand, was a bitter woman who was depressed most of her adult life because all of her three sons had to go abroad. This was not unusual for Paštrovići families at that time. By 1907, so many Paštrovići young men had immigrated that the government quit keeping track of them. Years of hunger, disease, economic depression, and repression from the Austro-Hungarians had taken their toll. It was estimated by one historian that as many as 70 percent of all their young men left between 1890 and 1917. All were hoping for a better life and, in the Paštrovići vernacular, their "piece of the sky." Few ever returned. They hoped that with the money and goods they sent back, the "house fires would not go out." Paštrovići families were in conflict. Family was

15 It was named after Stefan Štiljanović (1498-1543), a Paštrovići who served as a clan leader and head of the Reževići monastery. He went on to become the last leader of the Serbs before the Ottoman conquest.

most important, but there was not enough food. Additionally, if the sons were discovered, they would have to fight on the side of the occupying army.

According to Eva, my grandfather and his two brothers went to America—but not together. It is believed Andrija, the oldest, went first, Miloš second, and Filip, the youngest, third. Andrija felt he had to return to Montenegro to help his parents. Andrija came home and married Evica Pavolić. They had four children: Mata, born in 1914; Eva, born in 1919; Stefan, born in 1922; and Tomo, born in 1924. Again, due to economic pressures, Andrija soon left for work in Australia.

Before World War II, Mata worked as a financial officer for the hotel association along the coast. After the war, Tomo became a police officer in Bar and came down on the wrong side of Tito's changing attitude about Russia. He was put in prison on Goli Otok, the forced labor camp island off Croatia where the guards made the inmates torture each other. For two years, the family did not even know what happened to him. A neighbor found him wandering the streets of the village sometime after his release. He was too disoriented to go home on his own. The trial and tribulations had taken their toll on this entire generation. None of these four siblings ever married, much less had any children.

Andrija returned home from Australia after World War II. Eva did not even remember him from when she was a girl and now only remembers him as being sick. Andrija lived another fifteen years in Montenegro before he died in 1962. According to Eva, there was always someone to mourn. Eva took care of her mother, Evica, who died in 1972 at the age of 97.

During World War II, Eva and her mother would hide for weeks at a time in the mountain caves above the house to avoid marauding Nazi rape squads. When they would return home, at night, the women would sometimes hear soft taps on their windows. Upon opening them, members of Tito's Partizan fighters would pass their clothes inside. Mother and daughter would stay up all night doing laundry, returning the clothes before dawn with baked bread for the soldiers' breakfast. The many times they did this, they never saw who was outside the window. Eva was arrested by the Axis armies three times and imprisoned in the Citadel in Budva for collaborating with the enemy, but she was never convicted.

Here she was, at ninety-two years old, and Eva had somehow miraculously arranged for her only living relatives, whom she did not even know, to come all the way from America to see her in her old age—first her heir's daughters, and now the professor and his family.

•

I desperately wanted to know all I could about my Montenegrin heritage. Eva told us about the immediate family but not much more. I knew my great-grandmother was a Gregović but knew absolutely nothing about her side of her family. Conducting genealogical research in Montenegro is easy if you remember a few, simple rules. One, is that no one will help a stranger; but they will bend over backwards to help family or friends. Two, every subsequent conquering government sought to annihilate the archives and records of the previous government. (There was a day known as "White Day" where the sea was covered with official papers that had been thrown over the cliffs by the invading Nazis.) Three, both the Julian and Gregorian dates were used up until about 1919 (such that any given date could be off by as many as twelve days for over 400 years). And, lastly, most of the records of the last century will be in Cyrillic Serbian; but the records before that may be in German, Hungarian, or Turkish.

We thought it best to start our family search at the Reževići Monastery, as it was the closest one to the family home. As a rule, monks have their disciplined schedules, and do not like to be disturbed. One exception is the monks at Reževići. For centuries, they have left water, wine, honey, and bread in a shrine at the road for any traveler who needed to be refreshed. Named for the oldest tribe within the Paštrovići clan, the small complex sits on a bluff overlooking the sea, on the Adriatic Highway, about half a mile from the family house.

The monastery was constructed over a pagan temple of unknown origin, and it now contained three pale stone churches. Serbian King Stefan built the oldest, the Church of the Dormition of the Mother of God, and consecrated it in 1223. Beside it, King Dušan consecrated the Church of Archdeacon Stefan (in honor of, you guessed it) in 1351. It was on that occasion when Dušan presented the Paštrovići with his *Law Codex,* which can still be used to arbitrate disagreements between families within the clan. The largest and most stately church, with its sixty-foot bell tower, is the Holy Trinity Church erected by an Abbott, Nikodim Vuković, who was completely blind. That church was built in 1814 as a response to the ransacking of the monastery by Catholic French troops two years earlier. The monastery has been plundered and desecrated down through the ages—from the Ottomans in 1705, the French in 1812, the Italians in World War II, to the Communists in the 1950s. The adjacent refectory and sleeping quarters are perfect stone matches to the rest of the complex, but they were only constructed after World War II.[16]

---

16 The Adriatic Highway is the road that was used by the Crusaders as early as 1096 as they marched to the Holy Lands. It does not help that the monastery sat on the

We parked our car in the monastery's dirt lot, entered through the exterior arched doorway, and found ourselves in the middle of a lovely courtyard with flowers, shade trees, and the three churches. Behind the churches were vegetable and herb gardens with an apiary. Over the gardens were the ubiquitous grapevine trellises. To the right was an open door to a small stone kiosk that offered icons, votive candles, honey, and wine for sale. Behind the cash drawer was an elderly nun slumped over in a stiff wooden chair. She was snoring very loudly, and it irritated the cat that was curled up at her feet. Tip toeing softly out, I located a monk who was sweeping at the top of the exterior stairs. We could not communicate, but a local man who spoke English arrived just then to pay his respects. With his help, I found out this monk was just a utility player from the main monastery in Cetinje. He came to day-sit the churches, say Mass, and collect money from the shop. When I asked about Radovići, he shrugged his shoulders and said he didn't know anything about the local families but pointed outside to the Reževići cemetery and the Paštrovići Museum on the highway.

After walking through all the rows of tombs and monuments, there, in the back, we found the plot of Eva's family and her siblings. There were two crypts below a shiny marble headstone listing her parents and brothers with their birth and death dates. In the middle was a line that read, "Eva 1919—." It was quite possible there were other family members buried here. It was customary to bury family members on top of one another and then buy a new headstone that listed only the most recently deceased generation. Eva had told us her grandparents (my great-grandparents) were buried under a stone slab at the entrance to The Church of the Holy Trinity. As we walked back to view the chapels, we noticed there were no grave markers on the stones inside the courtyard, but we tread very lightly in that spot.

Built in 1856, the Paštrovići Museum next door was, until 1962, the village schoolhouse. Inside we met the charming curator, Olivera Franković, a woman of energetic enthusiasm for all things Paštrovići.[17] Inside the museum was a fine collection of native costumes and folk objects d'art. On the walls in the library upstairs, we found photographs of Eva and her siblings as students at the school. We confirmed this is where my grandfather had also attended primary before leaving his family. More than likely his father would have sat on the same

---

only road along the Adriatic coast. Thus, it was an easy and convenient target for conquering troops.

17 Olivera's house sat directly across the highway from the museum so she literally watches over the facility day and night. She invited us there for a drink where we met her cat. Because of his tendency to play around, she had named him Berlusconi. We laughed and she gave us a WEWYD look.

wooden benches as well. Over the course of several hours, Olivera told us many things about my family and what life was like for multiple generations of people who lived the Paštrovići life.

•

From Reževići, we headed south, past Petrovac, to Buljarica and the next nearest monastery, Gradište. We knew from Eva that my great-grandmother, Kata, was born in Buljarica. Access to the Gradište Monastery was via a tiny dirt road, which required a tight, five-point turn near a stone house. From there, we had to angle back and, then, up a 35-degree incline on the side of a densely wooded hill. This precarious path ended three hundred yards higher at the monastery entrance where there was just enough room to park two cars. Or, there would have been if it weren't for a monk filling his donkey's saddlebags from a large pile of sand in the parking lot. The monk could speak some English, and he said there were no Radovići buried here. However, there were Gregovići interred on the hillside above the church. We asked him what he was doing, and he said he was pouring a concrete slab for a café in hopes of bringing tourist dollars in order to support the monastery. He filled the bags, lashed the shovel to the donkey, turned him around, slapped him on the rump, and the two of them disappeared up a path into the woods. We spent the next two hours photographing all the Gregovići headstones in the cemetery not knowing if they were relatives or not.

When it came time to leave, it was apparent I could not turn the car around in such a tiny space; and we would have to back the car down the hill. Beth Lynn walked down, ahead of the car, in case another vehicle decided to ascend the single-lane road. I threw the car in reverse, my arm over the passenger seat, and my neck out of joint trying to drive very slowly backwards even though the incline was so steep I could not actually see the road out of the rear window. Creeping down the hill, everything was going smoothly until I hit a patch of wet leaves and lost control of the car. I yelled at Beth Lynn who jumped out of the way. The car began sliding down the road sideways barely missing the cliff on one side and large olive trees on the other. I stomped on the brake pedal while grabbing the parking brake. This, combined with the fact the car was now traveling perpendicular to the incline, created just enough friction so that it stopped a few seconds later less than six inches from a stone house at the bottom of the hill. I saw my entire stipend going to pay for a replacement car and repairing someone's newly ventilated living room. We spent the rest of the day finding, and being turned away at, the other two monasteries. It was clear we were going to need a new friend to provide introductions if we were going to find out about our family here.

Lights! Camera! Action! Hugs!

We were very worried we were going to leave Montenegro and not be able to find out anything at all about my Gregović relatives. This would have been the disappointment of a lifetime. In this effort, I told our family quest story to anyone who would listen—fellow faculty members, students, neighbors, waiters, and even my barber, who nodded understandingly through the entire narrative and then told me he did not speak any English. Nodding understandingly was just part of his job, he told me. He didn't really pay attention to anything his clients said.

We told everybody we met what little we knew about the family hoping someone might know them or at least know of them. Three weeks before we were supposed to leave, I spoke at the American Corner and ended by telling the audience about our quest. Four days later, I got a call from a woman who had attended the lecture. She told me there was a television show on *Crna Gora TV* (CGTV), the government-controlled network, about Montenegrin families. She arranged an introduction to a beautiful woman named Olivera Vukadinović, a television personality here in Montenegro. Olivera and her husband are both trained attorneys and work at CGTV. Among other television series, she produces a show on family history (mostly stories about the *diaspora*). We met at her office, told her our story, and she nodded though the entire conversation. Her son, Luka, a freshman at the University of Jacksonville, happened to be home for the summer, and he served as an excellent translator for us. She said she had a few phone calls to make, but she would contact us in a few days. We thanked her for her time, but I was not holding my breath.

I remembered what Alex Graham, the creator of the TV show, *Who Do You Think You Are?* told the *Friends* actress, Lisa Kudrow. He said, "Finding family might not be that easy. Let's just be aware that most of the time, the research comes to a dead end because there are no records or its just 500 years of sheepherders." My family still kept sheep.

A week later we got a phone call from Olivera. She had some news and invited us over to her house to share it with us and to also meet her husband and mother. We were giddy when we arrived. We wanted to know the names of our family members and where they were.

Olivera's search for Kata Gregović was a tough one. She started by trying to interview Eva who wanted nothing to do with anything related to television as she did not believe in it. However, the Bantulići did allow Olivera access to Eva's house. There, she found the trunk I had told her about. In it were all the letters Eva had received from my grandfather and his brothers. There were 104 of them. When Olivera began reading from the letters, she said they were full of pathos from an era that is almost lost in Montenegrin history because the people who played such a significant part never returned to tell their story. Now these letters must do all the talking for them. How much love and sorrow had travelled across the ocean in those small envelopes?

Dear Mother,

> *I hope you are well. It has been two weeks since I last received your letter you wrote on October 15 (1947). It took 45 days for it to reach us. I am glad you have received the packages and you got them all but two because there were seven packages. I am sorry the shoes are too small. You wrote about the meters of black material. If you have received my goods then you probably have enough to make black clothes. But, if you haven't received them both, write and I will send you more. A month back, I sent a package with food and it was 43 liters full. In the following days, I will send another one and the largest shoes I can find.*
>
> *I understood what you said about my late father and that you are 85 years old. With God's help, you will live a long time and we believe you would enjoy seeing us. We would also love to see you and everyone else. Anything is possible but our situation is poor. Therefore, a long voyage would be difficult. I told my daughter you wrote to her and her mother but she cannot answer, as she does not speak our language, only English. You do not understand English, but they send their love. Thank you for your kind letter. My son is now out of the Marines but is far away from here. He writes often and he is well. I often receive news from Filip. He is doing well, but has not yet fully recovered.*[18] *He also sends his love and when I write, it is from both of us.*

Much love,
Your sons

These letters ignited an emotional fire within Olivera. She was now determined to find our Montenegrin relatives. First, she had to find which

[18] Within the year, Phil would die of cancer.

Gregović family Baba Kata belonged to; but any family records would be over a hundred years old. Each conquering invader systematically destroyed records such as these. In the last purge, the Communists raided every parish church, burning marriage, death, and birth records (and imprisoning many of the priests). You cannot have any loose ends lying about when you have to re-write history in order to indoctrinate the next generation.

Olivera discovered the Gregovići were quite prolific. The family was so large she found Gregovići married to other Gregovići, and they were not even related. Many Gregovići lived in Budva, so she systematically began phone calling each one. It proved fruitless; none of them were my relatives. She travelled to several coastal towns and stopped people in the street to ask them if anyone could remember a Baba Kata. She searched through church cemetery records but to no avail. She then began searching real estate records from the Austro-Hungarian period dated from 1878. Needless to say they were in perfect order, but they were in German. However, one entry on the last page of a musty ledger showed a house in the village of Buljarica listing a little girl named Kata. Current real estate records showed a Vojo Gregović now owned that home.[19]

She paused here for dramatic effect (as all good Montenegrin storytellers do) and then burst out with the punch line.

"I have found your family, and they are anxious to meet you!"

"Are you *sure* they are *my* relatives?" (At this point, I didn't want any pretenders to the throne.)

"Oh yes," she said, "They have a family tree in their living room. On it is Baba Kata. This will make terrific TV!"

This was going to be a bit awkward. We were very grateful to Olivera for all her hard work, and we wanted to repay her by participating in the show. But, we were going to meet our new family under the harsh lights of a reality television show. Supposing they didn't like us? What if it was better we had not found them? Olivera had already arranged for us to meet them the next day at their house, along with a complete television crew.

•

The Gregovići home also sat on the Adriatic highway, just below the Gradište Monastery in Buljarica. A gate on the street opened to steps that descended to a lush garden hidden from the road. We were greeted at the street by Petar

---

19 I have no doubt that had Olivera not been trained as an attorney, she never would have been able to interpret the records in order to find our family.

Gregović, the spokesperson for the family, a stooped but distinguished man in his seventies who escorted us down the stairs to a pleasant home with wood paneling whose shelves were filled with books, keepsakes, and the objects d'art collected over a lifetime. Petar introduced us to his brother, Vojo, who is married to Danica, the woman who keeps the brothers and family together. Vojo has had a stroke and smiles a lot. Their son, Georg, was also there. Georg is a novelist and served as translator for their family with Luka serving as a translator for us. Petar lives next door to the couple and another brother, Nenad, splits his time between Beograd where his family lives and his own place next door. They all live together in typical Paštrovići fashion. There was another brother, Miloš, but he died a few years ago. He was represented by his widow, Nevenka, who spoke English very well and had a son who lived in Houston. These were my great-grandmother's grandnephews (or my second cousins once removed[20]).

It was a loud and joyous occasion with everyone talking at once and nobody understanding anybody. We finally slowed down long enough for the translators to catch up, but feelings do not need translation. On the Gregović living room wall over their sofa, was a family tree (an extremely rare thing in Montenegro) dating back to the 1600s. There, in the upper right corner, was Baba Kata. (In typical Montenegrin/Orthodox fashion, the tree followed only the male lineages—no mothers, no marriages, but there were daughters.) From this tree, we found Kata had one sister and five brothers.[21] Petar explained three of their uncles also left to go to America. Their father was the only one who stayed. As one of the brothers said, "The climate is wonderful here, but you can't live off animals and olives."

After introductions, libations, traditional Paštrovići cookies, and the thousand questions I had, they took us to the house where Kata was born. They believed the structure was built around 1700, as were most of the others above the village. It was a perfect specimen of a traditional Paštrovići house. The fact that it was still standing after so many disasters, both natural and manmade, was amazing. What was even more remarkable was the dedication of the Gregović family in keeping their heritage alive in this house. Danica produced a key that was eight inches long and placed it in an ancient lock in the old green door. We entered the top floor into the kitchen. The fireplace where Kata learned to cook from her mother was intact—complete with ancient kitchen implements hanging on the walls. There were pots on hooks over a clay tile ring around the fire pit and a rack for

20 Obviously, it was my grandfather who removed himself.

21 In typical Paštrovići fashion, I was *doubly* related to the brothers, as their grandmother was a Radović from Drobnići.

smoking meat. Built into the wall was a small, stone oven for baking bread. Every January 6th, since Baba Kata was a little girl, the family has cooked Christmas Eve dinner in that kitchen and then burned the Christmas log. The family still keeps that tradition and has done so for over 170 years (even when they had to do so in secret as celebrating Christmas was outlawed by the Communists). Outside of the second floor was a stone porch on top of a room extension. It was covered with a metal frame with the ever-present grapevines that were for harvesting as well as shade. The porch had stone benches allowing one to sit and survey the green Paštrovići hills dotted with other similar homes and glance down to a slice of the blue ocean at Buljarica beach. The floors were supported by large rough-hewn timber beams embedded into the stone walls. In the basement were large barrels for the homemade wine from the large steel still that was still in use.[22] The bare stone shelves were where bags of potatoes and onions had been kept.

There was a very strong feeling of pleasant spirits in the house. We had spent so much time searching for our family story; and here it was, preciously preserved in a living legacy by loving people dedicated to the honor of its heritage.

Meeting those family members was like holding your own newborn for the very first time. You immediately love that child, but it surprises you because you do not know where the love comes from. Nevertheless, you delight in it because now you know love can spontaneously erupt and at the most unexpected times. It is in you always, and it does not take a magical moment like finding family or having a baby to have it emerge and envelope you in a bonding warmth.

In one of the many ironies of our trip, we had driven directly in front of the Gregovići home at least seven times. Even eerier was the fact that the building I had almost hit with the car while sliding down the steep road from the Gradište Monastery was my great-grandmother's house.

We spent the rest of the time getting introduced to all the other branches of the family tree, those who had gone before and those who were still with us. We took many photographs in the garden before we had to say goodbye. There was additional hugging and more than a little crying, admittedly by the women. The men just happened to all simultaneously get something in their eyes. The television camera caught all of it.[23] They were all wonderful people. They had all received

22 Say that three times fast. Then do it after every drink.

23 When I returned to visit our Montenegrin family this past year, I asked our relatives if they had seen the television show. Cousin Georg replied, "Only eleven times! We are famous! When it first came on, we were celebrities. However, the show was so popular; the station ran it as filler when they didn't have anything else to broadcast. Now we get comments from friends like, 'You are in our living room more than you are in your own'."

educations, had productive careers, raised families and had not only survived during the vicissitudes of the times, but had thrived and were very happy.

Dear Mother,

> *When you write, tell me what you need. Do you have something warm to cover yourself with when you go to bed? Please receive our deepest affection. Do not worry and do not anger yourself because we are apart. It does not do you any good. Give our greetings to those who do and those that do not ask about us. We will always be your sons and we wish you well,*

Miloš and Filip Radović

(The others that are here from our hills send their love, too.)

Leaving with So Much More Than We Brought

The day before we left was spent packing up everything and, again, Beth Lynn knew the exact weight of every piece of luggage. That night we threw a dinner party at a restaurant for the new friends we had made and to repay all the social engagements we owed. We had to thank everyone for all of their hospitality and kindness they had shown us since we arrived. It was difficult to acknowledge everyone for the innumerable favors they had all done on our behalf. (I am sure there were many we did not even know about). Without all of these people, we would not have had the wonderful adventure of discovery coupled with the deep meaning that our experience had for us.

Our flight left at 9:10 a.m. the next morning, and our good friends from the embassy took us to the airport. Having them with us helped ease the emotional trauma. Both our suitcases and hearts were heavy. We drove one last time through the dreary streets that have so much life, and out the long road past the dirty, semi-dormant aluminum plant. When we first arrived, this road was dilapidated, full of potholes the taxi had to serve to avoid. Now it was a new four-lane freeway welcoming guests into a capital city that so wants to impress the rest of the world.

Beth Lynn and I sat in the airport waiting room; looking at each other not believing the experience was really over. We got teary-eyed if we talked about anything or anybody from the last six months, so we found ourselves in a very stunted conversation. We did not want to leave, but it was time to go. How do you thank an entire country for teaching you so much about its culture, your family, and yourself? How do you express the gratitude you have for the deep feeling of acceptance and belonging in a world that was so strange just six months ago?

•

After traveling westbound and down for twenty-three hours, we arrived home to a dark house. With the dust covers all over the furniture, I felt like Pip coming back in *Great Expectations*. It was a gloomy reminder that the trip was really over and we were returning to the reality that was our normal lives.

I took a much-needed shower and, then, Beth Lynn climbed into a hot bath. I heard her sigh a few times, then she yelled at me through the door that she would not be coming out for several days, and could I arrange to have all her meals sent in? That evening, we collapsed into our own bed, which made just laying still a blissful pleasure. *Flollopy* is a word we purloined from a favorite Britcom. It describes that blissful state of laziness when you do not have the energy to do anything coupled with complete ambivalence. We floated in that state staring at the ceiling knowing the other was thinking about our experiences. I, myself, was subversively scheming about how to get us back to Montenegro.

Even though we had been awake for almost thirty-six hours, for some reason we could not get to sleep, *again*. It dawned on us that the house was too quiet. We opened the windows to let in the distant din from the traffic in the valley, the nearby summer backyard parties, and the even nearer crickets. With the addition of that ambient noise, it did not take long for us to fall into a heavy slumber. This was good, as I had to be back at work the next day and Beth Lynn had to begin the arduous process of getting the house back in order.

•

The next morning, when I unlocked my office door at the university the next morning, I was immediately overwhelmed with, what I now understand to be, a bad case of post-partum depression. I sat at my desk and stared out of the window for almost an hour not really wanting to do anything. The adventure was over, so there was really not much to look forward to anymore.

This was ridiculous! I had come back to some new and welcomed challenges. While I was gone, my colleagues had elected me department chair. (Which taught me never to miss a faculty meeting again.) I cannot be feeling this way! There was too much to do and a new exciting semester to prepare for. Yet the morose feeling was real and it weighed on me as though I was trying to breathe and couldn't.

I tried to shake off the languor as I unwrapped the few souvenirs that I had brought back. I placed them on my desk where I could examine them once more. There was the Karadžić watercolor, the Vevčani passport, the Yugoslavian trillion-dinar bill, the tuna two-Kuna coin from Croatia, the Orthodox saints trading cards, and a photograph of my grandfather's house lit by the setting sun. Simply putting them on the bookcase would not be satisfactory; I had to place these precious items where I could always see them. In order to able to do that, I spent the rest of the day rearranging all the furniture in the office—probably as unconscious re-entry therapy. The photograph of the house I placed on my desk so it would be closest to me. The watercolor of Lake Skadar, I hung by my door so that I could look at the twin mountains called Sophia Loren every time I left. If that wouldn't make me smile, nothing would. Slowly, over the next few days, the internal gray cloud lifted and my disposition began to match the warm summer days once more.

Returning to our old routines, Beth Lynn and I realized how the experience had affected us in a thousand little ways and how we were changed because of it. Things that we just accepted before, we now found we didn't like at all—like going to the grocery store on one-item errands. We now loathed jumping in the car, rushing two miles to the grocery store, finding the shortest checkout line, and rushing back home. We longed to be able to mosey across the street to a small, family-run market, linger over window-shopping, and get back when we got back.

When we drink the same fruit juices that we used to enjoy, they taste just like sugar-water, with no body or real content. A few days after returning, I stood at the kitchen window drinking my usual morning pick-me-up and looked at the hummingbirds outside on the feeder. I recognized that there was no real difference between what each of us were drinking except theirs was free. I raised my glass to the birds, and poured the rest of my juice down the sink.

Our daily routine, which had been a very acceptable lifestyle before, became mundane to the point of monotony. We deliberately decided to overcome this by first appreciating together the little things in our life. Beth Lynn cherished our children that we loved (and even liked), the potential grandchildren on the way, and strolling as an entertaining activity. I thought more along the lines of having water pressure, guardrails on roads, and cuts of meat that I could identify.

In our return to reality, three main themes emerged that demonstrated how our lives and life perspective had changed. One was a new sense of looking for adventure in the everyday. We found that making an effort (and time) for small explorations paid off immensely in reenergizing ourselves and our lives.

This produced delightful and sometimes surprising results. Having spent the previous six months eating olives with every meal, we were delighted to find that our neighborhood grocery store had installed an olive bar that offered twelve different succulent varieties. Filling up a quart container, I asked the manager when they had had this feature installed.

He thought a minute and said, "I don't really know. It was here when I got here and I've been at this store for ten years."

Another example of us not even noticing something wonderful because we were caught in our myopic life rut and had walked right by it every time we had gone to that store.

We strived to expand our intellectual horizons. We sought out small art gallery openings, attended lectures, and went to events we never would have before the trip. We found that we slept less. Now it was not unusual for us to rise at 5:30 or 6 a.m. and begin some enjoyable task before breakfast.

I recognized I would spend an entire day working in front of a monitor, come home, and try to decompress by spending hours in front of another monitor. Yet, there were trails and streams on the mountain where we live that I had not yet explored. That was going to change.

Another theme was the acknowledgement that our lives were too fast-paced, which was not healthy for our bodies or our psyche. Not too long after returning, I found I had booked myself a day with solid appointments and only a fifteen-minute break for lunch. It was day where I had to leave meetings early, rush out in order to be late to the next meeting. As I was nuking some corny dogs at the campus convenience store for my lunch, I realized this is exactly the way I lived my life before the trip and I hated it. I thought about my friends in the corporate world that allegedly complain about entire weeks like this when, in fact, they were bragging about how busy, and, thus, how important they are. Perhaps, I was falling back into that trap myself.

In Montenegro, I had learned that afternoons were best spent with colleagues and friends with cups and glasses in our hands and plenty of conversation to go around. The English indulge in elevenses and teatime. Each of these agreeable activities slows down the pace of the day and provides time for companionship, which tends to lead to discourse and understanding. I began to find that I not only faced the difficulties of busy days more congenially, but it actually strengthened relationships and increased collegiality among my colleagues.[1] Occasionally, it even provided opportunities to produce some profound thinking among my department members, which resulted in scholarly collaboration.

---

[1] Something necessary for having a *college*.

Under Tito, Yugoslavians were told to take naps in the afternoon. I saw this as another opportunity for cultural adaptation. I bought a small sofa, wedged it into my office, and rediscovered the lock on my door. The unintended consequence of this piece of furniture was not the power naps that I had hoped for, but the additional seating the couch provided at the afternoon *kaffeklatsch* when people would crowd into my office.

I also discovered that being trapped at my desk under a large pile of administrivia made it impossible to court the muse. There was no quiet time for contemplation and, thus, no oxygen for thinking. I realized that there were buildings on campus in which I had never even been. As much as I love and appreciate all aspects of commerce, Business Administration buildings, as a rule, are very boring. I found that wandering over to the Fine Arts building and viewing the student work on display in the hallways or reading the cartoons and bumper stickers on the doors of the Philosophy faculty was cerebrally rejuvenating.

The final theme that emerged was the fact that we now saw our own American lifestyle through other cultural lenses. We became our own diagnostic anthropologists, dissecting our previous behavior with a fairly critical eye and not necessarily liking what we saw.

We found that walking after dinner through our little patch of suburbia was less than satisfying. People in our neighborhood tended to stay indoors; they are not front porch sitters. The neighborhood is calm and peaceful with front yards of delightfully groomed gardens that their owners share with the rest of the world. It is soothing, but it does not have the vitality of urban life where there are groups of people gossiping in front of the green grocer, men hanging out while waiting for haircuts, or the clinking and conversation created by the customers in the sidewalk cafés.

We found that strolling around the local open-air shopping mall was as close as we could come. There, shops had sidewalk displays, fragrances from foreign foods wafted through open doors, and families milled about. Some of the restaurants had a few outdoor tables around a center stage where local musicians shared their talents filling the evening air. Beth Lynn and I would walk holding hands, try the offered food samples, shop for gifts for the grandchildren, and even dine occasionally. However, we could read all the signage, understand all the conversation, and we still had to drive to get there. So, it was not quite the same.

More than anything, we realized that there was a fundamentally different approach to life in Montenegro than in the United States. Americans have to have rationality and logic. When things go wrong, they cannot possibly be inexplicable. Americans have to have a reason that something happened or, in some cases, someone to blame. Not so with folks from the Balkans. Any given event might have been caused by the gods, serendipity, or simple fate. Thus, the explanations for the occurrences of such events have much deeper spiritual meaning and require much more contemplation. The fault that Americans seek might be due to our over litigious society, but I think it goes deeper. To comprehend the world, American's have to force it into causality and reason.

Before we left on our trip, our son spotted a news article from Podgorica about flooding in Lake Skadar that had accidently set free a pet hippo that was kept in a private animal reserve. He was spotted at a neighboring farm with a herd of cows waiting to be fed. After the surprised farmer recovered his composure, he gave the hippo some grass, and called the owner.

The animal's owner said to a television reporter, "There is nothing that we can do until the spring flooding subsides." (Accompanied by the WEWYD look.) "It is good that the hippo is with the cows. Otherwise he would be very lonely as he misses the pats he gets from the visitors to our reserve."

In America, news about an escaped exotic animal would have resulted in charges of negligence, filing suits for damages, and set the authorities off on a bounty hunt. In Montenegro, it is nice that the hippo has new friends.

Just before we left to return home, I got the unwanted news I had a new boss. While I was gone, our previous Dean had ascended to sitteth on the right hand and had been named Vice-president of Academic Affairs. As such, we needed a replacement and our President had found one with local ties, extensive international experience, and a great academic pedigree. Not only had my supervisor changed, but also, much to my dismay, he and his family had moved in across the street from our house. As I spoke to my American colleagues, their response was, "What are you going to do? You want to be careful, keep your distance. Don't let this get personal, keep it professional."

When I lamented my tale of woe to my Teaching Assistant in Montenegro, he exclaimed, "This is wonderful! You will become best friends!" The exact opposite approach of the Americans (and myself).

When I finally did meet our new Dean, I told him I was going to take the Montenegrin approach and had already decided that he and I were going to become best friends. I now had previously undiscovered family that I barely know; yet I love them dearly. Why couldn't this be true for non-relatives as well? I think because of the new Dean's own experience of living abroad and knowing how fast friendships can form among ex-pats, he and I have had a mutual bromance ever since. The Montenegrin way works. Based on this experience,

Beth Lynn and I decided that the arbitrary probationary period that people subconsciously place on new relationships was too long for us and we would make friends with people faster and deeper than we ever did before.

Beth Lynn and I also made a solemn promise to one another. We decided, no matter where we were going (or how late we might be), if there was a rainbow, we would pull over to the side of the road and spend a few minutes in aesthetic admiration. Driving home in the evening after work, sometimes there will be a rainbow that connects the two nearest mountain peaks and arches directly over our house. After our trip, this rainbow now has a special meaning to us that was previously only known to Dorothy.

•

A month after we returned, I traveled to Texas to visit my mother. I had spent time compiling all the family history and labeling the snapshots with everyone's name so I could introduce her to our long lost, and now found, family. I typed up a manuscript to capture all the impressions, thoughts, and feelings about Montenegro and our family so she could get a glimpse into her mysterious heritage and the previously unknown story of her father's childhood. I chose a few photographs that best depicted the wild beauty of the country and the natural beauty of its people. I narrated our visit with anecdotes about our travels and included some regional history to put her, and our, story into a perspective she would appreciate. I placed all of these in a binder as a gift.

When I arrived at their home, the house was dark. Her husband, Sam, met me at the door and welcomed me in. Mother hugged and kissed me without getting up from her chair in the living room. This was not like her. We exchanged greetings and then I took out the binder and placed it in her lap. I pulled up a chair next to hers so I could read her the text. She oohed and ahhed over all the pictures and asked who everyone was three or four times. Photographs that depicted things she had never seen before had to be reviewed multiple times. Events or stories that referred to things on previous pages were lost to her memory forever. About halfway through the book, she started coughing. I got up to get her a drink of water from the kitchen. When I returned, she had moved the binder to the coffee table and had returned to her crossword puzzle.

"Oh, there you are. Come here and tell me all about your trip!" she said, smiling.

I was a year too late.

Now, when I visit her, she thinks I have just returned from Montenegro; and she wants to hear all about our adventure and discovering our family. I get the binder off the shelf, and I read her the same stories all over again. Her eyes light up and she gets just as excited as when she heard it the first time. It reminded me of reading the same bedtime stories to my children numerous times and them always getting enthralled.

Mother particularly wanted to know about her father's story, as he never spoke to her about it. After piecing together what I could about his early life, I speculate there were several reasons he never mentioned his childhood or family. He might have been tightlipped because he was hiding from the authorities. His brother, Miloš, applied for U.S. citizenship four times; but Phil never did. It might have been because he was a very stoic man like his father and casual conversation did not come naturally. He may have worked so hard that there was never any time for heartfelt chats. He also could have been ashamed because, as a son, he could not fulfill the traditional responsibility to take care of his parents. Whatever the reason, a rich legacy was lost and never passed down to subsequent generations—a legacy that took over a hundred years to regain.

When I re-read the story to my mother, it takes me back to that small apartment on the busy street filled with the friendly people I learned to understand and adore. It reminds me of the excitement of seeing the land of my family and the thrill of meeting wonderful relatives for the first time. I think about being in my classroom looking out over the students who were trying to make sense of their history and bring their future into focus. I look at the pictures of the places we traveled, the people we met, the family we found; and I get teary eyed and emotional. I understood that the trip had been made for many reasons—for my country, my students, my relatives, my mother, and myself. But, more than anything, the trip was for my grandfather, a man I never knew. A man I had learned to appreciate and love by living in the land he cherished and with the people he had to leave. A man who had lived a life filled with so much sacrifice and separation so that I could have the opportunities that were made available to me.

My Fulbright experience had taken me to a place I had never been before—physically, emotionally, intellectually, and even spiritually. The intersection of those four dimensions probably converges only once in a lifetime. I got to experience it. I realized that once you arrive at that unique place—it is impossible to return where you were before. That door is closed. You can only go forward onto a new path. I understood I owed so much to the legacy of Senator Fulbright and the entire scholarship program. From our experience, we made a promise to take our understanding and try to enrich the lives we encountered in the future in hopes of creating a fuller and brighter tomorrow.

After hearing our stories people ask us if they should travel to Montenegro so they can see the mountains that cascade down to the sea, or experience absolute silence in a primordial forest, or straddle the boundary between two ancient civilizations.

Without even hesitating, Beth Lynn and I look at each other, shrug our shoulders in unison, and give them our best WEWYD look.

Acknowledgements

This project began as a labor of love for my mother, but blossomed into a much larger project that ended up taking three years to complete. I would like to thank all the people who encouraged and contributed to our experience and the project and in so many helpful ways.

The Bantulić family, and especially their son, Nenad, made it possible to communicate with Cousin Eva and translate the love that we have for one another. Their continued hospitality is a cherished gift.

Bethann Boatright Freeland traveled part of the trip with us and provided a laugh track the entire time. Her considerate suggestions helped me convey the more emotional parts of the experience.

Laurie Bott provided lots of encouragement, proofing, and made valuable editorial suggestions.

Marija Bulatović provided wonderful assistance in helping us both understand our new world and discover the delightful students at the University of Donja Gorica.

Randy and Debby Eggleston provided logistical and security support on the home front that provided immense peace of mind.

James and Michelle Fowler (and their entire family), who, due to their extensive international experience, knew how to make our experience just the right combination of adventure and wonder. Their presence in Podgorica provided a deep sense of family and home away from home.

Olivera Franković, curator of the Paštrovići museum, taught us so much about the daily lives of my ancestors and my clan.

Ted Fulmer, the one man in the world with whom I would trust with my sense of humor, gave valued comments along with suggestions on sharpening and setting up punch lines.

Dennis Heaston reviewed the manuscript and made significant suggestions for clarification and historical context.

Danijela and Vladimir Ivanović made us feel so welcome and have become dear friends.

Jean McPeek was a patient and invaluable resource at the Council for the International Exchange of Scholars.

Paul and Kaye Martino read the manuscript and provided very helpful comments and corrections.

Ann Mecham, my administrative assistant with the editing eagle eye, compiled all the editorial and proofing comments for review. She read and reread the manuscript searching for all my errors and mistakes.

Richard McDermott gave great counsel for improving the flow and structure of the book.

Duane Miller provided professional proofing corrections and appreciated editorial suggestions.

Ambassadors Roderick W. Moore and Miodrag Vlahović graciously provided personal insight into the country and its culture.

Valentina Perović took to heart our desperate desire to find my family and did something about it.

Eva Radović and the entire Gregovići family welcomed us as long-lost family and gave us a sense of belonging and a living window into our family heritage. They gave us the best gift that we could have ever brought back from the experience—their love.

Mary Radovich-Miller, my wonderfully talented cousin, proofed the manuscript, corrected family stories, and insured that the truth be told.

Slavica Rosić served as the cultural liaison at the American Embassy and provided numerous doses of assistance.

Mike Swenson and Ned Hill provided friendship and encouragement for the Fulbright application.

Joel Swenson told us to venture out more and we did—more than we would have otherwise without his sage advice.

Anica Vujnović and all the staff at the American Corner were very helpful and kind to a bewildered scholar.

Professors Veselin and Milena Vukotić at the University of Donja Gorica provided a wonderful teaching experience and introduced me to some of the most inspiring students in the world. All of the UDG staff including Marija, Sonja, and Luka made the experience professional and very pleasant.

I am deeply in debt to Olivera Vukadinović for believing in our quest to find our family and making it all possible. She was the diligent catalyst who brought our family together. We are forever in her debt. Luka, her son, and scholar in his own right, provided an invaluable translation service (with a slight southern drawl).

Chris and Jill Willeke's friendship and helpfulness provided a cushion of comfort during times of confusion.

Ian Wilson, Janice Gygi, and Liz Hitch at Utah Valley University took a chance on a new employee and provided the opportunity for this enlightening and life-changing Fulbright experience.

Lastly, and most importantly, I want to thank my wife, Beth Lynn, for a variety of tasks such as compiling the family genealogy, double-checking my notes, and remembering things I didn't. She saw the trip through an entirely different perspective that gave experiences and new relationships their proper importance. I want to thank her for being such a gracious and patient traveling companion while I would stop in the middle of whatever we were doing to take notes and photographs. She gave up so many evenings and weekends while I completed this project. But, most importantly, thank you for making us a home wherever we are in the world and in whatever circumstances we find ourselves. With you, dear, traveling together through life has been a wonderful experience. I love you.

About the Author

Paul Dishman is the Chair of the Marketing department in the Woodbury School of Business at Utah Valley University. In 2010, he was named by the U.S. State Department as the Fulbright Scholar to Montenegro. Dishman holds a master's degree in Marketing and a doctorate in Marketing Research and Psychometric Measurement. Before returning to academia he served on the sales and marketing staffs of both Apple Computer and IBM. He has taught marketing for twenty-five years and has consulted with industry for over two decades. Dishman is a Past-president of the international Strategic and Competitive Intelligence Professionals (SCIP) and has been named a SCIP Fellow. He is also a Fellow of the Academy of Marketing Science. He has held visiting faculty positions at the University of New Brunswick in Canada, the University of Donja Gorica in Montenegro, and Shanghai Normal University in China.

Dishman has lectured on market strategy to a variety of companies, organizations, and conferences. He has spoken and conducted training programs in China and Japan as part of a United Nations invitation, as well as for the American Marketing Association, Microsoft, 3M, IBM, Amgen, American Airlines, KPMG, Deutschebank, Westinghouse, Unilever, professional groups, and various government agencies. He has also lectured in Taiwan, the United Kingdom, Belgium, Italy, France, Canada, Montenegro, Croatia, Albania, and Kosovo. He has also published academic articles in *The European Journal of Marketing, Market Planning and Intelligence, the Journal of Personal Selling and Sales Management, Industrial Marketing Management, the Journal of Competitive Intelligence and Management,* and *Competitive Intelligence Review.* He was also a columnist for the *Idaho State Journal.*

Made in the USA
Lexington, KY
03 December 2019

58088441R00168